To Nancy + Curtis
From your N

Awad + L
عوض + ليلى

December 16, 1994

Temples and Tombs of
ANCIENT NUBIA

Temples and Tombs of ANCIENT NUBIA

The International Rescue Campaign at Abu Simbel,
Philae and Other Sites

General Editor: Torgny Säve-Söderbergh

with lll illustrations, 43 in color

THAMES AND HUDSON

UNESCO

First published 1987
by the United Nations Educational,
Scientific and Cultural Organization,
7 Place de Fontenoy, 75700 Paris, France
and Thames and Hudson Ltd, London

First published in the United States in 1987 by
Thames and Hudson Inc., 500 Fifth Avenue,
New York, New York 10110

Library of Congress Catalog Card Number 86–50517

Printed and bound in Great Britain

Contents

Introduction

When it was decided in 1954 to build the Aswan High Dam, the governments of Egypt and Sudan were confronted with what was immediately recognized as a major problem: economic development, which had become absolutely essential, was jeopardizing the very existence of a large portion of their historical heritage, the sites and monuments of Nubia, in danger of being submerged for ever by the future artificial lake whose length would extend 500 km along the Nile valley, from Aswan in Egypt to the Dal Cataract in Sudan.

Aware of their responsibilities to their contemporaries and to posterity, the two governments immediately took the most urgent measures but soon realized that without substantial international aid they would be hard put to solve the problems, which were becoming more numerous every day.

In 1959, therefore, Egypt and Sudan considered it imperative to submit, independently of one another, an urgent request to Unesco which, under the very terms of its Constitution, is responsible for assuring "the conservation and protection of the world's inheritance" and which alone was capable of mobilizing men and resources throughout the world to safeguard the monuments of Nubia.

This was the first time since its foundation in 1945 that the Organization had received such a request. But the international community, already aware of the universality of art, had gradually become receptive to the novel idea of a common and indivisible heritage to be respected and handed on to posterity at all costs.

It was in this spirit that the Executive Board of Unesco authorized the then Director-General, Mr. Vittorino Veronese, to launch a solemn appeal on 8 March 1960 "to governments, institutions, public and private foundations and all persons of goodwill", requesting technical and financial contributions to save the Nubian monuments and sites from certain destruction.

The appeal was a milestone in Unesco's history: it ushered in the International Campaign to Save the Monuments of Nubia, which was to last for 20 years, ending on 10 March 1980 as a complete and spectacular success.

This work retraces those 20 years of close co-operation between the Organization and contributing Member States, on the one hand, and between the Organization and the Egyptian and Sudanese Governments, on the other, with a view to carrying out properly the excavation work in Nubia and transferring the threatened monuments to safety, especially the temples of Abu Simbel and Philae; the book accordingly recalls, from chapter to chapter, the inevitably hesitant beginnings of this entirely new undertaking, then the more confident advances by all parties concerned, culminating in the final victory, the dogged determination of the Egyptian and Sudanese Governments to save their cultural heritage, the generosity of Member States, the enthusiasm of the experts on their excavation sites, the skill of the engineers and the know-how of the workers.

The importance for Egypt of the building of the Aswan High Dam is generally acknowledged. But people are less aware of the material and financial efforts made by Egypt and Sudan to safeguard their monuments, the work carried out by some 40 archaeological missions sent to Nubia from Africa, America, Asia and Europe, the financial contributions earmarked by several states with a view to saving certain endangered temples, and the voluntary contributions made by some 50 Member States of the Organization to a total of nearly $26 million. The purpose of this book, of course, is to shed light on all aspects of the undertaking, which must be considered as one of the most successful achievements of the international community in a peaceful cause.

Looking back on this campaign, all those involved can, then, be proud of the work that has been achieved thanks to a movement of worldwide solidarity without precedent in the history of mankind. Although Northern Nubia has now lost its previous character and beauty, at least all the remains of the successive civilizations that flourished there have been rescued; the heritage has been preserved and will be handed down to posterity.

With three exceptions (the temple of Gerf Husein, the chapels of Qasr Ibrim and the temple of Abu Oda, of which only fragments could be removed), the monuments were all dismantled or carved up, moved to another site and reassembled in six groups, the first five of which may form the nucleus in Egypt of tourist and even agricultural centres. The sixth has been re-erected in Sudan. The six groups consist of:

1 the temples of Philae island on the island of Agilkia near the former Aswan dam;
2 the temples of Beit el Wali and Kalabsha and the Kiosk of Qertassi near the High Dam;
3 the temples of Dakka, Maharraqa and Wadi es Sebua near the former site of Wadi es Sebua;
4 the temples of Amada and Derr and Pennut's Tomb at Aniba near the former site of Amada;
5 the temples of Abu Simbel *in situ* but 60 m above their original site;
6 the temples of Aksha, Buhen, Semna East and Semna West in the museum garden in Khartoum.

In addition, Egypt donated four temples as tokens of its gratitude (grants in return): Debod to Spain, Taffa to the Netherlands, Dendur to the United States and Ellesiya to Italy.

Egyptian Nubia, which had already been explored and excavated on three occasions, during the building of the old Aswan dam (1898–1902) and each time it was raised (1907–12 and 1929–34), yielded less of spectacular interest than the excavations in Sudanese Nubia (although very important finds were made at Ballana and Qustul in the fortress of Qasr Ibrim); these brought to light a wealth of documents and information of the first order concerning the successive civilizations which flourished in that part of the Nile valley, clarifying and even adding to our knowledge of Nubia's historical past.

As early as 1977 the bibliography published by Unesco listed over 700 books or articles concerning the Nubia Campaign and its results; since then the number has increased considerably, so that we are now in a still better position to appraise the efforts and contributions of all the scholars who responded to the Organization's Appeal (prehistorians, anthropologists, Egyptologists, Coptologists, Arabists and ethnologists) and who became Nubiologists as a matter of course.

Unesco has therefore every reason to rejoice in the material success of its campaign, but it can also consider with satisfaction the moral and intellectual significance of the happy outcome of this large-scale and pioneering undertaking.

The emergence of a dual awareness must first be noted. In our era of widespread industrial and demographic expansion, a country may see fit to incur cultural risks in the interests of economic development. Having carefully assessed those risks, it may find itself unable to face up to them singlehanded. Its only option then is to appeal to international solidarity. In 1959–60, when Egypt and Sudan requested Unesco's assistance in safeguarding the sites and monuments of Nubia, the Executive Board and the General Conference, already convinced of the existence of a common world heritage, had no hesitation in responding to an urgent call for a work of peace founded upon "the intellectual and moral solidarity of mankind".

In our age, for the first time ever, the idea thus gained ground, both in individual states and in the international community, that the works of previous generations scattered throughout the world must be seen as an indivisible whole constituting a single heritage, at a time when each nation, in search of its identity, is engaged in taking stock of the spiritual and material legacy of its historical past.

This first example of international co-operation to an essentially cultural end was not to remain unparalleled in Unesco's history. The Nubia Campaign had aroused public interest and, in view of its successful outcome, other equally justified requests were soon being made to the Organization. In Indonesia, for instance, the Buddhist temple of Borobudur was completely cleaned and restored between 1970 and early 1983 and thorough studies or urgent practical operations were carried out in Venice, the Acropolis in Athens and the ancient urban centre of Moenjodaro in Pakistan. The list of sites for which Unesco's assistance has been requested has been steadily growing and has become considerably longer over the years. Following its experience in Nubia, the Organization has now become the perfect intermediary, assuming a role which it alone can play between nations of different size in the interests of safeguarding endangered works of art, and considers any request submitted to it with added assurance.

The Nubia Campaign unquestionably led to renewed interest, in both Egypt and Sudan, in the artistic or epigraphic vestiges of different civilizations in that part of the Nile valley. In Sudan, all the monuments and documents exhibited in the new Museum of Antiquities in Khartoum and in its garden, as well as the intense archaeological activity under way at present to the south of the Dal Cataract, bear witness to this interest. In Egypt, the government has decided to build a Nubia Museum in Aswan and, more especially, a National Museum of Egyptian Civilization in Cairo covering the entire history of the country from pre-history up to the end of the 19th century. These two projects, for which I made an appeal for international solidarity on 3 March 1982, are currently being executed, and are benefiting from international assistance through the intermediary of Unesco. They are the logical culmination of the Nubia Campaign. It is thrilling to think that the present-day world community, thanks to a movement of solidarity generated by Unesco, mobilized in Nubia resources which, all things considered, can be compared to those used by the sovereigns of Egypt to build the temples of Philae island or Kalabsha, to carve out those of Abu Simbel or to erect the fortress of Buhen. How many centuries separate the quarrymen who hewed the sandstone blocks for Philae in the quarry of Qertassi from the workers who reassembled them on the island of Agilkia or the scribes who solved the architectural problems presented by the sanctuary of Ramses II at Abu Simbel from the engineers who planned and effected the transfer of the monument under a reinforced concrete dome virtually unrivalled on the face of the earth! There is, however, an undeniable continuity here, for what is revealed in each case is a striving after perfection, whether it be to honour a king or gods, or to conserve for those who have inherited them, monuments that bear witness to man's creative genius and to offer them up to the admiration of as many people as possible.

Many sovereigns of Ancient Egypt erected imposing stelae on which they proudly recorded that they had paid tribute to the gods, their ancestors, by having sanctuaries or temples built in their honour. Unesco likewise felt it useful to give an account of its role in that extraordinary adventure which resulted in the safeguarding of the Nubia sites and monuments, and it entrusted preparation of a work on this subject to an eminent Swedish Egyptologist, Professor Torgny Säve-Söderbergh, who was the leader of the Scandinavian mission to Sudanese Nubia in the 1960s and who represented his country on the Executive Committee of the Campaign.

The Nubia Campaign could not have succeeded without Unesco's close co-operation with Egypt and Sudan, on the one hand, and with Member States on the other. I should therefore like to thank all those in the Nile valley, both from Egypt and the Sudan, who took the initiative and assured the smooth working conditions during the entire course of the project. Our gratitude is also due to all the Member States who heeded the two Appeals that Unesco made to the international community on 8 March 1960 and 6 November 1968. The spontaneity of their responses and the generosity of their contributions made it possible to accomplish a task which seemed a very difficult one from the outset.

Initially, valuable assistance was provided by the Committee of Honour, headed by H.M. King Gustav VI Adolph of Sweden, and the Action Committee. Also the effective measures taken by Prince Sadruddin Aga Khan proved extremely helpful.

I am also deeply grateful to the successive members of the Executive Committee of the International Campaign to Save the Monuments of Nubia, an organ of the General Conference chaired for 20 years by Professor Paulo E. de Berrêdo Carneiro. It was the main body responsible for advising my predecessors and myself throughout the Campaign, whose success was celebrated on 10 March 1980 at the inauguration ceremony to mark the completion of the preservation of the Philae monuments.

In conclusion, I wish to take this opportunity to thank all those who worked on the project at many different levels, as experts, archaeologists, engineers, technicians and manual workers, and staff members in the Secretariat who enthusiastically carried out the tasks assigned to them, with a special word for all those who are no longer with us, especially René Maheu, my immediate predecessor, who was the first to mobilize energies under Unesco's auspices and who launched the Appeal to Save the Temples of Philae on 6 November 1968.

Amadou-Mahtar M'Bow

1 Prelude

Nubia – Gateway to Africa

GEOGRAPHY AND LANDSCAPE

Nubia is the part of the Nile Valley which stretches between 18° and 24° N. Its northern limit is immediately south of Aswan in Egypt at the First Cataract, and its southerly boundary is in the Sudan at the district of Debba some 80 km downstream from the Fourth Cataract where the Nile makes a bend northwards, but geographically speaking, the natural boundary is the Fourth Cataract itself; here splintered rocks and torrents dramatically punctuate the open landscape and placid river of the so-called Dongola Reach.

If, however, Nubia is defined as the country inhabited by a Nubian-speaking population, the northern boundary is, and has long been, slightly further north of Aswan in the neighbourhood of the village of Kubaniah. In this area typical Nubian villages can be found, albeit somewhat Egyptianized as a result of the influx of people from the north drawn to Aswan by the industrial development. In the Wadi El Arab, however, about 160 km south of Aswan, there is also an Arabic-speaking population.

Still further north a "new" Nubia has been established at Kom Ombo, where the population of Egyptian Nubia was settled following the inundation of their villages by the High Dam Lake or Lake Nasser as it is also called.

The name "Nubia" appears for the first time in Strabo's Geography to designate a land which the Greeks called Ethiopia. "Nub" (nbw) in the language of the Pharaohs means "gold", and indeed Nubia was formerly a rich source of this precious metal. Whether this is the real origin and explanation of the name of "Nubia" is, however, uncertain. The ancient Egyptians, in Pharaonic times, usually referred to the land as "Ta-seti" (the "Land of the Bow"), or simply as the "Southern Land(s)". First, though, a description of Nubia as it was before the advent of the High Dam.

Nubia is often subdivided: Lower Nubia, reaching up to the Second Cataract, roughly corresponding to Egyptian Nubia, and Upper Nubia, extending further south into the Sudan. Whereas Lower Nubia can be regarded as a homogeneous geographical zone, Upper Nubia consists of several well-defined areas each of very different character. Almost immediately south of the little town of Wadi Halfa just across the political border between Egypt and the

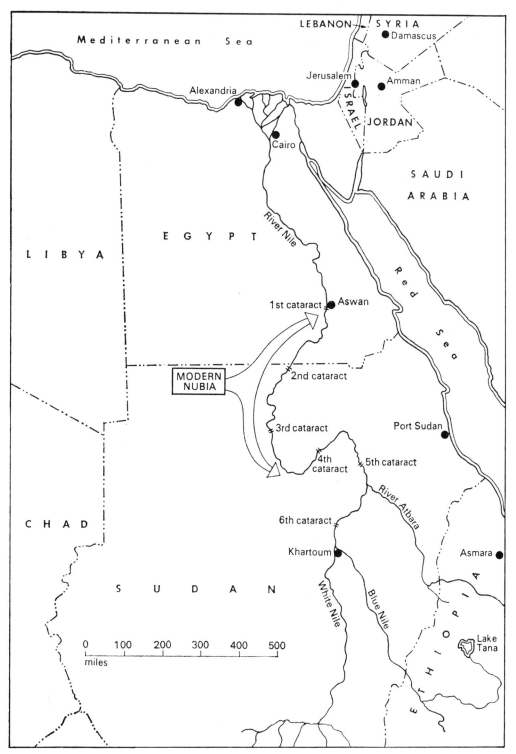

Fig. 1 *Location of modern Nubia.*

Sudan begins the desolate scenery of the so-called "Batn el Hajar", the "Belly of Rocks", where the Nile in breaking through a barrier of black igneous rockbeds, fragments into a labyrinth of tumbling waters and islets. This type of landscape continues upstream to the Dal Cataract where the more open Abri-Delgo Reach begins, with sandy plains opening between the rocks. Its southern boundary is the rocky barrier of the Third Cataract; thereafter the valley broadens into a featureless plain as it traverses the extensive area of Dongola Reach to the Fourth Cataract.

Most parts of Nubia were affected by the dramatic events of the 20 years following 1960 when the construction of the High Dam at the First Cataract effectively drowned some 500 km of the Nile Valley south of Aswan beneath the waters of the new lake. This was the period when world attention was drawn to the urgent necessity to rescue from destruction the unique monuments and historical remains of an ancient land. The part of the Nile Valley stretching from Lower Nubia in Egypt to the Dal Cataract inside the Sudan thus became the scene of a remarkable international salvage project unique in the history of archaeology.

The construction of the dam at Aswan completed in 1902 and its subsequent raising in 1912 and 1934, followed, later, by the building of the High Dam has transformed the character of the First Cataract. Nowadays it is very different from the Cataract so admired by the fashionable visitors of the 19th century when it formed a continuous stretch of turbulent rapids among an archipelago of rocky islands. Only a small section of the river between the Aswan dam and the town of Aswan remains to give an idea of its former aspect, when it was a natural barrier at the southern boundary of Egypt. Remains of ancient fortresses bear witness to its importance as a defence zone while numerous inscriptions carved on the rocks above the Cataract express the relief felt by the members of Egyptian expeditions on their safe return from arduous and often dangerous journeys in the lands up-river.

Geologically all the cataracts are formed by outcrops of a basement complex of pre-Cambrian age, consisting of hard igneous rocks, mainly granite. Elsewhere the basement complex is overlaid by layers of soft Nubian sandstone through which the Nile flows unhindered, but in the cataract zones the Nile forces its way through faults and fissures, plunging into a labyrinth of gorges and steep rocky islands. It is a landscape of dramatic beauty, fascinating in its wild desolation. The narrow wadis and gorges are filled either by the foaming waters of the Nile or by fine wind-blown sand, its greyness in startling contrast to the coarse yellow sand of the higher surrounding plateau.

Some 50 km south of Aswan the hard rocks surface again to form a narrow passage for the river, the "Kalabsha Gate". Thereafter comes an opening out of the landscape as the river flows placidly through a region of sandstone as far as the Second Cataract in the Sudan. (This is a horizontally stratified continental deposit of Nubian sandstone of Jurassic to Cretaceous age.) The river is now broad and easily navigated, with a floodplain of alluvium which at the river's

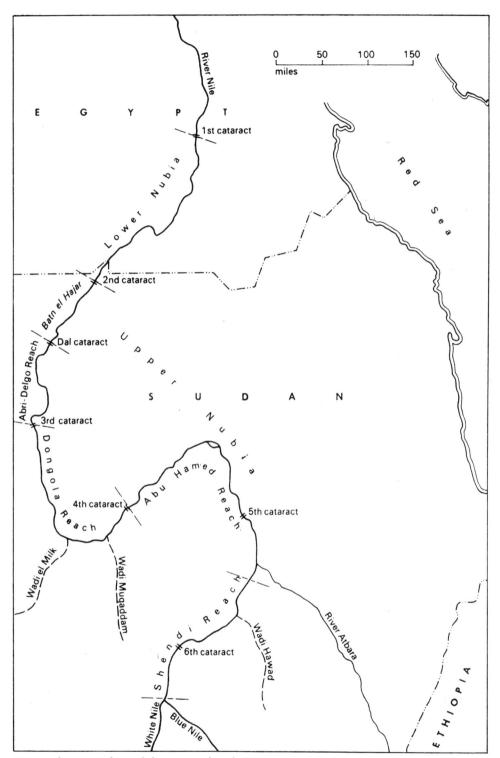

Fig. 2 Physiographic subdivisions of Nubia.

edge supports a strip of cultivated fields and groves of palm trees. In Egyptian Nubia this type of landscape more or less disappeared with the heightening of the Aswan dam in 1934, but further south in the Sudanese districts north of Wadi Halfa it was still preserved in all its natural beauty.

Here and there, especially at the mouths of the desert valleys, were extensive cultivable alluvial deposits. Back from the floodplain is a series of terraces, the lowest consisting of silt deposited in geological and prehistoric times by the Nile, which then flowed on a higher level. The higher are remains of the sandstone layers spared by the river in its process of erosion and especially of its prehistoric tributaries which once formed and filled the desert valleys of our day. The still-higher terraces or platforms are usually capped with layers of harder stone (quartzite or "ironstone") which protected the softer lower layers from erosion. The pyramid-shaped hills that remain are what the geologists call "Inselberg". This landscape of terraces and isolated hills progressively increases in elevation, eventually conforming to an extensive plain covered with sand dunes and pebbles.

From the surrounding heights the fertile floodplain is seen as a narrow green belt of life in a boundless expanse of aridity which in ancient times the inhabitants of the valley regarded as the realm of ghosts and death – but which for the roaming bedouin was a land of freedom and purity.

CLIMATE AND NATURAL RESOURCES

That part of the Nile Valley known as Nubia is, in effect, a narrow oasis in an immense desert which stretches more or less uninterrupted from the Red Sea in the East to the Atlantic in the West, and it is this vast and sterile continental mass that determines the extremes of the Nubian climate.

A few drops of rain may fall very occasionally and, exceptionally, a thunderstorm will bring a short torrential fall with catastrophic effects upon the mudbrick houses of the villages. Otherwise the northern parts of Nubia – Lower Nubia and the Batn el Hajar – are practically rainless. Thus the air is very dry, less than 10% humidity, and this makes the extreme temperatures more bearable.

The average daily summer temperature is about 30–35° C, and the daily maximum is as a rule over 40° C in the shade which is often non-existent. In wintertime (November to March) the average daily temperature falls to 15–20° C, agreeable enough one might think except that at nightfall it drops to near freezing-point while in daylight hours the prevailing north wind may be icy in the shadow of a hill, whereas the sunny leeside may be too hot for comfort. Thus Nubia is a land of extremes, where one may feel tempted to follow the habits of the Nubian workers, huddling over a small fire at dawn and working half-naked in the noonday sun.

The prevailing wind is from the north and is often extremely cold in winter but blows as a cooling breeze in the heat of summer. Sometimes a violent sandstorm erupts, hot as an open furnace. If the wind veers to the south then the heat becomes unbearable, even to Nubians. Generally speaking, the Nubians themselves prefer the heat of summer to the cold spells of winter.

The extreme climate and the geophysical characteristics of the land make Nubia an unproductive country, difficult to live in and capable of supporting only a small population. The natural resources are few and limited.

The deserts surrounding northern Nubia are more or less lifeless except for the narrow cultivable zone bordering the river. A brief flowering of desert shrubs and plants will follow the rare rainstorm and as for animals such as gazelle, foxes, jackals and hyenas, they live in the desert near enough to the cultivation to come down to drink and feed there by night. At some places, especially on the Wadi Allaqi and in the Batn el Hajar, gold, and to a lesser extent copper, mines were exploited in Pharaonic times giving an economic importance to the Nubian desert, but they are long since exhausted with the exception of the Duweishat gold mine in the Batn el Hajar. The desert traffic of camels from Kordofan and Darfur in Central Sudan to the meat markets of Egypt as a rule follows the Darb el Arba'in (the "Road of Forty Days") distant from the valley except at the frontier check points; it was a traffic which brought little revenue to Nubia.

The region of the Batn el Hajar was always very poor with negligible natural resources, apart from fish and the occasional crocodile. Here and there, as at Gemai and Sarras, an irrigated plain among the rocks would yield a crop or two and along the river banks pathetically small plots were cultivated at low water with a few vegetables and tobacco. The small population gained a livelihood from fishing and hunting or from passing trade. In former times of unrest tolls were exacted; early travellers have described how they passed through these parts of the valley in fear of being robbed or held to ransom.

Before the final inundation of the valley, the flora of Lower Nubia was dominated by agriculture and especially by the date palm, although other trees and shrubs grew in the cultivable zone along the river banks and bordering the fields, trees such as *dom* palms, acacias, tamarix and sycamores. They yielded wood for roof timbers, doors and windows, furniture and, of course, boats. However, wood has become a scarce commodity in modern times in contrast to the Pharaonic period when it was even exported from Nubia to Egypt. After 1934 when the agricultural zone was inundated by the Aswan Dam reservoir, these natural resources were of little or no importance in Egyptian Nubia, but for the Sudanese districts immediately south of the border they retained their importance until 1964 when the waters of Lake Nasser began to rise. Even in the richest district, Debeira, the agricultural zone was so constricted and resources so limited as to be insufficient to support the population without external assistance.

Thus Nubia was always a poor country, with few assets, a harsh climate, limited resources and hemmed in by barren deserts. Nevertheless, those outsiders who lived or worked there for shorter periods came to love the indefinable charm of this arid land as well as its inhabitants, whose traditions and remarkable social organization will be described in a later chapter.

The Nubians themselves, when forced to leave their beloved country, resisted their fate with all possible means; to this day they hold fast to the hope of abandoning the richer and in some respects more promising resettlement areas to which they were sent and returning to the land of their ancestors.

THE MEETING PLACE OF CULTURES

Since prehistoric times the narrow river valley of the Nile was the only dependable route from the Mediterranean world to Africa, Nubia itself being the point of contact between these two worlds, one the cradle of western civilizations, the other the shadowy continent out of which came many desirable and exotic commodities. For the Pharaonic, Greek, Roman, Byzantine and Arab civilizations Nubia was the "Corridor to Africa", an apt term used by Professor William Y. Adams in his comprehensive and masterly study of Nubian civilization through the millennia, "Nubia, Corridor to Africa".

As the meeting place of civilizations, Nubia was for the historian an invaluable connection between the Mediterranean cultures and those parts of Africa where history can be reconstructed only on the basis of the interrelationships with the north via Nubia, in short a significant link in the chain from the known to the unknown.

Northern Nubia was the constant victim of invasions from north and from south although occasionally, as for example during the centuries of the Christian kingdoms, the "corridor", thanks to its trade, political and cultural strength, developed a rich civilization of its own and was even regarded as one of the great political powers of its time.

For the scholar, this meeting place of cultures, Mediterranean and African, is a fascinating subject for the study of acculturation phenomena, in other words the long-range effects of the close contacts and coexistence of cultures with different backgrounds, technical and political structures. Such contacts sometimes gave rise to peaceful trade, advantageous for all parties involved, or sometimes through military occupation to an annihilation of population, and between these extremes the many possible variants.

The study of such interrelations and acculturation phenomena is all the more interesting in our day when similar problems have become of fundamental importance in the search for a better understanding of the complex interrelationships between the industrialized countries and their developing counterparts in the Third World.

The legacy of Nubia's geographical position as a highway for differing cultures and political powers during thousands of years is one of the most fascinating open air museums in the world, endowed with a wealth of impressive monuments in the shape of Pharaonic temples and fortresses, towns and settlements, Christian churches with galleries of frescoes, and tens of thousands of tombs illustrating the development of the indigenous population over the millennia and how they came to terms with the many invaders and traders from north and south.

What better reason for the scholarly and cultural interest of a whole world to become focused on this barren stretch of the Nile Valley?

The results of the international campaign launched by Unesco in the 1960s have caused much of the history of Nubia to be rewritten and many aspects, formerly unknown, studied in the light of the overwhelming wealth of finds and facts which have emerged.

This new development of Nubian history will be described later; first the main outline of the fascinating history of this border zone between Africa proper and the Mediterranean world should be sketched in as a necessary background to the many problems encountered during the work of salvage.

The main prehistoric development of Nubia from the earliest stone age down to the beginning of historic times around 3000 B.C. was already known before the Nubia Campaign, in particular through the investigations made in the 1930s, especially the basic study by Sandford and Arkell. However, the overall picture has changed so much thanks to recent research both in Nubia and in other parts of the Nile Valley and its surroundings that it seems superfluous to enter upon that stage of the Nubian cultural development here. Suffice it to emphasize that conditions for research are favourable to a rare degree in Nubia and that the deposits tell their story in a way which makes the expert's mouth water. Thus the environmental variations through the millennia can be studied, and the ways in which man adapted his patterns of living to the changing ecological circumstances.

The cultural development of this part of Africa during the end of the prehistoric period and the beginning of history, that is to say the end of the 4th millennium B.C., is far better understood now that Nubian development can be combined with that of the neighbouring zones in the north and, especially, in the south. Here also the picture has changed so fundamentally that a description of our earlier notions would be pointless.

What was known and remains correct is that when Egypt created the first great state in world history, by uniting the Egyptian stretch of the Nile valley into a single political, economic and cultural entity, the Pharaonic culture was born and developed with an unparalleled intensity. The more we learn about this formative stage of the Pharaonic civilization, the more we appreciate its importance in shaping the centuries to come.

There was no similar development in Nubia which remained on a more primitive level, illustrated by a complex of finds which archaeologists term "A-Group". Previously known only in Lower Nubia, A-Group traces have now been found in a far wider area southwards.

This Lower Nubian civilization was by no means negligible, although it cannot compete with that of Early Dynastic Egypt. Its pottery is among the

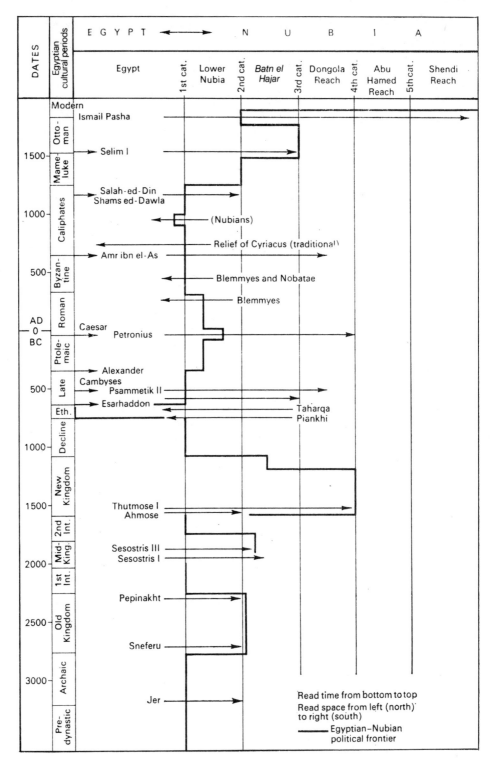

Fig. 3 *Major invasions across the Egyptian–Nubian frontier.*

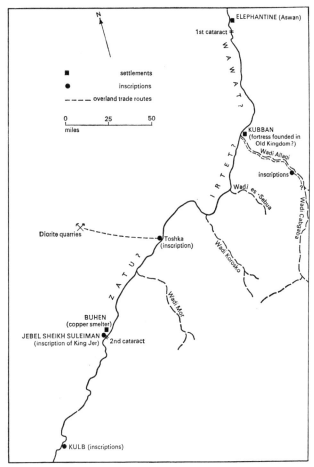

Fig. 4 Lower Nubia showing Egyptian activities in the Old Kingdom.

most perfect ceramic products of the Nile valley. The A-Group enjoyed a lively trade with Egypt to judge from the occurrence of imported goods, in the form of wine and beer jars, and of copper tools and weapons as well as luxury objects of gold. Egypt's imports, on the other hand, were mainly raw materials such as ivory and ebony.

Finds of A-Group type can be dated no later than to the end of the Second Egyptian Dynasty, *c*. 2700 B.C.; the causes of the disappearance of this culture, whether brought about by political, economic or ecological conditions, are unknown as yet.

Egypt's apparently peaceful exploitation of the raw materials of Lower Nubia continued during the Pyramid period of the Fourth and Fifth Dynasties (26th and 25th centuries B.C.), although occasionally warlike conflicts are mentioned in the texts. Thus king Snofru claimed to have captured 7000 Nubians and 110,000 cattle in a single expedition.

Colour plates

I

II

III

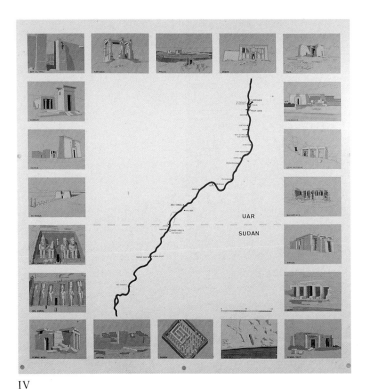

IV

V

VI

VII

VIII

IX

X

XI

XII

XIII

XIV

XV

XVI

XVII

XVIII

XIX

XX

XXI

XXII

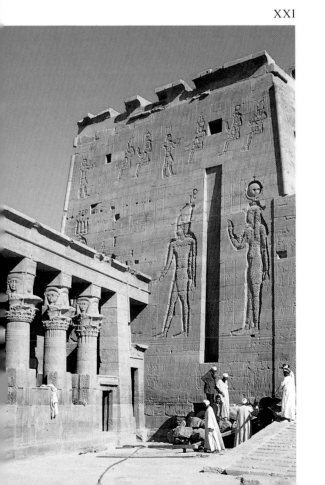

Colour plates

The famous diorite statues from the valley temple of the pyramid of Chephren near modern Cairo were quarried in the desert northwest of Abu Simbel, a quarry which continued to be used by other kings of the Fourth and Fifth Dynasties.

The archaeological enigma is that practically no finds can be related to a Nubian population of this same period. It is only towards the end of the Old Kingdom, in the Sixth Dynasty, that we find the first evidence of a new Nubian civilization, called "C-Group" by the archaeologists. (The so-called "B-Group", at one time assumed to have been contemporary with the Pyramid builders and to have been a poorer successor to the A-Group, has proved to have been non-existent.)

This change in the population of Lower Nubia may well have been a reason for the growing resistance of the Nubians to trade with Egypt which now becomes manifest. The inscriptions preserved at Aswan in which the leaders of the Sixth Dynasty trading expeditions describe their adventures in the south indicate that the Nubians had united to form larger political units and that the Egyptians found it necessary to negotiate with the chieftains of Lower Nubia before they were allowed to pass through to the richer regions further south, to the country called "Iam" in the Egyptian texts, possibly corresponding to the fertile areas of today's Dongola.

One of these expedition leaders, named Herkhuf, who records the growing difficulties in the Nubia trade, in importing ivory, ebony and frankincense, also states that he brought back a pygmy from the south, an acquisition which was much valued by the young king in Memphis.

As a rule there seem not to have been full-scale wars between Egypt and Lower Nubia – the so-called "peaceful Nubians" served in Egypt as a kind of police force – despite the increasing difficulties met by the trading expeditions. King Merenre (c. 2250 B.C.) in a newly discovered inscription on Elephantine tells that he came there in person "in order to slay the chieftains of the foreign countries" and a contemporary text says "The King himself came and stood on top of the mountain and the chieftains of Medja, Irtjet, and Wawat (Lower Nubian districts) kissed the earth and praised him greatly".

But the 94 years' reign of Pepi II, last king of the Sixth Dynasty, seems to have led to increasing difficulties and in his reign an expedition from Aswan led by Pepinakht perpetrated a massacre in Irtjet and Wawat and brought back to Egypt their royal children and nobles as prisoners together with cattle as booty.

Shortly after this episode a weakened Egypt lost its unity and broke up into several spheres of power. Henceforward Nubia could develop undisturbed by its northern neighbour. Yet the Nubians continued to be influenced by the nearby Egyptian civilization and the importing of goods and objects from Egypt persisted. Nubians also served as soldiers in Egypt in the country's internal conflicts; a wonderful model of a Nubian troop, found in a tomb at Asyut, gives a vivid illustration of the armed and disciplined C-Group Nubians of this period.

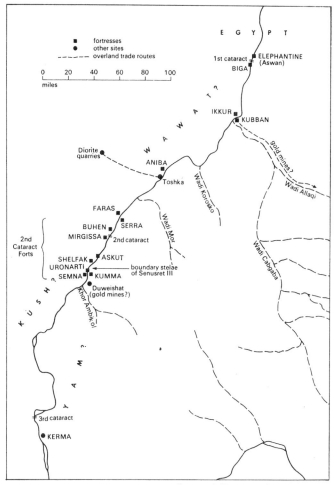

Fig. 5 Egyptian occupation in the Middle Kingdom.

When the Eleventh Dynasty reunited Egypt and restored economic and political stability shortly before 2000 B.C., one result was a series of conflicts in the south, after which Sesostris III of the Twelfth Dynasty subdued Lower Nubia and occupied it with garrisons housed in a number of strong fortresses sited at all strategic points.

The fortresses were located partly in the vicinity of the Nubian population centres in order to maintain control, partly at the entrance of desert wadis leading to the gold mines which were now being exploited on a large scale for the first time, and partly at the new southern frontier along the Second Cataract. In the cataract area a chain of forts culminating in the town and fortress of Buhen formed a defensive system against the Nubian kingdom in Dongola with its capital at Kerma, south of the Third Cataract. The Kerma culture was closely related to that of the C-Group but nevertheless clearly distinguishable from it.

The Egyptian texts tell a clear tale of a purely military occupation and the exploitation of rich gold mines. The reaction of the Nubian population can be seen in the fact that now practically no new Egyptian elements are accepted into their material culture. The C-Group develops along its own lines, building on a purely African cultural tradition.

The Egyptian occupation of Lower Nubia lasted from about 2000 B.C. to just after 1700 B.C. In Egypt foreign rulers, the so-called Hyksos, had gained power and the control of Lower Nubia was lost. In Nubia itself, possibly under the rule of a king from Kerma, a free state was formed which had friendly relations with the Hyksos in northern Egypt, but did not make common cause with them against the Egyptians in Thebes in Upper Egypt, who eventually succeeded in driving the foreign intruders from Egypt. In these battles between the Egyptians from Thebes and the Hyksos rulers in the town of Avaris in the delta far to the north, a Nubian group, the so-called Medja (corresponding to what archaeologists call the "pan grave" people), fought as mercenaries on the Egyptian side.

Freed from Egypt's domination, Nubian aversion to Egyptian culture now disappears and the Nubians, or at least some important elements amongst them, became more and more Egyptianized, to a degree that no longer can one decide with certainty whether a tomb belongs to a Nubian or to an Egyptian immigrant.

This state of affairs continues even after Egypt's re-conquest of Lower Nubia *c*. 1570 B.C. Several of the Middle Kingdom fortresses were restored and reoccupied, growing into towns on which the Egyptian administration was centred. An Egyptian governor, with the title "Royal Son of Kush" (Nubia) was appointed and made directly responsible to the Pharaoh. This official also ruled the southern part of Nubia which through the conquests of the kings Tuthmosis I and Tuthmosis III had come under Egyptian control as far as the town of Napata at Gebel Barkal near the Fourth Cataract. It is likely that Tuthmosis III penetrated even further south, but in principle the southern boundary of the rich Nubian province was at the Fourth Cataract.

Within the Egyptian hierarchy at the disposal of the "Royal Son of Kush", were also Egyptianized Nubian officials; local kinglets were retained, having been educated at the Egyptian court alongside the royal princes.

Lists of tribute and pictorial representations of Nubian goods provide us with a fair knowledge of the economic importance of the province. The most valuable export now was gold, then came cattle, hardwoods and various exotic goods and specialities.

However, apart from the gold production, Lower Nubia diminished in importance assuming more the character of corridor between the territories to the north and south. With the gradual decline of Nubia's economic importance, the centre of interest in the 14th and 13th centuries B.C. shifted further south, to the more fertile region of the Dongola province, where during this period large towns came into being, towns which had no counterparts in the north.

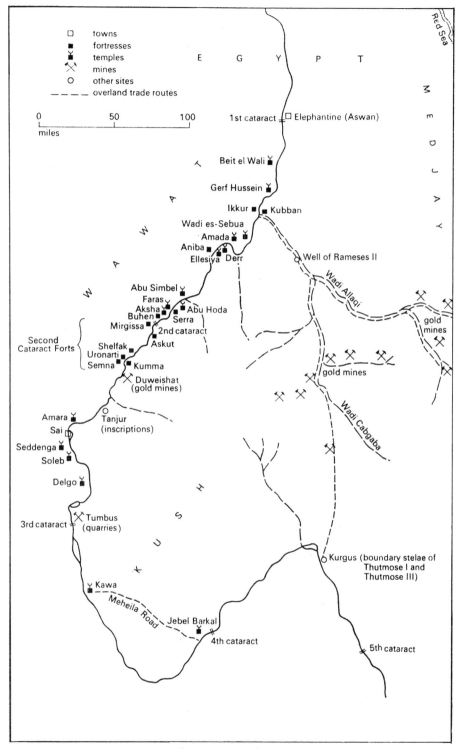

Fig. 6 Egyptian occupation in the New Kingdom.

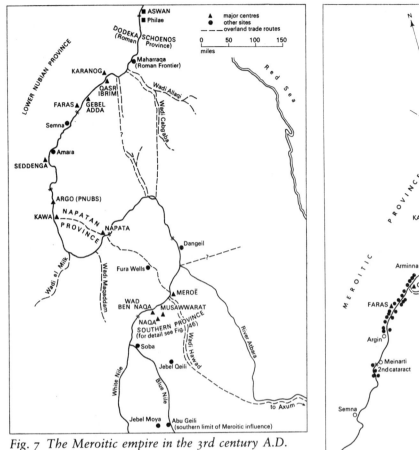

Fig. 7 *The Meroitic empire in the 3rd century A.D.*

Fig. 8 *Lower Nubia in Meroitic and Roman times.*

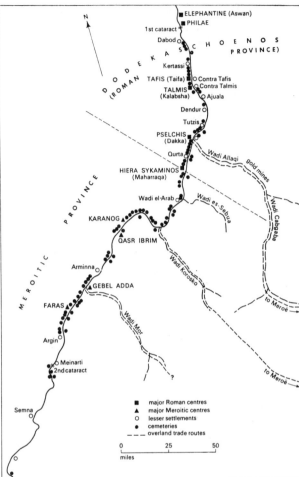

It is true that in the reign of Ramses II a series of imposing temples was built, among them the two rock-cut temples of Abu Simbel, but to judge from the archaeological finds and the small number of cemeteries of Ramesside date in Lower Nubia, this region seems to have been increasingly depopulated. It must be assumed that settlements of some sort near the temples would have existed, necessary adjuncts for the continuance of the cult, but so far investigations have failed to locate any considerable remains of such settlements. Egyptian officials of higher status were probably buried in Egypt, rather than Nubia, but this is not enough to explain the diminishing number of burials of all kinds. There is little doubt that the indigenous population also declined from the 13th century B.C. onwards.

Hardly any archaeological remains from the first millennium B.C. have been found in Lower Nubia, one plausible theory being that the level of the Nile over a number of years was so low that effective irrigation became impossible with the methods then in use.

According to this theory, confirmed during the Nubian campaign, it was only with the introduction of the waterwheel (*saqia*), an invention of Hellenistic times, that Lower Nubia began to recover, and the population to return; typical clay pots (*qadus*) of the kind used for irrigation waterwheels are characteristic finds from the period following the archaeological lacuna.

Lower Nubia was thus a corridor between Egypt and the south, where a kingdom arose in the 8th century B.C. Its capital was Napata at the Fourth Cataract, later removed further south to Meroë, not far north of modern Khartoum.

The kings of Napata conquered Egypt and ruled there for about half a century, until driven out by the Assyrians in 660 B.C. The next contact up-river was when the Pharaoh Psammetik II (595–589 B.C.) of the Twenty-sixth Dynasty made a raid in the south, probably to the neighbourhood of Napata. This was the campaign in which Greek and Carian mercenaries carved their names on the legs of one of the Abu Simbel colossi.

Later, in the 3rd century B.C., friendly relations were established between north and south especially during the reign of the Meroitic king Ergamenes. In the northern part of Lower Nubia, the Ptolemies, the Greek rulers of Egypt from 332–30 B.C., built a series of temples, sometimes in collaboration with the Meroites.

Thus the building of the temple of Dakka was started by King Ergamenes and completed by Ptolemy IV Philopator (221–205 B.C.). Ergamenes was active too in the construction of the earlier temple of Kalabsha. His successor King Azekher-Amun (Adikhlamani) erected the temple of Debod which was later enlarged by Ptolemy VI.

The temples in the northern part of Nubia were probably connected with the yearly pilgrimage to Nubia of the goddess Isis of Philae, which was a complex of temples where the Meroites habitually maintained a delegation.

Ergamenes is said to have had a Greek education and, according to written tradition, Greek scholars lived and worked at the Meroitic court, where a local Meroitic script was now introduced.

Following the Roman conquest of Egypt (30 B.C.) the Meroites attacked and sacked Philae and Aswan. In triumph they carried home statues of the Emperor Augustus erected at the Roman boundary; one such statue was in fact discovered by archaeologists at Meroë, buried beneath a pavement.

A Roman punitive expedition under the general Petronius sacked the city of Napata in 25 B.C. but the Meroitic queen, the "kandake", retaliated, advancing as far north as the Roman fortress of Primis (Qasr Ibrim) in the heart of Lower Nubia. The frontier between Romans and Meroites was then established further north at Hierasykaminos (Maharraqa), some 110 km south of Aswan. So with the exception of its northernmost part, the whole of Nubia was ruled by the Meroites for about 250 years, a period which produced a rich culture and considerable wealth, reflected also in Lower Nubia, which profited from the transit trade.

About 350 A.D. the Meroitic kingdom drops out of the historical record. It disintegrated in the south, and in losing its political centre, lost control of the northern regions. There a new and aggressive desert population, the Blemmyes, had settled, from the middle of the 3rd century A.D., losing no time in raiding north even as far as Upper Egypt itself. It is a measure of their strength that the Emperor Diocletian (284–305 A.D.) withdrew the Roman frontier to Aswan and, according to later texts, allowed another people, the Nobades, to form a buffer state against the Blemmyes. Both the Blemmyes and Nobades received subsidies from Rome in return for keeping the peace, but in the event failed to fulfil Roman expectations. Indeed around 450 A.D. they made common cause and attacked Philae. They made peace, however, after a punitive expedition in 453 A.D., handing over all prisoners and paying an indemnity. In return they were granted permission to attend the temple festivals of Isis on Philae and, on certain occasions, to borrow the sacred image of the goddess to bestow blessings in their own land.

It was this peace treaty that enabled the temples of Isis on Philae to continue to function as a centre of pagan worship long after the rest of Egypt had been converted to Christianity, and it was not until the years between 535–7 A.D. that the Emperor Justinian closed the pagan temples of Philae. By this time the whole of Nubia had embraced the new faith. An inscription in barbaric Greek in the temple of Kalabsha relates that God gave Silko, the king of the Nobades, a victory over the Blemmyes and after this defeat the Blemmyes seem to have played no further part in Nubian history. Silko's text may well be a testimony to the final triumph of Christianity among the Nobades in Lower Nubia, a conversion which, according to other written sources, occurred officially in the year 543 A.D. The conversion of Makuria, the Nubian kingdom south of Nobadia, situated between the Third and Sixth Cataracts, is said to have been in the year 569 A.D. and in the same year the southernmost kingdom, Alodia, in the neighbourhood of Khartoum, accepted the sign of the cross.

In reality the conversion was a slow process taking maybe a century and the role of King Silko is not clear; his claim to have been the first Christian king is now disputed.

Christian Nubia had lively connections with the north. A rich indigenous civilization based on native traditions mixed with influences from the rest of the Christian and, later, Muslim world, now developed in this part of the Nile valley south of Egypt.

In 640 A.D. the Arabs invaded Egypt and in the following year also attacked Nubia. The fierce resistance of the Nubians both then and during a war 10 years later resulted in a mutually advantageous peace treaty, the famous *baqt*, which continued to be respected for many years.

With the advent of King Merkurios of Makuria and the unification of the two northern kingdoms of Nobadia and Makuria (about 700 A.D.), a new era in the history of Christian Nubia begins. Merkurios' successor Kyriakos, called the "Great King", had no less than 13 kinglets under his command.

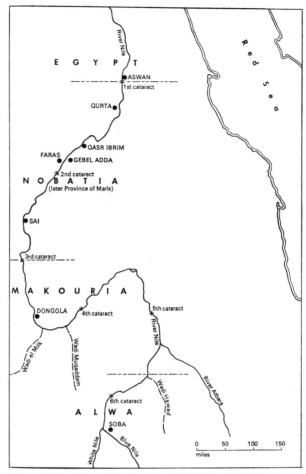

Fig. 9 The three kingdoms of Christian Nubia.

With the accession of the Abbasid Caliphate in 750 A.D. relations deteriorated: problems arose on both sides in fulfilling the terms of the peace treaty; the delivery of wine to Nubia via the monasteries in Egypt ceased and payment of their dues by the Nubians became delicate because of wars with the Bega desert tribes.

Nevertheless, Nubia continued to flourish. Now Alodia in the south joined the union of Nobadia and Makuria and Nubia became one of the great powers of its time; the Nubian Crown Prince Georgios was received with great honour both in Cairo and Baghdad when he visited these capitals to negotiate better terms for a new treaty.

With expanding trade came increased prosperity. The numerous churches in Nubia developed a standardized form, and it is possible to discern a growing urbanization. The relationship between state and church was one of complete harmony, the king being a devout Christian responsible for his moral behaviour to God and to the church. The liturgical and political languages were three – Nubian, Greek and Coptic, while Old Nubian, the ancestor of the modern Nubian tongue, had become a fully acknowledged literary language.

Alodia resumed its independence around the year 940, but this defection does not seem to have weakened Nubia's political strength. Indeed Nubia took advantage of Egypt's weakness when King Kubri ibn Surur in 962 invaded Egypt, penetrating as far north as Akhmim. For nearly a century thereafter the southernmost part of Egypt remained in Nubian hands.

A Muslim minority which had immigrated into Nubia seems to have lived in peace with its Christian neighbours, playing no significant role in political affairs.

The decline of Christian Nubia, which had now become an enclave in an otherwise Muslim world, began in the 12th and 13th centuries. The Nubians intervened in Egypt on behalf of the Fatimids against the conquering Ayyubids, but after an initial success the Ayyubids drove them back and Turan Shah, the brother of Saladin, captured the fortified town of Qasr Ibrim after a short siege in 1171 A.D.

After this event the Ayyubids lived at peace with Nubia for a long period, but Nubia was now threatened instead by tribes of the western desert, the Arabized Demdem and Zagawa, who had converted to Islam. These tribes were a constant danger to Nubia, but the final disruption of the Nubian political system was the result of internal dissension and of conflict with the Mamelukes who had come to power in Egypt.

King David I of Makuria, to which Nobadia still adhered, raided first Aidhab on the Red Sea and then, in 1272–3, Aswan. These adventures provoked a series of retaliatory attacks from Egypt and the consequence was internecine strife in Nubia, in which the Mamelukes intervened from time to time to enthrone or dismiss the Nubian kings.

In 1315, Kerenbes, who seems to have been the last Christian king of Nubia, was imprisoned by the Arabs and replaced by a Muslim, Abdallah ibn Sanbu. The majority of the population embraced Islam, although a Christian minority continued to be tolerated by the Muslim rulers. No longer did Nubia play a political role in Nile affairs and in the centuries that followed it was a more or less deserted land, significant only as a corridor to the more southerly parts of the Nile Valley and Africa.

Alodia in the south was overcome at the beginning of the 16th century by the Fung dynasty coming from the southwest and soon these new conquerors were pushing northwards, as far as Lower Nubia which meanwhile had been seized by the Turks. Selim I had invaded northern Sudan in 1517, and in 1528 Soliman the Magnificent installed a Bosnian garrison in the fortified town of Qasr Ibrim.

Except for this town and a few other centres used as strong points by the Turks, there are practically no archaeological finds from other sites or parts of Nubia which are datable to the long period down to the beginning of the 19th century, when Nubia re-enters history, once again a corridor for the passage of fighting men and the scene of battles between the Anglo–Egyptian forces of the Khedive and the Mahdist power of the Sudan.

The Valley – Gift of the Nile

HYDROLOGY

"Egypt is a gift of the Nile": this statement by Herodotus following his predecessor Hekateus is an apt description of the character of the country. It was the Nile that eroded and formed the valley and it is only thanks to the river and its yearly flood that Egypt became habitable and a cradle of civilization.

Until the industrial development of modern times the population depended almost exclusively on agriculture and in a country which is for all practical purposes rainless the river was and remains the basis for an agrarian way of life.

The annual Nile flood, laden with the silt which fertilizes the fields of Egypt, is the result of the tropical rains that drench the Ethiopian plateau from June to September causing the Blue Nile, Atbara and the Sobat rivers to swell prodigiously. The flow at the peak of the Nile flood is usually some sixteen times the volume obtaining at the lowest level of the river. Thus the annual fluctuation of water in the Nile is on average more than one thousand percent. The White Nile's contribution to the flood is barely one tenth of the volume, the bulk of its water from the equatorial lakes of East Africa being lost in the immense swamps of the "Sudd" region of the Sudan.

According to Pharaonic tradition, the Nile flood should start on 19 July of the Julian Calendar, the moment when the star Sirius or Sothis could be observed for the first time, shortly before sunrise. These two events, regarded as being of vital importance for the welfare of the country, marked the New Year's Day.

Before the modern regulation of the river by dams and barrages the level of the water started to rise at Aswan in the last week of June, reaching its full height at Cairo in September; by April the river had again sunk to its lowest level.

The flood plain of the Nile is not flat but convex with the lowest areas distant from the river, usually near the desert margins. Along the river itself are natural levees constituting the banks of the channel at low water. The alluvial plain is divided by minor levees, partly the remains of older abandoned Nile channels, into a system of natural flood basins which filled with water when the rising river spilled over its banks. Thus in normal years the whole alluvial plain was transformed into an immense lake where the levees or parts of them plus the higher levels of old deposits (the so-called "turtle-backs") and the tells (mounds) consisting of the ruins of earlier dwellings, offered safety for the modern villages perched precariously above the waters of the flood.

THE EARLIEST IRRIGATION

The first peasants of the valley – possibly even as early as about 12,000 B.C. according to the latest investigations – combined agriculture with cattle breeding, fishing and hunting. The river and its flood basins were rich in fish and the present desert areas in prehistoric times were during long intervals a savannah containing all the wildlife nowadays typical of, for example, Kenya and Tanzania. The game could be hunted when the animals came down to the river to drink and feed. Agriculture and cattle breeding were in the beginning presumably only an additional part of the sustenance pattern, but later became all-important when the deserts degenerated into barren areas. Migratory birds, passing through the valley in huge numbers, remained an important resource, and hunting and fishing never ceased to play a role in the life of the valley's inhabitants.

Originally, the peasants presumably lived with their cattle mainly on the levees and planted their crops on the wet soils of the flood basins when the water receded. The basins could be sealed off by simple means through artificial dykes becoming in effect reservoirs. The water was thus retained after the flood and was used for additional crops on adjacent fields.

By constructing a system of dykes and ditches, by deepening the overflow channels and by lifting water manually from residual ponds and channels, the first primitive artificial irrigation began, improving the natural conditions so as to expand the cultivated areas and increase the yield of the fields by several crops a year.

This primitive irrigation system seems to have prevailed during most of the Pharaonic times. Water lifting was done with buckets carried on a shoulder yoke, until the introduction of the *shadūf*, where the bucket is attached to a pole with a counterweight. This technical device, which is capable of lifting for slightly more than 1 m rather small quantities of water adequate for the irrigation of about half an acre, is testified in pictures for the first time in the Amarna period (14th century B.C.).

The next improvement was the *saqiya*, the waterwheel turned by animals, by means of which larger quantities of water could be lifted continuously more than 3 to 8 m, enough to water up to five acres. The waterwheel was introduced in Persian or early Ptolemaic times (4th century B.C.) in Egypt, and in Nubia in the 1st century B.C., where it coincides with the resettlement of the country. It was perhaps the waterwheel that made it possible to start agriculture again after centuries of decay due to low Niles that required a more efficient system to lift the water over the higher river banks.

The next technical device for water lifting was the so-called Archimedes' screw (*tanbūr*) which is efficient only for very low differences of levels, as for example between two garden plots.

44

After this, there was practically no development until the 19th century, when modern technology with low-water canalization, large dams and motor pumps was introduced.

The earlier irrigation technology was very vulnerable and functioned efficiently only when the Nile floods were more or less normal, or, rather, of the height required. The Nile floods are (according to Butzer 1976) "more predictable and reliable than that of any other world river". Nevertheless, the Nile is capricious, and as stated by Vercoutter: "hardly three times out of ten does it deliver the amount of water necessary for cultivation – the other seven, it brings too little or too much" (quoted by Adams, 1977, 35).

The early irrigation technology was quite inadequate to cope with excessive or deficient floods, or with long-term or regularly increasing occurrence of low Niles.

Excessive floods had catastrophic consequences. If the river went out of control through a sudden and sharp rise, its torrential mass of water, surging high over the alluvial plain in the valley, would destroy everything in its path, breaking and demolishing the dykes; villages would be razed to the ground and, if isolated by the sudden rise of water, the inhabitants and their cattle would drown in large numbers. Moreover, the food and seed stock reserved for the next season's planting would also be destroyed, leading to a disastrous lack of food in the year or years following. To construct efficient artificial levels along the main river, and its additional channels such as the Bahr Yusuf in order to hold back the flood water was beyond current engineering capacity, even down to the 19th century A.D.

The catastrophes caused by high Niles have often been described in dramatic terms by the early travellers to Egypt, especially the flood of 1818/19. Even after the modern regulation of the river excessive floods could be cataclysmic; in 1946 an exceptionally high Nile demolished more or less all the villages in the northernmost part of Sudanese Nubia.

Deficient floods or a series of low Niles over a long period were equally fatal. The result as a rule was starvation and destruction of the cattle livestock. In despair the population would be forced to eat the seed stock necessary for the next planting season and, in extreme cases, the consequence would be the depopulation of large districts, or at the very least a sharp diminution of the number of inhabitants – the importation of food was often impossible.

Thus the somewhat primitive irrigation system could not master the capriciousness of the river and the recurrent disasters through excessive or deficient floods led to economic disruption and to the death from starvation of a high percentage of the population. On the other hand it had the cruel advantage of regulating it and the explosion of population which today is the most crucial problem of Egypt, was avoided.

INTRODUCTION OF MODERN IRRIGATION

From all points of view, human, economic and political, the primitive irrigation system had become intolerable and had to be remedied as soon as technical development made it possible.

The introduction of cotton cultivation, which became one of Egypt's main assets, necessitated irrigation all year through which was impossible while based only on the capacity of the flood basins. So Mohamed Ali deepened the old canals and started work on the Nile barrage (el Qanātir el Khairīya) north of Cairo in 1835, an immense construction which was not completed until 1890. By means of this barrage the water level south of the barrage could be heightened so as to feed the main canals of the Delta with a volume of water big enough to make irrigation of the adjacent fields possible throughout the year.

In 1902 a barrage at Asyut was finished through which the Ibrahimiya canal and a large system of canals improved the irrigation of the northern part of Middle Egypt. Similar barrages at Esna (1909) and Nag'Hammadi had the same effects further south.

The most drastic change in the irrigation pattern was, however, the construction of the Aswan dam at the First Cataract. This was a great blessing to Egypt since it cushioned the negative effects of excessive flooding and, particularly, of deficient floods; it also dramatically increased the irrigation potential, especially for the cultivation of cotton in larger areas.

On the other hand, the new dam initiated the doom of Egyptian Nubia as its reservoir gradually drowned the cultivated areas and thereby dealt a fatal blow to the continuation of a normal life for the Nubian population in their country.

The dam was started in 1898 when a huge granite barrage was built just north of the island of Philae, "the Pearl of Egypt" with its impressive Pharaonic temple complex. The length of the dam is about 2 km and in the first stage of its construction was 30 m high with a width at its base of 30 m. This first stage was completed in 1902 by British engineers and its reservoir inundated Lower Nubia up to Wadi es Sebua, about 160 km south of Aswan. It was in its time one of the largest dams in the world, but subsequently was heightened twice, first in 1907–12 by 5 m, and a second time in 1929–34 when it was brought to its maximum height of $41\frac{1}{2}$ m. The surface of the reservoir was now 121 m above sea-level and the flooded area reached the Sudanese border, at times affecting some areas even further south.

The earlier irrigation system was now fundamentally changed. The flood basins were no longer needed as reservoirs and could be cultivated more or less all through the year. As the dam could not, however, store the flood from one year to another, more water than before had to be released northwards during the high flood, bringing a risk of swamping large areas of cultivated land in the Delta, while more than 30 billion cubic metres flowed into the Mediterranean sea each normal year.

In Egypt large new areas could now be cultivated and the additional land yielded up to three harvests a year. The big reservoir also secured a more adequate volume of water in years of low Nile and made possible a more economical use of the available water.

In November the openings in the dam were closed and the stored water in Egyptian Nubia was then successively released from the end of March when a lack of water was beginning to be felt in Egypt. In July, before the arrival of the next flood, as much water as possible was emptied from the reservoir in order to give place for the new flood and Egypt was thus as a rule transformed into a large lake. On the other hand, Nubia had the lowest water in the year; the date palms and the highest fields emerged from the water, though only very restricted areas could be cultivated; also the temples, as will be described later, were again visible during the hot months of summer. When the flood had arrived and the openings in the dam successively closed, the fields, palm trees and temples of Egyptian Nubia again vanished under masses of water.

Egyptian Nubia was thus very largely ruined. The Kenuzi Nubians lost their villages, most of their arable land and the majority of the palm trees which played such a dominant role in their lives, much more than the purely economic considerations.

The Egyptian Government offered them as compensation resettlement north of Aswan, but they firmly refused to leave their country. They built new villages higher up on the desert terraces and lived on in their inundated land. The able men among them went to Egypt and the Sudan to work and earn money in order to send food and other essentials to their wives, children and old people back in Nubia. This strange life and the remarkable social structure it gave rise to will be described later.

Monuments and Sites in Danger

As already described Nubia was for millennia a meeting place of cultures and an important part of the Pharaonic empire, and in Christian times a great power, politically and culturally, so the inundated areas were full of historical monuments and other remains pertaining to different cultures of Mediterranean and African origins.

When the first dam was built at Aswan the Egyptian Government was well aware of the dangers implied for the cultural values of Nubia and did what it could to minimize the losses.

THE TEMPLES

The most famous was the temple complex on the island of Philae, sacred to the goddess Isis and one of the most important shrines for worshippers and tourists in Roman times. The temples on Philae were mostly from the Greco–Roman period, and the temple of Isis was the last pagan temple in Egypt, closed and transformed into a church about 540 A.D. It was situated immediately south of the Aswan dam and was submerged for the greater part of the year. This caused the loss of the once vivid colours on its walls and some of its structures were also damaged. The Christian town which surrounded the temples, being built of mud brick, disappeared totally. The sad fate of the temples of Philae was described and lamented by Pierre Loti, who styled the island as the "pearl of Egypt, a wonder of the world" in his work "La mort de Philae".

From the same period as the Philae temples were the small temples of Debod (15 km south of Aswan), Qertassi and Taffa (45 km), followed by the larger temple of Kalabsha (50 km), built by Augustus to the local god Mandulis. In its vicinity was the temple of Beit el Wali, carved in the rock in the reign of Ramses II (13th century B.C.). Seventy kilometres south of Aswan was the small Dendur temple of Augustus, the rock temple of Ramses at Gerf Husein (87 km), the Dakka temple (106 km) dating from Ptolemaic times, the Roman period temple of Maharraqa (125 km), and at Wadi es Sebua (160 km) a temple of Ramses II.

After the big bend of the Nile at Korosko the Amada temple, the oldest one, built in the reigns of Tuthmosis III and Amenophis II (in the 15th century B.C.), was situated in an exceptionally beautiful landscape, 205 km south of Aswan, and on the opposite, right bank of the Nile, Ramses II had carved the rock temple of Derr. At Ellesiya (228 km) was a rock-cut chapel of Tuthmosis III, just north of the fortified town of Qasr Ibrim, which was one of the most important political centres in Roman times and later.

Finally, at 280 km south of Aswan were the most imposing sanctuaries, the two rock temples of Ramses II at Abu Simbel, followed on the opposite, right bank of the Nile by the small rock-cut chapel of king Horemheb (end of the 14th century B.C.) at Abu Oda, near the other big fortified town of the late period in this part of Lower Nubia on the rock of Gebel Adda.

With a few exceptions, for example the temples of Abu Simbel, all these temples would be submerged during the greater part of the year and exposed to the wearing and chemical effects of the flooding water. The temples therefore had to be consolidated if they were not to collapse into ruins of fallen and eroded stones. Evidently the protective works involved were extensive and the not inconsiderable costs were included in the estimates for the Aswan dam.

The work done was a technical achievement of great efficacy as the buildings resisted more than half a century of submersion and were able to be rescued when threatened with final submersion and being lost for ever in the huge reservoir of the High Dam.

The constructions survived with all their marvellous reliefs and inscriptional records of the past, but the vivid colours, preserved through millennia and still by a miracle possible to admire in the temple of Derr, were largely washed away by the water.

The temples to be submerged were also carefully recorded, especially from an epigraphic point of view, and were published by the Egyptian Antiquities

Service in the series "Temples immergés de la Nubie". Unfortunately, the photographic records of the time were not of a high enough quality for a proper study of details, and the colours extant at the time of the recording could not be reproduced in the publications.

The intentions were, however, laudable and, for example, the technical records and documentation of the works on the island of Philae, especially by Lyons, proved of great value for the final salvage operations during the Nubian campaign sponsored by Unesco more than half a century later.

ARCHAEOLOGICAL SALVAGE CAMPAIGN

"The Archaeological Survey of Lower Nubia has been undertaken by the Egyptian Government in order to discover and record the historical material which would otherwise be lost when the district is submerged by the filling of the new Aswan Reservoir to the level of 113 m above the sea. It is peculiarly fitting that this work should be undertaken by the Egyptian Government, . . . with whose history that of Nubia has been intimately connected since the Old Empire."

With these words G.A. Reisner introduced his first report (of 1909) on the first great Archaeological Survey, rightly styled by H.G. Lyons in the Preface as a formidable task. It explored in detail both banks of the Nile from Shellal, opposite Philae at Aswan, upstream to Wadi es Sebua, a distance of some 160 km. The work lasted four seasons (1907–11) and was directed by Reisner in the first season and then by C.M. Firth.

It was Reisner who established the scientific programme and the archaeological methods. His approach was rigorous: "As the work could never be done again, it was necessary that nothing of importance should be overlooked, either in the finding or in the recording", says Reisner in his report and continues "it was fortunately possible to make reasonably sure of this."

As stressed by Adams (1977, 71) "at that time the challenge of salvage archaeology (i.e. the systematic and non-selective excavation of all sites which are threatened by destruction) was unprecedented" and the methods of Reisner have, to a large extent, been accepted and adopted ever since.

Archaeologists were (and to some extent still are) prejudiced in favour of trying to find objects which are beautiful or interesting museum exhibits. As a result the excavation of tombs tends to have priority over investigations of other sites such as settlements, towns and fortresses, where such objects are less likely to be found. Thus some sites and settlements were left unexplored – although with expressions of regret – by Reisner and Firth, and later archaeologists even during the last Nubian campaign sometimes adopted similar priorities. "As a result, we often seem to know more about how the early Nubians died than how they lived" (Adams 1977).

The first cemetery (No. 7) excavated gave the main outlines of the cultural history of Nubia and after the first survey Reisner and Firth were able to establish the characteristics of the different periods and cultures of Lower Nubia, on the basis of their excavation of some 8000 tombs in 151 cemeteries.

Their work was supplemented by other expeditions to Lower Nubia: University of Pennsylvania (1907–10), Amada, Faras, and Buhen; Oxford University (1910–12), Faras; the German Sieglin Expedition (1910–12), Aniba; and Vienna Academy (1911–12), Toshka, Ermenna.

The next archaeological campaign in Lower Nubia was in connection with the final heightening of the Aswan dam. W.B. Emery and L.P. Kirwan extended the archaeological survey and excavations down to the Sudanese border.

In the years 1929–34 they excavated over 2000 tombs on 76 sites, 2 fortresses (Ikkur and Kuban) and also some settlements and town sites. The tombs, however, still dominated the picture, culminating in the discovery and excavation of the royal tombs at Ballana and Qustul, near the Sudanese border. These very large tumuli contained the burials of local Nubian rulers in the 5th century A.D., with an overwhelming richness of regalia, adornments, weapons, etc., and horses buried with costly silver harnesses.

The salvage operations of 1929–34 also included a renewed German expedition to the Pharaonic Centre at Aniba, while Ugo Monneret de Villard surveyed the literary and archaeological documentation concerning Christian Nubia, which he published in his magnificent work "La Nubia Médioevale".

An exploration of the oldest remains in Lower Nubia and Egypt from palaeolithic times was made by Sandford and Arkell for the Chicago Oriental Institute.

Egyptian Nubia was thus rather well explored before its submersion, but the surveys and the excavations left untouched, intentionally, the higher parts of the valley which at that time were not endangered. The exploration of these higher levels was of course imperative before the final submersion and the results obtained in these areas during the Unesco Campaign in the 1960s proved to be of great importance for our understanding of the cultural history of Nubia and its links with Africa.

The High Dam – A Hope and a Threat

The first Aswan dam had dramatically improved the use of the Nile for irrigation but as the years passed it proved insufficient for Egypt's needs.

A considerable amount of water was wasted, as in an average year some 30 billion cubic metres ran off into the Mediterranean. The negative effects of high floods were not yet fully controlled while low Niles could not be supplemented by means of stored water. Thus the maximum potential of the Nile was by no means exhausted. However, the main factor that led to the decision to change the water situation fundamentally was a population explosion in Egypt.

Before the first dam at Aswan was built Egypt had some 6 million inhabitants (1882), a number which had risen to 9 millions in 1897, to 12.7 millions in 1917, and to 16 millions in 1934, a figure which still left a margin of time and

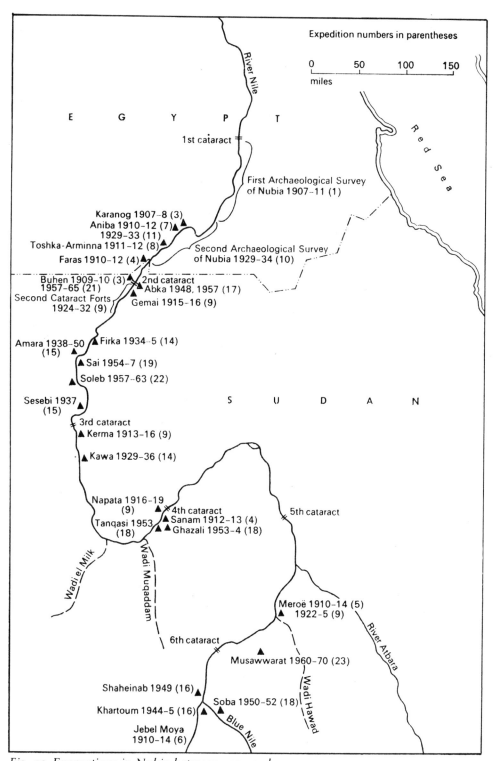

Fig. 10 Excavations in Nubia between 1907 and 1959.

resources for adaptation. But after the Second World War the population increased at a startling rate, partly because of an improved health service with its resulting fall in infant mortality. Efforts to control the burgeoning population through an ambitious family planning programme had only limited success and in any case could lead only to a long-term solution. Moreover, in common with most developing countries of the Third World, Egyptians now had a higher expectation of life. In any event the possibility of a further deterioration in an already very low standard of living was unacceptable, especially after the revolution of 1952.

Demographic statistics showed clearly the necessity for drastic action. In 1947 the population was 20 millions, and by 1961 had risen to 27 millions. Estimates, which later proved correct, showed that by the early 1980s, the population would be some 40 millions and increasing by more than one million each year. The consequent imbalance between the increased population on the one hand and the development of the country's agriculture on the other, resulted in Egypt, long an exporter of food, having in 1960 to import food for the first time.

It was evident that this growing population could no longer live exclusively on agriculture. The imperative need for industrialization could be met only if cheap and plentiful energy was available. The obvious solution was electricity through water power and although some was already generated by the hydro-electric power station at the old dam (constructed 1953–60, it was mainly used for the fertilizer factory at Aswan), a far bigger installation was required and for this a high dam was essential. It should be borne in mind that at this time very little oil had been discovered on Egyptian territory, nor of course was nuclear power available.

The need to make full use of the Nile for a compelling expansion of agriculture and for producing energy for an equally imperative industrialization led to an inevitable conclusion: the feasibility of a high dam had to be investigated.

In 1954 an international committee of experts met to study the problem and they recommended the proposal for a high dam as both feasible and advisable. On this basis the government decided to implement the project.

It was a decision not dictated mainly by political ambitions and to fulfil revolutionary expectations, as has been frequently represented. The reasons were "basically humanitarian" (Keating, 1975) in order to avoid human suffering, starvation and a no longer tolerable dependence on the vagaries of nature and international politics and on external economic pressures. The feeling in the 1950s of a pending catastrophe which had to be avoided explains why Egypt took immense risks in order to be able to build the High Dam, the Sudd el 'Ali.

CONSTRUCTION AND FUNCTIONING

The site chosen for the High Dam was 7 km south of the Aswan dam. The dam as built has a length of 3600 m, a breadth of 980 m at its base and 40 m at its crown. It consists of rockfill, clay and sand with an impermeable screen in the centre, injected down to the rock, about 180 m below the base, and an impermeable covering of the dam face upstream. Its total volume has been calculated to be seventeen times that of the Great Pyramid and to build it about 30,000 men worked round the clock for five years often under extremely hard conditions, especially during summer when the normal daily temperature is around 40°C. in the shade. The immense pit dug for the water inlets to the power station looked in the heat and choking dust, despite the installations of modern ventilation, like an opening to hell.

The dam raises the high water level by 63 m to 180 m above sea level, and the reservoir is a huge lake extending upstream to the Dal Cataract in the Sudan, 500 km long and with an average width of 10 km. The total capacity of the reservoir is 157 billion cubic metres. If a figure of 30 billions is deducted to allow for silting during 500 years (the silting per century amounts to barely 5% of the reservoir's volume), 37 billions as a safety capacity against inundation catastrophes and 10 billions for annual evaporation and infiltration, some 80 billion cubic metres are left to be divided between Egypt and the Sudan, in accordance with special agreements and rules drawn up between the two countries. Compared with the 5 billion cubic metres retained by the old Aswan dam this is a dramatic improvement. Compare also the former average annual flood of some 80 billion cubic metres: of this, 50 billion cubic metres were available for irrigation and 30 billions were let out into the Mediterranean – an amount no longer a wastage but now stored in the lake. With an evaporation factor of about 10 billion cubic metres (Lake Nasser is located in one of the hottest and driest regions on earth) the High Dam leaves a net surplus of 20 billion cubic metres a year as a reserve against low Nile floods.

As a rule the level of Lake Nasser is maintained at 170 m above sea level with normal yearly variations of some 6 m which, however, can rise under extreme conditions to 30 m.

From the outset the High Dam was planned as a generator of electric power and the hydro-electric power station at the eastern end of the dam has a yearly production of 8 billion kwh. With the completion of the power station in 1970 the available output of electricity in Egypt was doubled; modifications to the installation can increase its capacity. Most of the power is used for the country's rapidly developing industry, especially in the Aswan and Cairo regions and in the Delta.

IMPACT OF THE HIGH DAM

From its inception the High Dam Project was the object of much criticism. It was the first large-scale attempt to regulate a major river system and it was always understood that the ecological and environmental effects would be profound. To interfere with any ecologically balanced system always implies great risks and the consequences are often difficult to predict. Some of the more harmful may indeed appear only after some time has elapsed.

Deeper understanding and closer analysis of the complexity and diversity common to all ecological systems have led technical planners to adopt more cautious attitudes towards environmental considerations in latter years. In the 1950s and 1960s large dams were almost obligatory in economic development plans everywhere, but nowadays they are viewed as less acceptable – the heyday of the big dam seems to have passed.

In the case of the High Dam, the Sudd el Ali, the gains are clear enough but the more important losses are difficult to assess in purely economic terms. Nevertheless, and contrary to what is often stated, most of the likely negative effects were foreseen and as far as possible quantified, and were taken into consideration before the Egyptian Government decided to implement the project. Essentially, a balance had been struck.

Even the loss to over 100,000 Nubians of their beloved homeland has been balanced against the fact that the High Dam would provide sustenance for an additional 10 million inhabitants of Egypt, with its overwhelming population problem.

The official estimate of the national gains from the project was as follows:

1 Increasing the present cultivated areas by about 1 million *feddans** and converting 700,000 *feddans* in Upper Egypt from basin to perennial irrigation
2 Guaranteeing water requirements for crops even in years of low flood, improving drainage, and guaranteeing the cultivation of 1 million *feddans* of rice annually
3 Protecting the country against the dangers of high floods, preventing seepage and inundation of small islands and river banks
4 Improving navigation conditions on the Nile
5 Producing electric power annually of about 10,000 million kwh

*one *feddan* = 4,200 square metres

The impact of the output of the hydro-electric station was evaluated by Mansfield (1969, 218) before the installation and distribution network was ready: "The cheap electric power should help Egyptian industry to expand more rapidly and to become more competitive. The improved incomes of the rapidly increasing numbers of industrial workers in the towns should enable them to pay more for the food produced by the *fellahin*, who, at least for a few years, will have substantially more land to cultivate ... it is possible to foresee the creation of a new atmosphere and outlook in the Egyptian countryside."

On the other side of the coin, it cannot be denied that the human and cultural losses have been high. Over 100,000 Nubians lost their homeland and in so doing risked losing their cultural identity when moved to alien tracts – in Egypt to the Kom Ombo region and in the Sudan to Khashm el-Girba in the Kassala region – to strange environments and ways of life.

As for the endangered historical monuments and archaeological sites of Nubia, these have already been described; the losses were minimized as far as was humanly possible through the efforts of the international Unesco Campaign in combination with the indispensable efforts of the Egyptian and Sudanese authorities. Nevertheless, something was inevitably lost. All these are matters which are the main subject of this book and will be described fully in due course.

Meanwhile, what follows is a brief outline of the environmental effects of the High Dam.

The Delta, with its rich alluvium, is the kernel of Egypt's agricultural economy. This is the true "gift of the Nile". Over the millennia the river has shed its silt, estimated at between 50,000 and 100,000 tons annually, extending the land ever further out into the Mediterranean – in short, the natural process of delta formation. The High Dam has reversed the process. No longer does the vitalizing silt pass through the sluices and the water which flows into the canals is clean and fast running. The result has been coastal erosion and a threat to the string of freshwater lakes that border the sea. To halt the sea's encroachment has been for years the preoccupation of an international, multi-disciplinary team of scientists and engineers, and the signs are that the battle is being won. A relevant problem in the coastal region is increased salinity in the soil brought about by a rise in the ground-water level. Since nature's fertilizer, the mineral-rich Nile silt, is no longer available, artificial fertilizer has to be applied to the land in increasing quantities.

Yet another result of the river being cleansed of its silt is the near-extinction of a lucrative sardine fishing industry. The nutrients which feed the plankton which in turn feed the fish stocks are no longer carried into the Mediterranean. However, this loss has been largely offset by the establishment of a considerable fishing industry in the High Dam Lake where the annual volume of fish is expected to approach that of the defunct Mediterranean catch.

The effects of the higher ground-water level, and difficulties in introducing an effective drainage system present a serious problem. The development of drainage has lagged behind and this has resulted in local damage through swamping and the concentration of salts in the cultivated soil. The ancient monuments also suffer from the lack of proper drainage, while salt incrustations threaten their reliefs and decorations with destruction.

A serious health consequence of the new perennial irrigation is the spread of schistosomiasis (bilharzia), a debilitating disease which drains away the energy of its victims. The shallow irrigation channels in which the *fellahin* work are ideal breeding places for a species of snail that is host to a parasite whose larvae emerge in great numbers and bore their way into the human body through the skin. Now the irrigation channels no longer dry out for any part of the year, the scourge of bilharzia has spread, and medical control is extremely difficult. Fortunately bilharzia does not occur in the High Dam Lake and stringent precautions are taken to ensure that it never will.

Finally there is the new and dreaded possibility of earthquakes, especially in the Aswan region; the immense weight and volume of the water contained in the High Dam Lake exerts seismic pressures on the surrounding rock strata, a phenomenon which is closely monitored and studied by seismologists.

To sum up, Egypt's only great natural resource, the Nile, is the mainstay of the country's existence. Faced with the problem of runaway population expansion, no responsible government could have done otherwise than expand industry, develop new sources of energy to drive it, and, above all, grow more food. All these things the High Dam has made possible.

A Doomed Heritage

NUBIAN CULTURE THREATENED

Hassan Dafallah was District Commissioner in Wadi Halfa over the period of the Campaign. His book, "Nubian Exodus", published posthumously, was dedicated thus: "To the Nubians with whom I lived for six years over the crucial period of their emigration and resettlement and to their future generations." It was Hassan Dafallah who was charged with the distressing task of evacuating the 53,000 Nubians of his district, compensating them for their material losses and overcoming their sometimes desperate opposition to the move from their beloved homeland. Of the Nubian character he had this to say:

"In spite of the hardship and poverty of their area, the Nubians are among the most friendly tribes in the Sudan. They are generous and courteous to aliens and foreigners. Guests are treated hospitably and with consideration, and entertained with the best food and drink available. . . . It is also a characteristic of the Nubians that they are clean. They sweep out their dwellings frequently and collect the rubbish in the proper place, where it is burnt; the roads to their villages are also clean. The clothes they wear are always washed, and their children are free from dirt. They are truly fond of cleanliness and domestic order. . . . The Nubians are also famous for their honesty and love of peace. They respect the right of property, and do not trespass or enter the property of others. They do not know stealing or fraud. It is normal for them to fit the wooden bolts to the main gates of their houses on the outside rather than on the inside. Perhaps the real reason why dishonesty has not crept into their society is mainly that they are all related to each other, and no foreign element settled with them."

That description, specifically of the Sudanese Nubians, is valid throughout Nubia. Hassan Dafallah's characterization is echoed in the many publications and descriptions of Nubia and its inhabitants, and his love and esteem for this admirable people was something which was felt by all those who were drawn to Nubia during the Campaign years. Also it should be understood that despite the emotional upheaval forced upon them by the exodus, the Nubians became an essential element in the salvage operation. Indeed, it is true to say that without their able and dedicated assistance the moving of the temples and the archaeological field work would not have been possible.

The outer and visible form of Nubian culture which first struck visitors was the architecture. Their houses, built in adobe, often showed a monumental grandeur and beauty. In the northern districts of the Kenuzi Nubians the dwellings were characterized by vaults and cupolas, skilfully constructed in the ancient Egyptian fashion without scaffolding or supports, and white-washed walls often decorated with geometric patterns in vivid colours. Since all the original villages had been destroyed following the construction of the old Aswan dam this architecture was of recent date; nevertheless, it echoed old traditions, even if they did not go very far back in Nubia itself but presumably had been reintroduced from Egypt. Their creative powers and capacity to adapt old forms to changed conditions are characteristics of the Nubian people.

It was the architecture of northern Nubia, its elements dictated by the lack of wood and complete with cupolas and vaults, that inspired the Egyptian architect Hassan Fathy in his well-known attempt to create in Egypt what he termed an "architecture of the poor", as demonstrated in the "New Qurna" village experiment. That it unfortunately failed was in no way due to the architectural ideas inspired by Nubia!

Further south – among the Fedija and Mahasi Nubians – where palm trees were available, the houses had flat roofs of palm beams and mat coverings of palm leaves. This architecture was not only aesthetically pleasing in its simplicity of volumes and lines and frequent decoration with painted reliefs; it was also well adapted to the harsh Nubian climate. The thick walls of sun-dried brick had only very small openings – they could hardly be called windows – the rooms being ventilated in the main through the roof where the mats let the air percolate. It was a simple yet ingenious arrangement that kept out the heat of summer while retaining the interior warmth through the often bitterly cold nights of winter, where temperatures could fall to near freezing point.

Here too, the houses, skilfully laid out along streets following the natural terraces, or grouped among the rocks, were of recent date, most of the original villages having been destroyed by a disastrous high Nile in 1946.

Among Nubians there was a strong feeling of ethnic unity, based on common cultural traditions and language. The Nubian language, of which the earliest texts occur as early as the 8th century A.D., is an enigma in that it seems not to be related to any other linguistic group. Connections with other languages are restricted to loanwords, and neither Ancient Egyptian, Meroitic or other Sudanese languages belong to the same group as Nubian.

Another strange phenomenon is the distribution of the different dialects or variants of them within the Nubian linguistic family. There are four groups: Kenuzi Nubian in the northernmost part of Lower Nubia, Fedija or Mahasi Nubian south of the Arabic-speaking enclave at the Korosko bend down to and including the third cataract at Delgo, and finally the Dongolawi Nubian in Dongola. The fourth group is the language of the inhabitants of the Nuba Mountains in the western desert, much further south in Southern Kordofan province in the Sudan.

In the Nile Valley the northernmost group, the Kenuzi, speak a language very similar to that of the southernmost one, the Dongolawi, and yet these two groups are separated by the Mahasi Nubians who use a different dialect. How this distribution should be explained is still disputed among scholars and has given rise to fanciful theories. According to the, perhaps, most plausible explanation, proposed by that leading authority of modern Nubian culture, Robert Fernea, the Kenuzi represent emigrants from Dongola who settled near the Egyptian border zone at Aswan where they specialized in the transit trade, as did the Arabic-speaking group further south at Korosko for the transit trade through the desert from Korosko to Wadi Hamid.

The tragedy of the exodus from the Nubian homeland was the greater because of the social role played by two assets which could not be moved – the waterwheel (*saqia*) and the palm trees. They were jointly owned and because of this served as a social bond.

The waterwheels were owned by a number of "shareholders" who retained their shares through generations, even when they no longer lived in the neighbourhood. Thus the joint ownership represented far more than an economic interest; it was a symbol, a tie which held fast even if members of a group were dispersed abroad and could seldom meet.

Similarly the palm trees were jointly owned by groups and, like the *saqias*, kept the groups together. All the women who had tended and watered the trees from the day of planting owned a share of the harvest of dates corresponding to the labour they had contributed. Only the women concerned had knowledge of these shares and their common economic interest thus became another social tie. This social structure explains why the Nubians, for example in the Halfa district, especially Debeira, insisted on taking with them as many as possible of the young palm trees on the long journey to Khashm el-Girba in the Kassala province – a burdensome thing to do and which from a purely economic point of view seemed to make little sense.

That women cooperated in groups was all the more essential as the men even in the richest districts had no option but to emigrate in order to find a living for themselves and the families they had to leave behind in Nubia. Hassan Dafallah describes the destiny of the Nubian women as follows:

"Unfortunately the Nubians were attracted by remote enterprises: they knew they could sell their skills and craft in distant places like Cairo, and even as far away as England. This made it difficult for them to pay regular annual visits to their families, with the result that their wives had to suffer long periods of desertion. . . . Being left to face life alone with her children, the Nubian mother had to shoulder all the domestic responsibilities of her husband. So women cultivated the small plots of land left by their husbands, and supervized the harvest. They saw that their bins were full of wheat and that future supplies were assured. They pollinated the date trees in season, and harvested and marketed their produce. Moreover, they maintained and repaired their houses and looked after the livestock. . . . Nubian women play a considerable part in the social economy. They have a prominent place in society."

The economic necessity for the men to emigrate could have led to the break up of Nubian culture through a gradual transfer of whole families to the Arabic-speaking environments where they earned their living. However, so deep was the attachment of the Nubian to his homeland that to leave it for good was unthinkable. The ties between the villages and common interests were upheld and strengthened by the organization of *gamaᶜiyyas* in the countries abroad where the men worked. The *gamaᶜiyyas* were societies or social clubs which played a key role in maintaining contacts in the urban environment between migrants from the same village (*nog*) or group of villages (*nahia*).

The members of these "clubs" stood by one another in adversity, assisted newcomers from the village to find jobs, and took care of the interests of their fellow members in all problems relating to life and death; it was the club that organized the proper burial rites which assume such importance in Nubian social life. Should a member be accused of theft – a rare occurrence – the club would guarantee the employer of the suspected Nubian against loss and would deal with the case internally without resorting to any external court.

Their close contacts with the Nubian homeland enabled them to use food cooperatives for sending shipments of wheat and other foodstuffs to the villages in Nubia. The clubs were also centres of education and in the 1940s they founded elementary schools back in the villages with money collected from the cities.

According to Robert Fernea, who together with his team has made a detailed study of modern Nubian life, these clubs were a recent phenomenon, the first formal Fedija clubs beginning only in the 1920s. They were a means of preserving old Nubian traditions which in various ways always bound the members of the villages and districts with strong social and economic ties. The development of the clubs is one more proof of Nubian resourcefulness in meeting the demands made by changing conditions of life with methods that held fast to and even strengthened their cultural traditions, while at the same time advancing the interests both of the individual and of the community to which he belonged.

Modern society has much to learn from these methods and from the attitudes of life they reflect in a people whose main assets in a harsh and unproductive environment were cleanliness and honesty, a stability of character made manifest in their aversion to violence of any kind, and a social structure which recognized a truly democratic balance between social groups and between the sexes. The homeland of the Nubians was unusually vital in the upholding of their social and cultural structures.

The destruction of this ancient land of Lower Nubia and the dispersal of its inhabitants was a tragic event in the long, eventful history of the Nile Valley.

THE NUBIAN "OPEN AIR MUSEUM"

As already described, the earlier regulation of the Nile through the construction of the original Aswan dam had been combined with far-sighted efforts to counterbalance any ensuing damaging effects to cultural evidence and history.

The string of Pharaonic temples was consolidated and has survived with little damage the decades of annual submersion. They had, however, received comparatively little attention since, because most of them were submerged during the period of the year when tourism was at its height. This was especially true of the fantastic complex of temples on the island of Philae and the series of Greco–Roman temples in the northernmost part of Lower Nubia.

An earlier series of Ramesside temples was also comparatively unknown to the general public, apart from the miracle of Nubia, the two monumental rock temples of Ramses II, which never ceased to fascinate large groups of visitors when the regular steamer from Aswan to Wadi Halfa stopped at Abu Simbel for a short visit.

Now, in 1960, all these temples of Egyptian Nubia were threatened with final loss, and once more they received attention to evaluate their cultural, historical and aesthetic importance. Even though the submersion in most cases would probably not lead to immediate destruction they would nevertheless vanish under 50 or so metres of water and would disappear irretrievably under successive layers of silt deposited by the river.

In the case of the rock temples of Abu Simbel there was little doubt that their submersion would lead to total collapse when the water reached the soft friable sandstone of the lower parts of the temples.

Not only were the monuments of Pharaonic civilization under threat. The earlier archaeological salvage operations had been unable to cope with the sites on levels higher than those which would be submerged by the reservoir of the old Aswan dam, that is to say over 120 m above sea level; moreover, the towns and settlements had not received the attention they merited. Thus several big centres of the Late Nubian periods, from the 1st century A.D. down to the

Middle Ages, also risked destruction and consequently the loss of valuable information concerning those fascinating chapters of Nubian history when the country was ruled first by Sudanese Meroites, then by a large state with its heartland further south at Gebel Barkal and Meroë, and finally by Christian kings who created a Nubian state which counted among the great political and cultural powers of its time.

Especially, centres such as Qasr Ibrim and Gebel Adda and, further north, Ikhmindi, Taffa, and Sheikh Daûd had much to tell us about this remarkable chapter in African history. Their loss without timely investigation would leave a great gap in the history of Africa.

Otherwise the general cultural development of this part of Nubia was reasonably well known thanks to the earlier investigation of hundreds of cemeteries dating from different periods as well as of Pharaonic fortresses and townsites (Aniba, Kuban, Ikkur, etc.). Even so, large numbers of cemeteries and settlements on higher levels between 120 and 180 m above sea level remained to be examined. Also the prehistory of these parts of Nubia had been no more than outlined and investigations had concentrated on later prehistory. Little was known for instance about the palaeolithic development in Nubia, which in the event proved to be of paramount importance.

In the main, however, and especially when compared with the situation further south in the Sudan, it could be said that the most urgent problems to be dealt with in Egyptian Nubia concerned more the salvage of its temples, and that archaeological investigations there would be involved more with supplementing existing information than establishing entirely new, revolutionary conclusions.

It was, therefore, logical in the ensuing promotional activities to give priority to the salvage of Egyptian Nubia's wonderful collection of monuments, in what came to be known as the "greatest open-air museum in the world", otherwise doomed to be lost for ever beneath the waters of the High Dam Lake.

SUDANESE NUBIA

The problems involved in Sudanese Nubia differed from those of Egyptian Nubia, although here too several temples were endangered; however, their salvage did not present the same difficulties or technical complications.

Of a temple of Ramses II at Aksha, not far from the border between Egypt and the Sudan, only one wall with reliefs of greater interest remained and this could easily be removed. In the fortified town of Buhen where the Second Cataract ends, there were two smallish temples of the Eighteenth Egyptian Dynasty. Finally, two temples of the same period were preserved in the fortresses of Semna East and West, where the difficulty consisted less in their dismantling than in the transporting of them through a lunar landscape of rocks devoid of proper roads and with only the remains of the embankment of an abandoned railway.

In short, compared with the problems involved in the salvaging of the temples in Egyptian Nubia, including such items as the two rock temples of Abu Simbel and the complex of buildings on the island of Philae, the rescuing of the endangered temples of Sudanese Nubia was a minor issue.

It was the archaeological investigation of Sudanese Nubia which was of paramount importance. This part of Nubia was justifiably characterized archaeologically as unknown land in contrast to Egyptian Nubia which had been thoroughly investigated by the previous archaeological surveys of Nubia. However, those surveys had never gone beyond the border, since the Aswan dam reservoir did not then inundate any significant areas of the Sudan.

Various expeditions had excavated in sites of special interest, but theirs were isolated efforts and certainly did not exhaust the potential of any one site, nor did they expose an overall picture of the cultural development of this part of Nubia.

Before the First World War an English expedition directed by Griffith had excavated parts of the town of Faras, just south of the border, and at Serra East, a fortress and town further south. At Faras, during the Nubian campaign, not only was a large number of Pharaonic temples unearthed but a whole cathedral containing over a hundred frescoes which had escaped the attention of the earlier archaeologists. This example indicates how even sites which had been partly excavated could provide exciting surprises on later examination.

The fortified townsite of Buhen (at the northern end of the Second Cataract) had also been surveyed, by another English expedition directed by MacIver and Woolley, and its cemeteries had been at least partly excavated. However, Buhen, too, had much more to give and through the work directed by Professor Emery yielded sensational results during the later campaign, not least an Old Kingdom fortified town just north of the Middle Kingdom fortress.

The fortresses of the Second Cataract from Mirgissa to Semna had also been the object of archaeological investigations but few of them had been thoroughly excavated. Nevertheless, these fortifications were among the most spectacular of the monuments of this part of Nubia.

For the older periods of prehistoric date, Myers' investigations at Abka were important but could not be fully assessed at the time since comparable material was still lacking.

In the same neighbourhood of Abka one could also mention Oric Bates' excavations of cemeteries from various periods, including rich tombs from the so-called X-Group (*c.* 350–550 A.D.), with parallels at Firqa, south of the Second Cataract, where tumuli of the same period had been excavated by Kirwan. With these activities, the more important earlier archaeological expeditions in Sudanese Nubia in the reservoir area of the High Dam have been recalled. However, there were literally thousands of other sites, mainly cemeteries from all periods, but also settlements, towns, fortresses and churches containing frescoes, all more or less unknown or at least not excavated or properly recorded.

The millennial development of this part of the Nile Valley was the more important since here was the link between the known and the unknown, between the Mediterranean civilizations and the Egyptian history and culture on one hand, and the far less understood cultures further south in Africa on the other. Had this link been severed by the destruction of the archaeological sites in the Sudanese sector of the reservoir area, large parts of African history and cultural development would also have been lost to us or at the least very difficult to reconstruct.

Thus the archaeological investigation of the whole area to be inundated was the crucial problem in Sudanese Nubia and it called for a massive and urgent effort on the part of numerous archaeologists, and experts in other disciplines.

2 Launching the International Campaign

The Alarm is Sounded

The first major goal of the revolution of 1952 was to generate an economic and social renaissance of Egypt and one of the means chosen was the project for constructing a High Dam at Aswan. In April 1953 a group of experts had selected the site, 7 km south of Aswan, and already in 1954 it was clear that Lower Nubia and the Nile Valley up to the Dal Cataract would have to be sacrificed. The plans were finalized in 1956 by Egyptian and Soviet experts, and in 1960, on 9 January, the work officially started, to be completed 10 years later.

The Egyptian authorities responsible for ancient monuments and antiquities, the Antiquities Service, was at this time directed by Mr. Mustapha Amer. He communicated his anxiety concerning the monuments to his minister, M. Kamal El-Din Hussein, and as a result a mission of Egyptologists and engineers was sent to Nubia in December 1954. Their report was published in June 1955 and widely distributed. It mentioned a very restricted number of monuments which could be saved (Qertassi and Amada to be removed and some statues at Abu Simbel and Wadi es-Sebua to be cut from the rock) and included an inventory of archaeological sites which should be excavated. This report was sent to scientific institutes all over the world, soliciting urgent cooperation in research and excavation in order to save as much as possible of the endangered sites and monuments. However, the report and the appeal of the Egyptian Government had no great success. Only two foreign expeditions started work in Nubia – in 1958 – the German Archaeological Institute conducting excavations at Amada, and the University of Milan at Ikhmindi, both yielding interesting results but with restricted goals.

The University of Alexandria undertook some investigations at Gebel Adda, an important Late Nubian site not far from the Sudanese border, and the Department of Antiquities extended the successful excavations of Professor Walter B. Emery at Ballana and Qustul with their exceedingly rich royal tombs of the so-called X-Group (c. 350–550 A.D.). The tombs of Ballana were nearly all intact, whereas those of Qustul had been plundered. On the other hand, at Qustul other, earlier cemeteries were located, which later proved to be very rich.

So, even if the initial appeal for world-wide support and cooperation had no great success, it did lead to investigations which showed that the archaeological potential of Egyptian Nubia had by no means been exhausted by the earlier surveys.

Also in 1955 an important study was published by the Antiquities Service – Osman Rostem, "The Salvage of Philae". It stressed on the one hand the danger that this remarkable complex would be lost despite the fact that it was to the north of the proposed High Dam, while on the other it showed a possible method of avoiding the catastrophe by connecting the surrounding islands with dykes to hold back the waters.

An important event for the future of Nubia was the creation with Unesco support of the Documentation and Study Centre for the History of the Art and Civilization of Ancient Egypt in Cairo, in 1955. In November 1954 Mrs. Christiane Desroches-Noblecourt of the Louvre Museum went to Cairo at the request of Unesco and the Egyptian Government to look into the establishment of a Centre intended to document the monuments and antiquities of the Pharaonic civilization, and make available the data to scholars, starting with the documentation of the 400 and more private tombs in the necropolis of Thebes, the ancient capital on the west bank of the Nile opposite Luxor.

The development of the High Dam project made necessary a change of programme and the General Conference of Unesco, at its eighth session held in Montevideo in 1954, was told that the most urgent task for the new Centre would now be to record and document the threatened monuments and sites of Lower Nubia. These should be photographed and the most important monuments, Abu Simbel and Philae, registered by photogrammetry, the architecture analysed and measured by architects, all the scenes on the walls and pillars drawn to scale by designers trained to do archaeological precision drawing, the texts on the walls copied by Egyptologists or by specialists in other ancient languages and tabulated before being card-indexed and, finally, published in easily accessible forms. Thereby, the Nubian antiquities would not be entirely lost, even if the originals could not be rescued.

The then Director-General of Unesco, Dr. Luther Evans, visited Abu Simbel in January 1955 and an agreement between Unesco and the Egyptian Government was signed in the following May. Under its terms the Centre would be created by Egypt while Unesco would give technical assistance in the form of experts and materials. By September 1955, Unesco had sent the first experts and most urgently needed material and the Centre, under the direction of Dr. Ahmed Badawi, an eminent Egyptologist and Rector of Ain Shems University, sent its first field mission to Nubia to work in Abu Simbel.

With the creation of the Centre of Documentation, in which Mrs. Desroches-Noblecourt played throughout an important role both as an expert and an inspiring link between the Egyptian authorities and foreign institutions, several goals had been achieved which became decisive assets to the future salvage campaigns in Nubia.

The Egyptian Government had demonstrated its concern over the safety of the Nubian antiquities and its willingness to make its own contributions in saving as much as possible of scientific value. It had also shown its willingness to collaborate internationally, and specifically with Unesco, to find solutions, and this was done in the charged atmosphere of a tense international political situation which came to its head in 1956.

Unesco in its turn had, through the creation of the Centre, become involved in the fate of the Nubian monuments, an involvement authorized by the General Conference already at its 1954 session. The interest and concern evinced by the Organization was an encouraging pointer to future developments.

In the campaign to save the cultural heritage of Nubia from destruction or oblivion, architectural and epigraphic documentation became a vital element in addition to the salvage of monuments and excavations of sites.

Here the Documentation Centre played a dominant role. In a race with time and in close collaboration with their Egyptian colleagues a number of foreign scholars, covering with their expertise all the different scripts and languages of ancient Nubia – hieroglyphs, hieratic and demotic texts, Coptic, Greek, Latin, Meroitic and Old Nubian – succeeded in documenting all the temples of Egyptian Nubia. There was a similar collaboration in the preparation of the architectural documentation. This collaboration gave the younger and less-experienced epigraphists an opportunity to be trained under the supervision of the best experts, and the Documentation Centre became an important element in the training of Egyptian staff of the Egyptian Antiquities Organization.

The outcome of the activities of the Documentation Centre in Lower Nubia was an archive of thousands of copied texts and complete architectural drawings of the temples. The larger part of these documents have been published by the Centre in its series "Collection Scientifique"; for instance, the temples of Abu Simbel alone are covered by no less than twenty publications such as "The Battle of Kadesh", "Stèle du mariage", "Décret de Ptah", etc., in addition to the two magnificent de luxe volumes on the small temple by Christiane Desroches-Noblecourt and Charles Kuentz. The Centre also published a series of educational "Cahiers" on the most important temples as well as on different aspects of ancient Egyptian civilization.

The programme of the Centre was supplemented by the documentation work done by the archaeological expeditions in their respective concession areas. In the Sudan the temples were documented by archaeological expeditions and by some specialized missions; to mention just one instance of outstanding quality, Professor Ricardo Caminos copied the reliefs and texts of the temples of Buhen and Semna. The documentation of the rock drawings and rock inscriptions was done mostly by a mission directed by Professor Fritz Hintze from the German Democratic Republic. Also the Spanish expedition under Professor Martin Almagro, the Czechoslovak expedition under the late Professor Zbyněk Žába, the Soviet mission under Professor Boris Piotrovski and the Scandinavian Joint Expedition to Sudanese Nubia documented and published large numbers of rock drawings and rock inscriptions in their concession areas in combination with their other archaeological field work; and other expeditions also made their contributions.

Many of the most important rock drawings and inscriptions were cut out and brought to safety, in Egypt to Wadi es-Sebua and New Kalabsha, for later transfer to the planned Nubia Museum at Aswan, and in the Sudan to the National Museum in Khartoum.

The launching of large schemes and projects often depends on the combined efforts of creative and imaginative personalities who happen to come together at the right moment. Such was the case at the very beginning of the International Nubian Campaign.

In the first years, following the initial appeal of the Egyptian Government for international assistance in the exploration and salvage of Nubia, the situation remained stagnant. Then, in 1958, Dr. Saroite Okacha was appointed Minister of Culture and National Guidance in Egypt. In his book "Ramsès re-couronné" (pp. 3 ff) he described how the threat to the Nubian monuments was brought to his attention by the Director of the Metropolitan Museum of Art, Mr. James Rorimer, and how he decided to visit the scene of the threatening disaster. He was accompanied by Dr. Ahmed Badawi, then head of the Documentation Centre.

Dr. Okacha was deeply moved by this journey which brought home to him vividly the grandeur and cultural significance of the endangered temples: "I am seized by anguish when I think of the scope of the catastrophe and of my responsibility. Created only a few months ago, the young Ministry which I head is surely a symbol of the vitality of our Government and its interest in culture. To destroy such a heritage would be a disgrace to this Ministry and indeed to the Revolution. And what then would be the judgment of history and future centuries?" (*Translated from the French*).

Mrs. Desroches-Noblecourt experienced similar feelings. She too had for a long time been deeply concerned about the fate of the Nubian monuments, and she told Okacha that Mr. René Maheu, Assistant Director-General of Unesco, then on a visit to Addis Ababa, would be the right person to contact.

So these three, Saroite Okacha, René Maheu, and Christiane Desroches-Noblecourt, were brought together in January 1959 in an endeavour to save Nubia, and all three came to play a decisive role in future developments.

Mr. René Maheu arrived at Cairo Airport with a stopover of only four hours, and it was during those hours of the night that Okacha revealed that his only hope of saving the Nubian monuments was through Unesco. Maheu left Cairo convinced and 24 hours later the then Director-General of Unesco, Mr. Vittorino Veronese, called Okacha by telephone to tell him that he, too, had been persuaded and viewed the proposal with enthusiasm, and that he would submit it to the Executive Board of Unesco.

Having received confirmation of Unesco's response, in January 1959, Okacha went on to secure the wholehearted approval of Egypt's President, Gamal Abdel-Nasser.

This chapter of, or rather preamble to, the history of the Nubian Campaign is of more than passing interest from several points of view, but especially because it illustrates the crucial role of personalities endowed with vision and enthusiasm; through Okacha's description we learn – a rare occurrence indeed – details of the arguments they used to persuade others.

First of all, until that time it had been taken for granted that all monuments located within the boundaries of a state were a national concern and to be cared for by the state itself. It was an entirely new concept that they also could be viewed as part of the cultural heritage of mankind and should therefore be of concern to the international community of mankind and thus to Unesco. On the other hand, it was made clear that the state, in this case Egypt, should bear a reasonable part of the burden and should undertake to fulfil all the commitments it would have to make in the Campaign.

An objection sometimes raised, following the launching of the Campaign, was a reaction against protecting the past rather than caring for the present and future. Strange as it may seem, even a renowned archaeologist put forward the argument that Unesco ought to wage a campaign against illiteracy instead of involving itself in the salvage of temples and monuments of the past.

It is noteworthy, too, that at this time and during the initial discussions on the Campaign, the main emphasis was laid on the salvage of monuments. No mention was made at first of the urgent need for the archaeological investigation of the reservoir area to rescue remains indispensable for the understanding of African history, or the necessity and obligation to document and attempt to preserve the modern Nubian culture which likewise was threatened with oblivion.

The Request of Egypt

The ground thus prepared through personal contacts between Saroite Okacha and René Maheu now followed more official procedures.

In a letter dated 23 January 1959 René Maheu repeated the assurance of Unesco's positive attitude. In it he emphasized that the salvage of the Nubian monuments was an undertaking that, "both because of its nature and of the magnitude of the financial resources involved, would largely exceed the usual scale and norms of the assistance which international organizations have so far been able to give to their Member States". He further pointed out the necessity for an official request from the Egyptian Government which should include details regarding the nature of the assistance needed as well as information concerning the efforts to be made by the Egyptian Government itself.

It was regarded as self-evident that the work to be done was far beyond the resources of Egypt, both financially and in the field of expertise.

The official request for an international appeal to be launched by Unesco was contained in a letter dated 6 April 1959. In specifying the nature of the aid required, the coordination of archaeological excavations was now added, as well as the preparation of a photogrammetric map of Nubia. Other items were the documentation of the monuments through the offices of the Documentation Centre, removal of those temples which could be dismantled, and the preservation of rock temples impossible to displace. The details and modalities should be further examined by experts who would also prepare estimates of the likely costs.

The undertakings of the Egyptian Government would entail a financial contribution in addition to the ordinary budget of the Antiquities Service and the Documentation Centre. Funds should be made available from the budget set aside for the construction of the High Dam and these should be used not only for the indemnities to be paid to the Nubians as part of their resettlement but also for the needs of archaeological missions, for example, boats, labourers, etc.

Member States taking an active part in the salvage work would be offered all facilities for archaeological operations in Nubia, which should have first priority, and would also be granted concessions to excavate in Egypt outside the threatened area. The expeditions would be entitled to 50% of all finds for the museums of their respective countries.

The possibility of donating certain temples or other monuments or antiquities in return for foreign aid should be studied further in collaboration with an international committee.

This request thus broadened previous discussions in admitting the necessity for archaeological exploration, nevertheless the international appeal which came later, as well as Unesco's own undertakings, continued to concentrate on the salvage of monuments. However, archaeological investigation came to play an increasingly important role and here, too, international bodies were directly involved in collaboration with Unesco's own efforts. This development is one which will be reviewed later in the book.

Undoubtedly a key factor in the Nubia story was the declaration made at the outset that Egypt was fully prepared to participate in any salvage operations to the utmost of her resources; at no time was the impression given that the responsibility for salvaging the monuments might be shouldered by Unesco and the international community.

The Executive Board of Unesco at its 54th session in June 1959 affirmed its support for the scheme and recommended that a group of experts be sent to Egypt to study further the salvage operation requirements and that a meeting of experts should submit a report to the Board at its next session.

In July 1959 Unesco sent Mr. van der Haagen, head of its Museums Section, together with Mrs. Desroches-Noblecourt, to Cairo. Here they prepared a plan of action in collaboration with Dr. Anwar Shukri (Sub-Secretary of State for Antiquities at the Ministry of Culture) and Mr. (later Dr.) Shehata Adam, who subsequently became head of the office for safeguarding the monuments of Nubia. Their memorandum dated 22 July 1959 recommended the following actions:

– an appeal by the Director-General of Unesco to the Member States and relevant institutions to join forces with the Egyptian Government to save the monuments of Nubia, in particular the two rock temples of Abu Simbel
– a declaration by the Egyptian Government on the nature of the operations and the needs involved, as well as what Egypt could offer as recompense for participation in the Campaign
– a meeting of international experts in October 1959 to establish details of international action to be taken
– aerial photographs of Egyptian Nubia to be made by a Unesco mission to establish up-to-date maps which would facilitate the work of the various missions that would come to Nubia
– an office to be established with special responsibility for the safeguarding of the Nubian monuments.
The memorandum yielded immediate results.

In August, the French Institut Géographique National completed the aerial photography of Egyptian Nubia from Debod to Abu Simbel. The necessary funds were made available by Brazil thanks to its delegate Professor Paulo E. de Berrêdo Carneiro. Since Unesco's foundation Professor Carneiro had played an outstanding role in the work of the Organization, and he now put all his weight behind the project to salvage Nubia.

Also in August, despite the intense summer heat, missions of geologists, engineers and architects were in Nubia to study the many problems likely to arise in the rescue of the monuments.

The Documentation Centre, too, was fully occupied in preparing a priority list of archaeological sites to be excavated, together with a documentation programme and a plan for research into the prehistory of the area under threat.

In October 1959, a meeting of experts was convened in Cairo under the chairmanship of Professor Joe Brew, a prominent American archaeologist and leading protagonist of salvage archaeology. In his opening speech, Egypt's Minister of Culture, Dr. Saroite Okacha, again confirmed the Egyptian Government's undertakings regarding rewards to Member States and institutions participating in the Campaign, and in particular gave assurances that Egypt would award certain Nubian temples to States making the greatest contributions to the Campaign – a committee of experts from the Antiquities Service and the University of Cairo had selected what Okacha called "nouveaux ambassadeurs extraordinaires", the temples of Debod, Taffa, Dendur, Derr and Ellesiya. All this, together with the promise of concessions for archaeological excavations in Egypt, had a stimulating effect both on the meeting in Cairo and in the Campaign which followed.

The committee went on to visit the sites of Egyptian Nubia and debated practical methods of saving the monuments. At their disposal were the reports of the previous expert missions to Nubia, especially those of Coyne and Bellier which proposed constructing protective dams for Abu Simbel and Philae, and of Knetsch who submitted a geological analysis, stressing the dangers of chemical erosion through capillary-fringe-attack and warning of the risks involved in any scheme necessitating pumping. According to his report it was imperative to prevent ground moisture reaching the temples of Abu Simbel as it would sooner or later lead to collapse of the structures. Finally, in his report on methods of saving the temples, Piero Gazzola recommended that no temples should be left in place which could possibly be removed to higher, entirely dry levels. For Abu Simbel he therefore suggested a lifting scheme – a project which will be described in another chapter.

Despite these reservations and warnings the committee of experts recommended a protective dam for Abu Simbel, and for Philae a dam project along the lines suggested by Rostem in 1955. The committee considered it impossible to remove the rock temples of Abu Simbel, as had in fact been proposed by Gazzola. As regards the other temples the Committee recommended their removal to higher levels, also that the documentation work should continue and endangered archaeological sites be excavated.

Finally came the most important of the recommendations: having visited the sites, temples and other remains of successive cultures spanning thousands of years, the experts urged the Director-General of Unesco to launch a world-wide appeal for international cooperation to save the historic, archaeological and artistic inheritance of Nubia, it being part of the cultural heritage of mankind. In November 1959 these ideas and recommendations were adopted by the Executive Board of Unesco at its 55th session.

The Request of Sudan

"In our country, according to the Antiquities Ordinance, every excavator has always been, and is still, entitled to fifty per cent of the objects discovered by him; but this is the only counterpart we can offer. We do not possess important reserves in our museum which we could cede; we have no attractive sites like Sakkara to offer as a favour in return if the finds from an endangered site are insufficient; furthermore we do not have enough temples and chapels in the threatened area to allow some of them to be transported to foreign countries.

"So the only hope that is left to us, after the United Arab Republic's offer, lies in the fact that the prehistory, history and archaeology of the area endangered in our territory are much less known than Egyptian Nubia and for this reason might attract scholars to help us to undertake in the short time available the work of survey, prospection, excavation, removal and documentation, necessary to ensure that at least a part of the history of our country – and thus of the world in general – will be safeguarded for future generations.

"It is because we need considerable aid from abroad to accomplish the above-mentioned work that our Government applies to your Organization in order that they may launch an appeal for financial, technical and scientific participation in the action our Government is planning for this purpose.

"It would be of the utmost help to us if participants would be prepared to undertake – under the general direction of our Antiquities Service – a specific part of the work to be done."

That appeal, signed by the Sudanese Minister of Education, Mr. Ziada Arbab, was dated 24 October 1959 and was considered together with the appeal of the Egyptian Government by the Executive Board at its 55th session.

The background of the Sudanese request has been described by Professor Jean Vercoutter in a personal letter. He was, during the years before the Nubian campaign, Commissioner for Archaeology in the Sudan, and as such was responsible for the care of all monuments, antiquities and archaeological investigations in the biggest country in Africa:

"When I took up the post of Commissioner for Archaeology, in June 1955, well before the Unesco Campaign was officially launched, there was already talk of the possible construction of the High Dam and I became concerned with what was going to happen to the sites threatened by it.

"Early in 1956, I made contact with El Azhari, then President of the new Republic of Sudan, to submit to him my 'Preliminary Report on the Sudanese Monuments and Sites likely to be submerged by the Sudd-el-Ali Scheme'. I had drafted this report in haste, on the model of the 'Report on the Monuments of Nubia . . ., Ministry of Education, Egyptian Antiquities Department, Cairo 1955' which did not, of course, cover monuments on Sudanese territory.

"My intention in submitting my report was to request the President to make official representations to Unesco. El Azhari, an affable, agreeable man, received me most courteously. He heard me out, then concluded the interview by saying 'Don't worry. Sudan will never agree to the construction of the new Aswan Dam.' (A few months later General Ibrahim Abboud became President and one of his first acts was to agree to the construction of the Dam.)

"The result is that during the presidency of El Azhari and in the early days of that of Abboud – who had things other than antiquities on his mind – I was in an awkward position as it was impossible for me to make official contact with Unesco, by then busy with preparations for the Campaign. I therefore unilaterally redoubled my calls for help in various scientific journals. It was then, too, that of my own accord, I began the 'survey' in the north and commissioned the aerial survey (2000 photographs!) from Kosha to the Egyptian border (1955–7).

"By the time my appeals were heeded, thanks in particular to H.E. Ziada Arbab, the new Minister of Education, it was already very late in the day. As far as the preparatory work for the Campaign was concerned, therefore, Sudan 'jumped on the train just as it was going', so to speak, making a very late start compared with Egypt.

"With the support of Mr. van der Haagen and Mr. Daifuku at Unesco, I secured the assistance of William Y. Adams and then Hans-Åke Nordström and Jan Verwers, who continued the 'mini-survey' which I had begun back in

1955 with my own limited resources, between Faras and Gemai. Even before the Campaign was officially launched, I had managed to get Professor Kazimierz Michalowski to ask for the Faras concession . . . (It was at Faras that Michalowski made the wonderful find, among others, of a cathedral fully decorated with mural paintings dating from different periods.) Meanwhile, Emery had established himself at Buhen in 1957 (where he excavated one of the most interesting Pharaonic fortified towns in Nubia).

"At the very beginning of the Campaign, Sudanese government officials were much less sensitive to archaeological problems than the Egyptians, and were mainly concerned with evacuating the Nubians from the region of Wadi Halfa and Batn-el-Hajar. There were exceptions, however. For instance, H.E. Ziada Arbab and, particularly, the Director of Education, were extremely helpful. It was thanks to them that by 1958, the project was under way to build a new museum to house the objects discovered during the survey and the salvage operations, and that, in 1960, the first stone was laid. The museum was completed during the Campaign.

"On the spot, Hassan Dafallah, the District Commissioner, actively and efficiently supervized the evacuation of the inhabitants to Khasm-el-Girba, but at the same time he was extremely helpful, even before Unesco's appeal, and certainly afterwards, to the foreign missions working in the Sudan.

"The attitude of the Nubians themselves was bitter. 'We would be better looked after if we were statues', was a remark often heard. On the whole they were all against transferring the antiquities and temples to Khartoum. They would have preferred them to stay where they were, they said, near the new reservoir." (*Translated from the French*).

In the event, it was only thanks to the Nubian workers that the archaeological salvage work in Sudanese Nubia was after all a success. The Nubians themselves, with their profound love of their country, were in fact deeply interested in the history of Nubia and were willing to sacrifice much of their personal interests to assist in the salvage of their cultural heritage.

Unesco's Final Commitment

When the Executive Board met for its 55th Session in 1959 it had been given a series of studies and reports together with the official requests for assistance received from Egypt and the Sudan. Now the time had come for the final commitment.

The debates of the Board which lasted from 27 November to 4 December 1959 resulted in a series of decisions and recommendations through which Unesco officially embarked upon the international campaign to safeguard the sites and monuments of Nubia in danger of destruction. The Board expressed itself as conscious of the loss to the cultural heritage of mankind that would be caused by the submersion of these sites and recalled that "the conservation and protection of . . . works of art and monuments of history and science . . . " is one of the essential tasks laid on Unesco by its Constitution.

The Board therefore decided to grant the Governments of the two countries concerned the assistance asked for. The Director-General would launch an appeal in Unesco's name relating to the assistance to be afforded to Egypt and the Sudan, and take all appropriate steps to secure the widest publicity and maximum effectiveness for the appeal.

Before launching the appeal further steps were taken by the Director-General.

An honorary Committee of Patrons was established under the chairmanship of H.M. King Gustaf VI Adolf of Sweden. Among the prominent members of this committee may be mentioned Their Majesties Queen Elisabeth of Belgium and Queen Frederika of Greece, Their Royal Highnesses Princess Grace of Monaco, Princess – later Queen – Margrethe of Denmark (who took an active part in the archaeological fieldwork of the Scandinavian Joint Expedition to Sudanese Nubia), and H.H. Prince Mikasa, brother of the Japanese Emperor with his intense interest in Near Eastern archaeology. Other members were Mrs. Franklin Roosevelt, the Secretary General of the United Nations, Mr. Dag Hammarskjöld, the ex-Presidents of Italy, Federal Republic of Germany and Colombia, the Vice-Presidents of Poland and India, Mr. André Malraux, French Ministre d'Etat et Chargé des Affaires Culturelles, Sir Julian Huxley, Unesco's first Director-General, and many more notables. Together they represented practically all aspects of, and institutions involved in, official cultural affairs.

The Chairman, H.M. Gustaf VI Adolf, followed the development of the whole campaign with the greatest interest; Dr. Okacha has testified to the significant role played by the King ("Ramsès re-couronné", pp. 95 ff). Sweden was among the first States to contribute substantially in hard currency to the salvage of Abu Simbel.

The Director-General was also authorized to set up an International Action Committee of "eminent persons to assist him in the organization of a world-wide campaign . . . thus to ensure the fullest participation by Member States", as well as to cooperate in the establishment of the Advisory Committee which Egypt proposed to organize. In the meetings of the Action Committee the chairmen of national committees formed by individual Member States to take action at national level also participated.

The two advisory committees for Egypt and the Sudan, the Consultative Committee established by the Egyptian Government, and the Panel of Experts organized by the Sudanese Government, did not meet until after the official launching of the Campaign on 8 March 1960.

Finally, Unesco's Executive Board allocated $126,000 for (a) the preliminary studies on the salvage of Abu Simbel ($110,000), and (b) sending two archaeological experts to Sudanese Nubia in order to examine the problems involved there ($16,000). One of them was Dr. William Y. Adams from the USA who had special instructions to analyse aerial photographs of the reservoir area in the Sudan. The other was H.A. Nordström from Sweden. In time both became eminent figures in Nubian archaeology although they had little knowledge to start with of the special problems of Sudanese Nubia. The choice showed that scholars in archaeology and anthropology need not necessarily be specialized in the archaeological areas involved, but that basic scholarship and methodological expertise are the more important factors for a successful campaign.

In January 1960, René Maheu, Assistant Director-General, accompanied by Dr. Gamal Mokhtar, paid his first visit to the temples of Abu Simbel, travelling in the private plane that President Gamal Abdel-Nasser had put at his disposal. On his return to Cairo he was received by the President. This was a journey he always remembered with emotion and which he recalled in his last speech to the Executive Committee on his retirement from the post of Director-General in 1974 and shortly before his death.

In February 1960, the Director-General, Mr. Vittorino Veronese, was also received by Gamal Abdel-Nasser in Cairo. The President confirmed his resolve both to build the High Dam and save the historical heritage of Nubia, while Unesco's Director-General assured him of full international cooperation in the planned salvage operations.

The setting up of National Committees in Member States to stimulate interest in the Campaign at governmental level and among the general public was a cardinal step. Essential to the work of these National Committees was reliable documentation and above all the support of the mass media. Working in collaboration with the Egyptian and Sudanese authorities Unesco was able to secure such support from the very beginning.

The Nubian campaign would not have succeeded had it not paid attention to world public opinion. Therefore, already in February 1960, a number of representatives of the mass media were invited to visit Nubia. A charter plane took them from Cairo to Aswan and back, and a Sudanese boat carried them from Aswan to Wadi Halfa and back. Lectures on the history and civilization of Nubia were delivered every evening before dinner; Nubian folk dances were performed on board at Abu Simbel and visits were also made to Nubian villages, particularly in the Aniba region. American, Yugoslav and German diplomats as well as Unesco media officials joined in the trip to all the Nubian archaeological sites and monuments up to Semna in the Sudan.

The echo in the written and broadcast press was great. The photographs displayed later at Unesco's headquarters in Paris during the session of the General Conference in October–November 1960 aroused considerable interest among the delegates and among people outside the Organization, who were attracted both by these treasures and the problems involved in their salvage. Unesco and the Egyptian Government received numerous letters of sympathy, including different proposals on how to save the monuments; many were from school children.

The ground, then, had been well prepared when on 8 March 1960 Unesco's Director-General launched his world appeal.

Appeal by Mr. Vittorino Veronese *Director-General of Unesco*

Work has begun on the great Aswan dam. Within five years, the Middle Valley of the Nile will be turned into a vast lake. Wondrous structures, ranking among the most magnificent on earth, are in danger of disappearing beneath the waters. The dam will bring fertility to huge stretches of desert; but the opening of new fields to the tractors, the provision of new sources of power to future factories threatens to exact a terrible price.

True, when the welfare of suffering human beings is at stake, then, if need be, images of granite and porphyry must be sacrificed unhesitatingly. But no one forced to make such a choice could contemplate without anguish the necessity for making it.

It is not easy to choose between a heritage of the past and the present well-being of a people, living in need in the shadow of one of history's most splendid legacies; it is not easy to choose between temples and crops. I would be sorry for any man called on to make that choice who could do so without a feeling of despair; I would be sorry for any man who, whatever decision he might reach, could bear the responsibility for that decision without a feeling of remorse.

It is not surprising, therefore, that the governments of the United Arab Republic and Sudan have called on an international body, on Unesco, to try to save the threatened monuments. These monuments, the loss of which may be tragically near, do not belong solely to the countries who hold them in trust. The whole world has the right to see them endure. They are part of a common heritage which comprises Socrates' message and the Ajanta frescoes; the walls of Uxmal and Beethoven's symphonies. Treasures of universal value are entitled to universal protection. When a thing of beauty, whose loveliness increases rather than diminishes by being shared, is lost, then all men alike are the losers.

Moreover, it is not merely a question of preserving something which may otherwise be lost; it is a question of bringing to light an as yet undiscovered wealth for the benefit of all. In return for the help the world gives them, the governments of Cairo and Khartoum will open the whole of their countries to archaeological excavation and will allow half of whatever works of art may be unearthed by science or by hazard to go to foreign museums. They will even agree to the transport, stone by stone, of certain monuments of Nubia.

A new era of magnificent enrichment is thus opened in the field of Egyptology. Instead of a world deprived of a part of its wonders, mankind may hope for the revelation of hitherto unknown marvels.

So noble a cause deserves a no less generous response. It is, therefore, with every confidence that I invite governments, institutions, public or private foundations and men of goodwill everywhere to contribute to the success of a task without parallel in history. Services, equipment and money are all needed. There are innumerable ways in which all can help. It is fitting that from a land which throughout the centuries has been the scene of – or the stake in – so many covetous disputes should spring a convincing proof of international solidarity.

"Egypt is a gift of the Nile"; for countless students this was the first Greek phrase which they learnt to translate. May the peoples of the world unite to ensure that the Nile, in becoming a greater source of fertility and power does not bury beneath its waters marvels which we of today have inherited from generations long since vanished. (*Translated from the French*).

The Campaign under way

The appeal was widely publicized, following its distribution to all Member States and to all kinds of governmental and private institutions which might be persuaded to contribute.

The National Committees now had a firmer basis for their promotional activities, having available to them adequate explanatory material in the shape of booklets, pamphlets, slides, films, TV and radio recordings put at their disposal by Unesco and other agencies.

The world's mass media responded splendidly to the spectacular nature of the Campaign throughout the twenty years of its duration. A constant flow of press material, films, TV, and radio documentaries, much of it originating from Unesco and the two countries concerned kept the media alive to the drama as it developed month by month, year by year. Many television and radio companies assigned special teams and correspondents to follow the field of operations in Nubia with the result that the salvage work in all its phases was amply covered and publicized. The extraordinary nature of the campaign and its historical setting, so far removed from their everyday routine, fascinated many of those working in the mass media.

Undoubtedly these efforts of the mass media were fundamental in creating world-wide sympathy for and interest in the Campaign, which in turn encouraged direct contributions by governments and financial backing also for the work of scientific institutions which had shown previously little or no interest in the Nile Valley.

Of similar influence in arousing public interest abroad was the series of international exhibitions sent from Egypt to various Member States. The President of the Republic supported the proposal and the High Council of Antiquities gave its approval. So the exhibition "Five Thousand Years of Egyptian Art" left Egypt for its first destination, Brussels. It opened on 25 March 1959 in the presence of Her Majesty Queen Elizabeth the Queen Mother. A welcome aspect was the opportunity it afforded Dr. Okacha to meet the world press and many leading figures of the intellectual and political worlds who attended it and explain the nature of the Campaign and its conditions. The success of the exhibition prompted other states to ask for it.

During three years it toured the Netherlands, Switzerland, Denmark, Sweden and the Federal Republic of Germany. Everywhere it drew large crowds and the number of visitors was limited only by the time allotted to each country.

In the autumn of 1961 another exhibition, this time of Tutankhamun treasures, went to the United States of America, where it stimulated the interest of the American people in the preservation of the sites and monuments of Nubia. Through the efforts of Unesco and its emissaries – for example Prince Sadruddin Aga Khan – as well as through the work of the United States National Committee with such ardent supporters as Professor Wilson, the US Government was led to adopt a positive attitude. On 7 April 1961 President Kennedy had delivered a message to Congress concerning American participation in the international campaign. His proposals were approved and the United States contributed to the salvage of the temples of Wadi es-Sebua, Beit el Wali and the tomb of Pennut at Aniba as well as to the cost of US archaeological expeditions in Egyptian and Sudanese Nubia. The US contribution for Abu Simbel was not included, nor was that for Philae, which was postponed till 1968, when salvage operations there were scheduled to commence.

The Egyptian exhibitions, particularly those of Tutankhamun, caused wide and sensational publicity for the Nubian Campaign. Sometimes they were sent to countries in response to the requests of Heads of States, who, in some instances, inaugurated them, as was the case in Denmark and France.

The exhibitions were sent abroad with the object of arousing interest in the salvage of the Nubian monuments and at first Egypt and the Campaign received no revenue from them. Later, however, the net income was paid to Egypt to meet expenses for the Campaign and, at a still later stage, it was included in the international contribution to the Nubia Campaign. The sums derived from these exhibitions, especially from those of Tutankhamun, were impressive. In London the net income amounted to $1.6 million and the USSR paid a similar amount to cover the equivalent of entrance fees which do not apply in the USSR. In the USA the Tutankhamun exhibitions yielded still larger sums.

In the final accounts of the international aid for the salvage of Abu Simbel the proceeds from the exhibitions are entered as $1,582,336 (from Canada, France, Japan and Sweden) and the corresponding sum for Philae is $4,571,033 (from Belgium, Norway, Federal Republic of Germany, United Kingdom and USSR) (cf. Annex IV). These sums do not, however, represent the total net income, but only the proceeds which were booked as international aid to these two bigger projects, Abu Simbel and Philae.

A philatelic campaign initiated by Unesco, whereby Member States issued stamps with "Nubian motives", paying part of the revenues (for example first day issues) to the Campaign, proved less lucrative but was nevertheless significant as a promotional factor.

In 1963, in agreement with the Executive Committee, the decision was taken to impose a tourist tax of two dollars on each entrance visa to Egypt, the

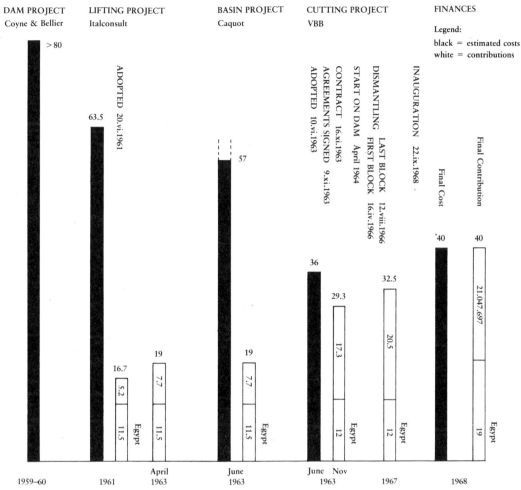

Fig. 11 *The salvage of Abu Simbel. Diagram of estimated costs of different projects (black) in relation to contributions pledged or paid (white). The first very expensive projects brought no substantial contributions; only the adoption of the more realistic cutting scheme resulted in a better balance. Note also the small difference between the first estimate and the final costs, less than 10% in five years. (Cf. Philae, fig. 17, below.)*

intention originally being to raise hard currency for Abu Simbel. Some objections, based on international conventions, had to be overruled by exempting diplomats from the tax. This tax, which was also regarded and calculated as an international contribution, was extremely useful in the financing of the salvage of Abu Simbel and later for the Philae operation and other expenditures of the Egyptian Antiquities Organization.

A Presidential decree of January 1964 authorized the setting up of a special independent fund for financing the Nubian salvage work and it thus became possible to keep all allocations separate from the regular budget of the Egyptian Government.

79

The Organization of the Campaign

UNESCO AND THE GOVERNMENTS OF THE MEMBER STATES

The promotional activities and the world-wide publicity bestowed on the Campaign over its 20-year span aroused lively interest among all Member States of Unesco – rich and poor, industrial and developing countries, East and West, North and South, irrespective of their political systems. The widest possible support of Member States was needed to demonstrate world-wide solidarity – which was achieved, even if with some delays. The interest among the general public and private contributions might have been adequate for more normal needs – the salvage of a smaller monument or some archaeological investigations on a restricted scale.

But when it came to the financing of the great works of salvage, such as those of Abu Simbel, Philae, Kalabsha and Amada and the exhaustive archaeological investigation of the whole reservoir area, solid governmental support became essential – administrative and, especially, financial. Most of the archaeological expeditions working in Nubia were almost entirely financed through government grants, examples being the missions from East Europe and the USSR, and those from the United States of America which drew on a common fund made available by Congress; in the case of the Nordic contribution it was an inter-Scandinavian governmental arrangement.

The securing of the financial guarantees from governments to cover the huge sums of money needed was a matter of great concern to all involved in the Campaign; the waters of the reservoir were rising month by month while the discussions to decide on which methods of safeguarding the temples – Abu Simbel in particular – should be adopted seemed to be interminable. Until decisions were reached no firm financial guarantees would be forthcoming nor could work contracts be placed.

The main financial contributions came from a few industrialized countries, the decisive role, of course, being played by the United States of America, not least because of the active interest of President Kennedy and his successors. But as already stressed the massive participation of all manner of Member States undoubtedly formed a valuable political platform for the decision-makers of the wealthier countries who could argue from the standpoint of universal cultural solidarity of the Member States of Unesco.

A more precise analysis of the impact of different arguments on the decision-makers of the Member States and their motives for a positive response is rather complicated for many reasons. Many of them no longer remember, others have passed away. Official documents are available in an overwhelming quantity, but they only report the acts and official motivations which do not always correspond to realities or cover the whole field.

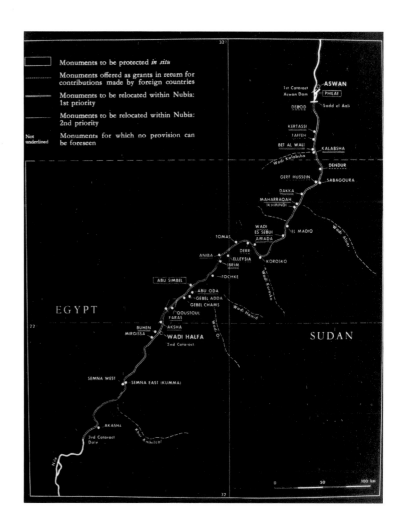

1 Geographical position and status of threatened temples.

2 Decorated Nubian house at Ashkeit, Sudanese Nubia.

3 (Opposite) Queen Nefertari's temple: life-size relief depicting the coronation of the Queen by the goddesses Hathor of Ibeshek (left) and Isis, "the Godmother" (right).

4 Work at Abu Simbel was carried on round the clock.

6 Covering the façade of the Great Temple with sand to protect sculptures during dismantling operations. Protected access tunnel to interior can be seen. In the foreground, cofferdam under construction.

5 Abu Simbel. Sawing the temple façade in blocks for removal.

7 Abu Simbel. Removal of small temple. Protected access tunnel to interior can be seen.

8 The Great Temple cut free from the surrounding cliff. To the left are the colossi of the façade still covered with sand. Two faces have been removed.

9 Abu Simbel, Great Temple. Removal of the face after cutting it free.

10 Abu Simbel. Face of one of the colossi after removal to storage area.

11 Abu Simbel, Great Temple. The protective dome over the reconstructed temple under construction.

12 Abu Simbel, Great Temple. Protective concrete dome nearing completion.

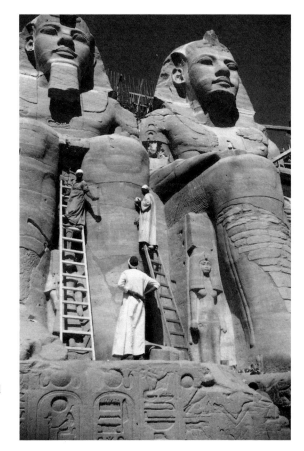

13 Abu Simbel, Great Temple. The final touch – filling the cuts.

14 Triumph – the inauguration of Abu Simbel after salvage.

15 Kalabsha temple interior before salvage operation.

16 The reconstructed temple of Kalabsha on its new site near the High Dam.

17 The Roman Kertassi kiosk moved to its new site alongside Kalabsha temple.

The sense of national responsibility towards international solidarity as a Member State of Unesco was, at least officially, the decisive element, especially perhaps in the case of States that had recently become members or for some other reason wanted to emphasize their ties with and support for Unesco. Solidarity could be strengthened by such factors as the feeling in Ghana of special obligations towards another African State or of India towards another non-aligned country. The thrill of participating in a great adventure far different from the usual more common place problems of political life undoubtedly was often an additional reason for active involvement.

In some cases commercial, diplomatic or other political interests concerning the relations of the Member State with Egypt or the Sudan played a role, but even a close analysis of such relations between the contributors and Egypt and the Sudan, at the time, would hardly reveal the nature of the motives for participating in the Campaign. For example, the United States' first contribution to the rescue of Philae (through a special emissary attached to the Spanish Embassy in Cairo as there were then no official diplomatic relations) was partly motivated by a wish for better relations, although President Kennedy's earlier declaration of solidarity undoubtedly was also a positive factor when the decision was made to contribute.

As to the way of demonstrating this solidarity, there was a choice between making contributions to the salvage of monuments, as for example, Abu Simbel or Philae, or making more individual contributions such as an archaeological expedition or the rescue of frescoes. The latter alternative was more attractive to some States than appearing as just another name in the long list of contributors. Several Member States, for instance, Italy and Sweden, made a substantial contribution to Abu Simbel and, in order to show impartiality towards both countries involved in the Nubia Campaign, also sent an expedition to Sudanese Nubia.

Of importance in this connection were of course the personal interests of the political decision-makers and their consultants or advisers, who were often leading archaeologists or Egyptologists with professional responsibility towards a museum wanting additional exhibits or an institute with specific scientific interests. They would naturally tend to advocate contributions in line with those responsibilities and interests.

THE ATTITUDE OF THE EGYPTIAN AND SUDANESE AUTHORITIES

When Egypt and the Sudan solicited international aid through Unesco it could be taken as a matter of course that they themselves would show a positive attitude towards international cooperation. Unfortunately experience has shown through similar projects that international cooperation cannot be taken for granted. National considerations and chauvinistic attitudes have all too frequently hampered such cooperation. Changes of government have often created difficulties, arising from shifts in policy and changing priorities in internal affairs and finances.

In the case of the Nubian Campaign, there were changes of leaders or governments both in Egypt and the Sudan, there were the political and financial upheavals – national and international – stemming from the wars of 1967 and 1973. Nevertheless the leaders in both countries made manifest their interest in the Campaign on more than one official occasion and their whole-hearted commitment to the cause never flagged. In Egypt it was the support of President Nasser and, later, President Sadat that gave impetus to the national effort. Similarly, the Sudanese leaders from Abbud to Nimeiri always backed the operational requirements of the Campaign and the allocation of national funds, at considerable sacrifice for a developing country with limited resources and political problems, was a remarkable response.

Political differences of opinion were on the whole kept out of the Campaign apart from the occasional effect of, say, a deterioration or even total rupture in diplomatic relations between countries. Compared with the global political history of the twenty years from 1960 to 1980 and the dramatic events of the period, the impact on the development and running of the Campaign was surprisingly small.

The attitude of the leaders concerned could be summed up in the words of President Nasser: "The preservation of the legacy of mankind is no less important than the construction of dams, the erection of factories and the greater prosperity of the people."

Active encouragement was shown likewise by the Ministers of Culture in both countries. Mention of the efforts of Dr. Okacha has already been made but cannot do justice to his influence in the early, decisive years of the Campaign. His example was followed by his successors, especially Dr. Abd El Kader Halem, both as Minister of Culture and Information and as Vice Prime Minister. This was also the case in the Sudan where the first Minister of Education, Mr. Ziada Arbab, was simultaneously active as a delegate of his country in Unesco.

The Egyptian delegations to the meetings at Unesco were led sometimes by the Minister himself but more often by his Secretary of State, assisted by the Head of the Nubia Office and the President of the Egyptian Antiquities Organization. A considerable asset to Egypt was the presence in its delegations of several highly competent personalities skilled in diplomacy, who in their various ways rendered great service to their country and to the Campaign, among them: Dr. Abd El Moneim El Sawi, Dr. Gamal Mokhtar, Dr. Ahmed Kadry and Dr. Shehata Adam.

The Nubia Office and, from 1973, the Egyptian Antiquities Organization benefited greatly from the professional and dedicated collaborators at their disposal, so many that space does not permit mention of individual names here.

In the Sudan the operations were less complicated and less difficult to handle financially, and as a consequence world interest and Unesco's own efforts tended to be less concerned with the development of the Sudanese area of the Campaign; it was a circumstance that sometimes aroused in the Sudanese a sense of receiving less than fair treatment, of unfair bias even.

It should be understood that the situation in the Sudan was very different from that in Egypt. There were no spectacular and costly salvage operations to fire public imagination as there were across the border. Moreover Egypt enjoyed a long, enviable tradition of archaeological discovery and experience in the care and preservation of great monuments of the ancient past. These assets were almost entirely lacking in the Sudan. The Commissioner for Archaeology, a post corresponding to that of Director of the Egyptian Antiquities Department, was in the opening days of the Campaign a Frenchman and well-known Egyptologist, Dr. (later Professor) Jean Vercoutter. He fought hard and skilfully for the Sudanese cause and had accordingly schooled his Sudanese successor, Dr. Thabit Hassan Thabit, who had to shoulder responsibility for the antiquities service of Africa's biggest country with only limited experience to draw on; moreover the number of Sudanese assistants at his disposal were few, the most important among them being his eventual successor, Mohammed Nigmeddin Sharif.

Against daunting odds these two managed to fulfil their responsibilities admirably. They were supported by the several foreign experts put at their disposal, among them in particular the Unesco expert, Dr. William Y. Adams who as the years passed became more and more the trusted adviser and helper among his Sudanese friends and colleagues.

The Sudanese authorities did their utmost to further the Campaign, granting all manner of priorities together with administrative assistance and financial contributions far beyond what could be expected of a country labouring under great financial restraints.

This unfaltering spirit of cooperation and loyal collaboration with Unesco and with the foreign experts and missions as well as with the various international committees created by Unesco and the governments involved – the so-called "spirit of Nubia" – was of fundamental importance to the ultimate triumph of the Campaign.

THE ROLE OF UNESCO

From the outset the role of Unesco was not clearly defined, indeed it could hardly have been otherwise given the constraints within which the Organization must work. However, in May 1960 the Director-General, Vittorino Veronese, convened the International Action Committee to assist him "in the organization of a world-wide campaign designed to ensure contributions in money, services and equipment and thus to ensure the fullest participation by Member States in the international action".

The meeting was chaired by the Director-General himself and the Assistant Director-General, Mr. Jean Thomas, acted as its general secretary. Mr.

Thomas' role was an important one, especially during the first part of the Campaign, as coordinator of the programme and representative of the Director-General.

The Action Committee was of the opinion that Unesco's action should cover the project in its entirety, that is to say, both salvage of monuments and archaeological field work. It recommended that "action in the archaeological field should be carried out with all possible energy", and that "a judicious division of financial effort and operations between the Egyptian and Sudanese parts of Nubia should be assured". Here it should be borne in mind that the salvage operations in Sudanese Nubia were largely concerned with archaeological field operations which will be described in due course; suffice it to say here that they played a minor role in the activities of Unesco headquarters.

The International Action Committee went on to recommend that Unesco should plan the whole programme, draw up an order of priorities and coordinate the work done for both countries. In the course of discussion several members emphasized that Unesco, in collecting large funds for the operations, would assume a heavy responsibility towards donors who would expect guarantees in the disbursement of their contributions. The recommendation that emerged read: "Unesco should not restrict its role to that of intermediary between the two Governments (Egypt and the Sudan) and the rest of the participating countries, and it was desirable that Unesco's responsibility should extend over the whole undertaking until the completion of the operations." The Director-General pointed out that this "would require Unesco to assume a role and duties far beyond those which had been envisaged by the Executive Board". He referred the problem with proposals for other different solutions to the two Governments concerned.

Dr. Okacha's reactions are revealing ("Ramsès re-couronné"p. 63): "After giving the matter a great deal of thought, we decided not to fall in with the opinion of the International Action Committee. However much we respected and admired the Organization, we could not fail in our obligations. . . . It was thus decided that we would continue to direct operations, which would remain entirely our responsibility, while Unesco would act merely as intermediary and adviser. In that way both national authority and the international character of the operation would be kept intact". (*Translated from the French*).

The management of a world-wide campaign such as that of Nubia could never have worked without the involvement of a series of administrative and advisory bodies both in Unesco and in Egypt and the Sudan.

In the summer of 1961, on the authorization of the Executive Board of Unesco, a "Service for the Monuments of Nubia" was formed within the Department of Cultural Activities. The new Service paralleled the Nubia Office in Cairo and the Special Nubia Campaign Bureau within the Sudan Antiquities Service. Its successive directors were often the Director-General's spokesmen at the meetings of committees and other international bodies connected with the Campaign.

In Egypt, Unesco's representative for Nubian affairs from 1960 to 1967, Mr. Louis Christophe, was an Egyptologist able to draw on many years of field excavation and scholarship. A long and profound attachment to Egypt and its people coupled with his memorable verve and enthusiasm made him an invaluable link between Unesco Headquarters in Paris and the Egyptian authorities.

Unesco's growing involvement in other salvage operations similar to that of Nubia resulted in a more efficient handling of the problems involved and clearer concepts of objectives. Thus there evolved more effective ways and means of arriving at the desired goals than were possible in Nubia. Nubia was for Unesco – a tightly structured organization – a move into uncharted waters. That such an outstanding success was achieved was very largely due to the devotion to the cause of the Unesco personnel concerned, that and the inspiration which comes from the feeling of belonging to a winning team.

The importance of the personal commitment of successive Directors General in bringing the Campaign to its successful conclusion cannot be over-emphasized. It was a tradition which began with Vittorino Veronese, as already described. René Maheu, first as Acting Director-General and then as elected Director-General, during his many years of office always manifested his deep involvement, as a skilled administrator coupled with an ardent devotion to the Nubia project. It became in his view one of the outstanding activities of Unesco. He never hesitated to make personal visits to Heads of State, or to send his emissaries in his stead, Prince Sadruddin Aga Khan, for example, whose sagacity and warmth never failed to impress those who had the privilege to meet him or collaborate with him. The Prince's visit to the United States of America at the beginning of the Campaign undoubtedly did much to pave the way for the favourable attitude later adopted by President Kennedy. Professor Paulo E. de Berrêdo Carneiro was another able emissary of the Director-General. René Maheu's example was followed by his successor Amadou-Mahtar M'Bow who immediately demonstrated his intention of continuing along the same lines by chairing the meeting of the Executive Committee in Cairo in February 1975 shortly after his nomination. Director-General M'Bow was able to overcome many a crisis in the latter part of the Campaign and had the great satisfaction of seeing the mission accomplished with the inauguration of the temples of Philae.

THE EXECUTIVE COMMITTEE

The thorny question of Unesco's role in the Campaign was studied by a Working Party at the eleventh session of the General Conference in 1960 and it recommended that Unesco should keep to the role of intermediary. "In order, however, to give the Governments, institutions and individuals taking part in the international action, particularly through financial contributions, the guarantees they were entitled to expect with regard to the allocation and employment of those contributions" the Working Party proposed that the Director-General should marshal an international body to save the monuments of Nubia. Resolution 4.414.2 of the General Conference accordingly authorized him "to set up, in consultation with the International Action Committee, an Executive Committee to advise and comment on the allocation and employment of the moneys collected and on the coordination and execution of the work".

Among the members of this Executive Committee when it was first convened were several archaeologists, M. Almagro, J.O. Brew and Sir Mortimer Wheeler, for example; other Committee members were representatives of the Governments of Egypt and the Sudan. The Consultative Committee of Egypt was represented by its chairman, and the Panel of Experts of the Republic of the Sudan by one of its members. Several other prominent persons sat on this Committee, including Prince Sadruddin Aga Khan, in the capacity of Special Consultant.

The membership and terms of reference of this, the first Executive Committee, were changed by the General Conference at its 12th session, in resolution 4.421.1. §8 (1962). The members were no longer chosen by the Director-General but consisted of persons drawn from 15 Member States elected by the General Conference. No longer would it only be an advisory body assisting the Director-General, but should "issue directions to the Director-General on all questions of a general nature which arise in the course of salvage operations".

Particular attention was drawn to the coordination of the work, the distribution of contributions between the programmes to be carried out in the two countries and the allocation to the two Governments of moneys drawn from the Trust Fund of the Campaign. Henceforward the Executive Committee would be directly responsible to the General Conference and should report to it.

Professor Paulo de Berrêdo Carneiro who had been President of the International Action Committee now became Chairman of the Executive Committee and continued to be so until the triumphant inauguration of the temples of Philae following their transfer to the island of Agilkia. His untiring efforts, diplomatic skill, persuasiveness and tact were matched by the firmness and determination he could exercise when critical situations so demanded. He had a warmth and kindness that made him irresistible. The success of the Campaign was due to him in no small measure.

The members of the Executive Committee were as a rule the permanent representatives of the Member States elected by the General Conference. The Swedish delegate, Professor Säve-Söderbergh, usually was the only one among them who by profession was connected with salvage archaeology and associated problems.

The Executive Committee thus changed from a body of experts and advisers to be a body of official representatives of governments and the Committee's main task now was to ensure that the Campaign and its financial allocations were implemented according to the resolutions of the General Conference and the stipulations of the donors. It is significant that this change was adopted when the Campaign was at a crucial stage, when despite all efforts sufficient funds had not been collected to save Abu Simbel.

By strengthening the guarantees towards the donors and by tying a larger group of Member States to the project through membership of the Executive Committee, the hope was that the Campaign would achieve a greater impact. In as much as the contracts covering the salvage of the Abu Simbel temples were able to be signed on 9 November 1963 on the basis of the contribution of some 17 million dollars from 45 Member States, the move could be considered as successful.

The newly constituted Executive Committee held its first session in December 1962, immediately after the 12th session of Unesco's General Conference. True to its role of guarantor to donors of the proper use of their contributions, the Executive Committee had perforce to follow all operations in detail, drawing on the technical and financial reports prepared by the governments and the international bodies set up by these governments in collaboration with Unesco. On the basis of such reports the Committee issued directives and made recommendations and, most important, authorized payments from the Trust Fund which had been established to receive contributions and other revenues for the operations in Egyptian and Sudanese Nubia.

The payments were mainly, and in the case of larger sums always, issued in accordance with certificates covering payments made to the contractors and receipts in respect of payments made to the consulting engineers, as well as other expenditure recommended by or decided on by the Executive Committee. Promotional activities and fund-raising were other concerns.

Naturally the work of the Executive Committee was not limited to financial operations, it had also to pass judgments on the methods and nature of the operations which gave rise to the expenditure. Thus the Committee was deeply involved in the choice of the major salvage projects of Abu Simbel and Philae.

The decisions of the Executive Committee were during its 29 sessions always unanimous despite the thorny topics and issues which arose from time to time. Of great value here was the fact that the Egyptian and Sudanese governments and their delegations were always loyal in their support of Unesco and thereby to the donor states, which in turn could be confident that the control of the use of allocated funds was in reliable hands, both with regard to expenditure and choice of methods.

INTERNATIONAL GROUPS OF EXPERTS

Such were the complications, diversity and extent of the Nubia operation that the calling into service of groups of specialists was paramount from the beginning. Of a consultative nature, these groups were brought together by Unesco and the governments of Egypt and the Sudan working in collaboration. Their members were drawn from many states and the criterion for selection was specialized expertise. Their reports were at the basis of the decisions and recommendations of the Executive Committee.

First was the Consultative Committee set up in February 1960 to advise on the offers received to undertake an archaeological survey, excavation, documentation and the removal of monuments other than Abu Simbel and Philae. Initially, there were 12 members, among them René Maheu, Assistant Director-General of Unesco, and Fritz Gysin, President of the Consultative Committee of the International Council of Museums. This Consultative body, with its sub-committee which dealt with questions arising between meetings of the full Committee, also had to decide on the grants-in-return to be offered by the Egyptian Government to the countries in recognition of assistance given in safeguarding the Nubian monuments.

Later, the intricate technical problems associated with the salvage of Abu Simbel and Philae, in civil engineering, geology, archaeology and landscaping gave birth to more advisory committees, two for each of these major projects of the campaign.

The first of these, named the Board of Consultants, was created in 1961 by the Egyptian Government in consultation with Unesco. Composed mainly of engineers, the Board's Chairman was Dr. Hassan Zaki, the engineer in charge of the High Dam construction and who was destined to become Egypt's Minister of Irrigation.

The other advisory body, the Group of Archaeologists and Landscaping Architects, was presided over by Professor Kazimierz Michalowski, a leading Polish Egyptologist. A voluntary body, its members – eminent scholars all – were drawn from the USA, Poland, Italy, France, Denmark, the Netherlands and Egypt. Theirs was a pivotal role in the execution of the gigantic and delicate Abu Simbel enterprise. Their discussions, usually held on board the Department of Antiquities boat "Dakka", ranged over such intricacies as the cutting of the reliefs and blocks from the mountain and their re-erection with the same orientation as on the original site, the protection of the façades of the two temples against the abrasive winds by the planting of trees and bushes and the shaping of the artificial hills behind and above the monuments in such a way as to harmonize with the surrounding landscape.

There were several other groups of specialists, such as the Panel of International Experts convened in May 1963 to study the various proposals for the salvaging of Abu Simbel, and the International Group of Experts for the Preservation of the Philae Monuments.

For the operations in Sudanese Nubia, a Panel of Experts was selected by the Sudanese Government in consultation with Unesco, charged with the task of drawing up final plans for the work to be undertaken. Then, in accordance with a resolution of Unesco's 1960 General Conference, the Director-General was authorized to give financial support to a more permanent group of advisers, to be established by the Government of the Sudan and Unesco; the functions of this body would be much the same as those of the Consultative Committee in Egypt. Unfortunately, apart from three meetings (October 1960, February 1962, December 1963) each with different experts, a permanent committee was never established for Sudanese Nubia, despite the protests of those who were especially concerned with this part of the project which had a more scientific emphasis than the spectacular and much publicized salvage of temples in Egypt.

Eventually an international meeting on the archaeological campaign as it applied to Sudanese Nubia was held in Venice in April 1966, in accordance with an Executive Committee resolution made in the preceding September. The main discussion centred on how best to persuade institutions to involve themselves in the archaeological investigation of this southernmost sector of the reservoir area, which was in danger of being neglected and this would have meant the abandonment of any hopes of uncovering evidence leading to a better understanding of the ancient connections between the northern civilizations and Africa further south.

3 The Salvage of Monuments

The Flagship of the Campaign – Abu Simbel

Christmas 1961 at Abu Simbel. A flotilla of tourist boats is moored by the beach fronting the two rock temples of Ramses II and his wife Nefertari. For the visitors it was a memorable occasion and one of them has left this account of the happenings.

"Christmas Eve was a social occasion with the different groups and parties visiting one another. The Nubian crews and servants danced and played their musical instruments – drums, flutes and strings. The visitors were caught up in the Nubian atmosphere and many of them joined in the dancing. The temples were there in the darkness, flooded in the soft radiance of the spotlights used by the Egyptologists in their documentation of the wonderful reliefs. On the beach several bonfires flickered.

Now it is the last hour of night and all of us are assembled in front of the Great Temple, in hushed silence. We are there to witness the moment when the first rays of the sun will fall on Abu Simbel. It is a spectacle described by many travellers a century or more ago. This is the hour when King Ramses the Divine, together with his fellow gods will meet their celestial *alter ego*, the sun, when it rises over the eastern horizon beyond the shining river.

The dimly-seen statues of the king seated before the temple – they are gigantic, all of 20 m high – seem to be awaiting the touch of the rays to bring them to life. The groups of visitors are silent, nobody dreams of disturbing this solemn moment. The guides too are silent, letting the monument speak for itself.

The crest of the mountain turns red, then to gold, and the first shafts of sunlight fall on the temple illuminating the row of baboons carved above the statues and façade, their hands lifted in adoration. The disk of the sun lifts higher and now the heads of the statues are bathed in warm light. It is an awesome sight. From the watching crowd comes a sigh as the silence is broken by the cries of a flight of hoopoe birds soaring from the temple to meet the new day. In triumph the revived sungod leaves the underworld, the realm of the dead. The sky turns crimson as the blood of the slain enemies of the god of light, justice and order. Each morning darkness and death are conquered and a new world is created, a cosmos out of chaos."

A detailed description of these two unique monuments bequeathed to posterity by User-ma-ré (Ramses II) is given in Annex V.

SALVAGE PROJECTS PROPOSED

Between the years 1960 and 1963 when the temples were still standing in their original sites, Abu Simbel experienced a veritable invasion of tourists drawn there by the descriptions of and debates on the fate of the temples, carried in countless articles and broadcasts world-wide. Such was the success of the opening press campaign and, inevitably, it provoked a flood of suggestions from experts and laymen alike on how to save these wonders of the ancient world, some impossibly fanciful, others down-to-earth and supported by detailed plans. Children, too, imaginations fired by the adventurous nature of the enterprise, offered both solutions and their savings in cash – a touching gesture!

Some of the proposals are described in "The World Saves Abu Simbel" (p. 91): those quoted below are typical;

"An American construction expert proposed salvaging the temples by building concrete barges under and around them, then waiting for the rising water level of the reservoir to float them up.

A Polish engineer suggested leaving the temples under water, protected by reinforced concrete domes: elevators operating in vertical shafts would then make the monuments accessible to visitors.

Another study of the project – also Polish – planned to surround the Great Temple with a semicircular reinforced concrete wall, the Small Temple being placed in a smaller concrete cylinder with glass roof.

A British film producer suggested sealing the temple rooms off against the reservoir and making them directly accessible from the top. His idea was to allow the temples to be submerged and then, by means of a curved membrane – a thin, non-supporting dam wall of pre-stressed concrete – separate the muddy waters of the reservoir outside from the clear, filtered water inside. From observation galleries in the membrane, visitors would be able to observe Ramses in a kind of aquarium – provided, of course, the brittle sandstone of Abu Simbel did not disintegrate in the water!

There were many other such plans and projects."

However, two basic requirements were overlooked in most of the proposals – the necessity to protect the temples from the encroachment of water and the effect of stress and fissures present in the rock itself. Were the waters allowed to reach the lower parts of the temple the brittle sandstone would disintegrate, leading to an explosive release of the stress-forces within the rock along the weakened lines of the fissures. The result would be catastrophic.

The rescue of Abu Simbel was indeed a highly complicated technical problem demanding thorough investigation and analysis, yet the whole operation was put at risk because four years were to elapse while possible solutions were discussed and what was then seen as the only feasible project put in hand. The period from October 1959, when the first expert studies were made, to November 1963 when the final contract was signed, was certainly not wasted, but too much time had been spent on unrealistic exercises and delays caused by conflicting interests.

All this resulted in a dramatic race between, on the one hand the threat of rising water once the High Dam had begun to function, and on the other the disappointingly slow growth of the moneys pledged or paid over as contributions. These financial difficulties were not unconnected with the fact that no entirely convincing solution had been found – a project, in short, realistic both from the technical and financial points of view.

Before embarking on an account of the sequence of events leading up to the final choice of project it is necessary to explain the "integrity of a monument" viewpoint, a concept which gave rise to much heart-searching among those concerned in deciding the most suitable method to be used in safeguarding the temples.

Nowadays the prevailing philosophy in the preservation of historic monuments is to regard them less as isolated works of art, but as being integrated with an environment which must be equally protected and respected.

It was during a meeting on the choice of project for the preservation of the temples on Philae that the archaeologists present explained their "integrity of a monument" concept as follows (Unesco/NUBIA/ 15, p. 11; 1968): "By the phrase 'integrity of the monument' is meant the preservation of the original geographic, architectural and cultural position and ambiance of the monument including not only the position of the various buildings vis-à-vis each other, but also their original relationship with surrounding physiographic and cultural features in the area."

This group, consisting of Professor Abdel Moneim Abu Bakr, Professor Joe Brew, Mrs. Christiane Desroches-Noblecourt and Professor Sergio Donadoni, held that "from the Egyptological and general point of view the maintenance of the integrity . . . is of utmost importance".

Following this view, any transfer of a monument from its original setting should be avoided if at all possible and then only under conditions which ensured the preservation of the monument's surrounding environment. To do otherwise would be to destroy "the integrity of the monument".

Thus, in the discussions concerning the choice of project for the salvage of Abu Simbel, any transfer of the monuments from their original setting was decried as vandalism and a breach of archaeological and scientific principles. However, neither archaeology as a science nor science as such can be the arbiters in such matters. Respect for the proper integrity of the monument and its environment is a question of cultural and human responsibility; on the other hand the choice made must be realistic, technically and financially. Should it come to a choice between preserving the monument at the cost of the original environment, or preserving the unity of monument and environment but at great risk to the monument itself, priority must of course be given to the safety of the monument proper.

In the case of Abu Simbel, to preserve the temples in their original location *and* keep their surroundings undisturbed was physically impossible. Any solution which permitted the temples to remain untouched in their original location would have necessitated a fundamental change in the character of their surroundings.

It was a dilemma which exposed conflicting views among the experts concerned. Indeed in the first report of 1959 the eminent authority, Piero Gazzola, had made much of the risks involved in keeping the temples in their original location because of the two fundamental factors already described, namely the necessity to protect them from water and the stresses and fissures within the rock. Nevertheless, the proposal to leave the temples in position and protect them with a huge surrounding dam was the solution recommended by this first group of experts though with some reservations.

THE FINAL CHOICE

Now follows the dramatic sequence of events which led to the final choice of project:

The dam scheme was proposed by the French Consultative Engineers Coyne and Bellier, who later carried out detailed studies on this project sponsored by Unesco and the Egyptian Government.

When the General Conference of Unesco met in Paris in October 1960, the Egyptian delegation received a new proposal from the Italian Government, based on an idea of lifting the two temples with hydraulic jacks. To some this new proposal seemed to be nonsense, but to others it appeared as a fascinating idea. It was therefore put to discussion and agreement was reached to submit both projects to a group of experts, to be convened by the Egyptian Government in consultation with Unesco, to give their opinion on the choice of project.

The group of experts from five countries (Egypt, USA, USSR, Switzerland and the Federal Republic of Germany) met in Cairo in January 1961. They pointed out the two main problems with the dam scheme: the first was the effect of the capillary water in the rock and consequently also in the monuments themselves. The second was the necessity to construct a pumping station to prevent the infiltrating water reaching the monuments. If the pumping were to stop in critical moments such as war or an economic crisis, it would entail serious danger to the monuments, probably destruction. It would thus be a constant worry to the Egyptian authorities who would be responsible for running the pumping station.

Obviously it would be extremely difficult, if not impossible to execute the dam scheme, and the group of experts finally recommended the Italian lifting scheme. Their report was submitted to the Consultative Committee which was meeting at the same time in Cairo and they asked the Egyptian Government to carry out further studies on the lifting scheme.

A realistic estimate of the costs of the dam scheme – excluding the capitalized yearly pumping costs as well as contingencies of a magnitude unknown – amounted to more than $80 million. At an early stage of the Campaign it was already obvious that such sums were out of reach, or at least were thought to be so by possible contributors. Consequently as long as the dam project was kept in the foreground only smallish sums were pledged – important donors, especially the governments of the Western powers, were not convinced.

The Egyptian Government therefore adopted the Italian lifting scheme on 20 June 1961. Owing to the technical complications involved in this scheme, a Board of Consultants was set up under the presidency of Dr. Hassan Zaki, and the consulting engineers VBB (Vattenbyggnadsbyrån, Stockholm) were nominated to prepare the detailed study for the new project and to carry out the technical supervision of the work.

The VBB started with the preparation of the tender documents and other studies, including a study of the rock stresses and the fissures in the monuments which was done by Professor Hast of Stockholm, and proved to be very valuable in the execution of the cutting scheme adopted later.

Time passed and not without criticism of the lifting scheme. The VBB affirmed however that this scheme could be executed. But the first stage of this operation would cost up to $58 million, a fact which caused financial worries since at this stage there was only a very restricted number of pledges, amounting to some $5 million in addition to the pledged contribution of the Egyptian Government totalling $11.5 million.

These worries increased as the General Conference of 1962 approached. Obviously, the lifting scheme might be a failure for financial reasons. Egypt therefore proposed an alternative project to cut out the temples and re-erect them on the mountain higher up. So the VBB was asked to prepare a preliminary project before the beginning of October 1962, the date of the General Conference. In good time a positive answer was received: the cost would be $32 million.

When the General Conference met in 1962 it was obvious that the international pledges were still quite inadequate to finance the lifting scheme. The Director-General proposed that Unesco should finance the project with a long-term bank loan, to be paid back by the regular budget of Unesco. Each Member State would thus bear, as an obligation, its usual proportional share on the basis of the United Nations scale of contributions. Another alternative of obligatory contributions to Abu Simbel was also proposed, but the General Conference rejected these proposals. Contributions to the salvage of Abu Simbel should remain on a voluntary basis.

The General Conference fixed 31 March 1963 as the deadline for receiving further contributions for the Italian lifting scheme, but when that date came it proved impossible to finance this scheme and it was therefore abandoned. The pledges were still low, amounting to $7.5 million. The Egyptian authorities then officially announced the cutting scheme to Unesco and to the Executive Committee at its session of 24–5 April 1963.

At the meeting a number of archaeologists and Egyptologists, who were not members of the Committee, had been called in and they opposed the cutting scheme, which the technicians and engineers present regarded as the only realistic one because of the financial situation and the extremely short time available. The cutting scheme was decried as "butchery" and in sharp conflict with archaeological and scientific principles.

At the same time the French National Commission for Unesco submitted an alternative scheme. The temples should be placed on a concrete platform or raft and floated into the desert in a basin constructed with the aid of a dam higher than any so far constructed, built on a river bed of unknown quality and with an unknown thickness of silt before the rock level was reached. This little lake would be on a higher level than the High Dam Lake. The costs had not been adequately analysed, but were stated to be approximately of the same magnitude as that of the cutting scheme, an estimate which was doubted by many experts.

Following the usual procedure, the Executive Committee referred both projects for analysis to a committee of experts. However when this committee met a difference of opinion arose and the members were unable to reach a decision or to recommend definitely either one of the projects as the most acceptable.

The matter was then referred to the Board of Consultants for Abu Simbel to pass judgment on the technical and financial points, which seemed to be more complicated than those of the Italian lifting scheme previously rejected. The Board gave its recommendation in favour of the cutting scheme.

Consequently the Egyptian Government adopted the cutting scheme on 10 June 1963. The Government was convinced of the feasibility of the project, technically and financially. All ideas to save Abu Simbel had been exhaustively studied and discussed at great length. Time was pressing and it was necessary to proceed with no further delay with the studies needed for the execution of the new scheme.

It was now hoped that more Member States would participate in the salvage of Abu Simbel. If the USA Government could be persuaded to participate, the project would be realized. However, the USA Government seemed to have some doubts about the cutting scheme and sent an eminent engineer, Mr. Johnson, head of the Engineering Division of the US Army, to Egypt to report on the matter. His report was favourable and the USA Government decided to contribute to the salvage of Abu Simbel. At a meeting with the delegates of the donor states on 5–9 November 1963, the USA representative announced his Government's promise to contribute $12 million in Egyptian pounds.

The Executive Committee approved the texts of the agreements between Unesco and the Member States and between Unesco and the Egyptian

Government, and the contract with the "Joint Venture" was signed by the Egyptian Government on 16 November 1963.

The "Joint Venture" was a consortium comprising firms from the Federal Republic of Germany (Hochtief A.G.) acting as General Manager, Italy (Impregilo), France (Grands Travaux de Marseille), and Sweden (Sentab and Skånska Cementgjuteriet). This Joint Venture also included the Egyptian firm Atlas, which lowered the amount of hard currency required and which also gave an Egyptian firm the chance to participate in this gigantic international project. This solution was also submitted to the Executive Committee and was agreed upon by Unesco.

After these negotiations the Egyptian Government agreed to execute the project, accepting the risk of completing it, even if international contributions should not suffice to cover the total cost.

The cost of the project had been estimated at $36 million, of which Egypt had pledged to pay one third, that is $12 million. Of the remaining $24 million, $17.5 million were covered by international pledges, so the financial risk involved amounted to about $6.5 million.

If the estimate of the costs were to prove correct, this still implied a considerable risk. At that time no one could know that the VBB estimate was so accurate that the actual costs came to only $40 million, that is to say, an increase of only 9% in the $4\frac{1}{2}$-year period of the project's execution. This was well below the inflation percentage over the same period.

The willingness of the Egyptian Government to take this risk and to bear so large a part of the financial burden undoubtedly eased the continuation of the Nubia Campaign, not least the financing of the rescue of the Philae temples, at a much later date.

By virtue of the agreement signed between Unesco and the Egyptian Government, Unesco was committed to continue fund-raising through all appropriate means in order to fill the gap between the sums pledged and the actual cost of the project.

Another financial difficulty for the Egyptian Government was to meet the contractual obligations in convertible currency, since part of the contracted sum had to be paid in US dollars. For the advance payment in hard currency to the contractors the Egyptian Government obtained a loan of three million pounds sterling from the Kuwait Government, a loan to be repaid over twelve years from 1966 onwards in equal annual payments.

The largest contribution, that of the United States of America, was the equivalent of $12 million in Egyptian pounds. This amount, as well as other sums pledged by the USA for the transfer of some smaller temples and for archaeological missions to Egyptian and Sudanese Nubia, was drawn from the funds held in Egypt in the name of the US Government as part of the costs of grain shipments delivered to Egypt as aid.

This and other contributions in non-convertible or national currencies had largely to be converted into US dollars, and lodged in the special Trust Fund of

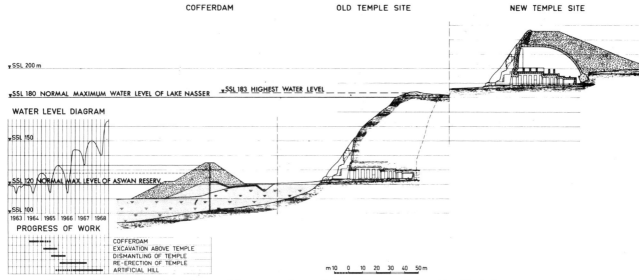

Fig. 12 Section showing the working procedure of the salvage of the Abu Simbel temples. Originally the temples were situated a few metres above the Nile water, but from 1964 onwards the water level was to rise year by year. The temples were to be dismantled behind a temporary cofferdam and then re-erected at a higher level.

the Nubia Campaign, and kept apart from the regular Egyptian national budget. All contributions and revenues were put into this Trust Fund and all financial operations pertaining to it were regularly reported to the Executive Committee, which authorized payments for specified purposes, as already described.

In this way, throughout the Campaign, the hard currency problem was solved. But it was always a delicate point because a certain percentage of the payments had to be met in hard currency, whereas the majority of the pledges were in restricted currencies, in other words, funds that were blocked in Egypt.

THE EXECUTION OF THE CUTTING SCHEME

What follows is a concise account of the cutting scheme as described by the Consultant Engineers, VBB, in "The Salvage of Abu Simbel" (December 1971).

As already mentioned, the main contractor for the work was a consortium of six contractor firms, named Joint Venture Abu Simbel. The work was supervised by Dr. Anwar Shukry, as Resident Archaeologist, as well as by two engineers/architects representing the Egyptian Antiquities Service.

The Scheme. The two temples at Abu Simbel consist of huge carvings on the cliff faces, forming outer façades, and of halls and rooms hewn inside two sandstone hills. The plan of the salvage operation required that the sculptured and decorated surfaces of the cliffs and rooms be cut from the rock in blocks of suitable sizes to be handled. These blocks would then be moved to a new site, some 65 m higher up, on the top of the cliff from which they were originally taken and re-erected there. To provide similar settings for the temple façades, entire sections of the original cliff faces adjacent to the façades were also to be moved to the new temple sites and used to cover the artificial hills that were to be built over the temples in their new positions. In this way the temples and their settings would be preserved.

The cofferdam. When work was started at the Abu Simbel site at the beginning of 1964, the Aswan High Dam works were already well advanced, and in August that same year, the level of the Nile upstream of the dam site began to rise. In order to keep the temples dry during the dismantling period, a cofferdam had to be built in front of them to hold back the flood waters. This cofferdam, in itself an achievement, was only completed after a dramatic race against time. The height of the cofferdam above the lowest river bottom and the underlying rock bed was 27 and 37 m respectively. The length of the crest was 370 m, and the total volume of sand and rock fill used in the dam was 380,000 cubic metres. A cut-off wall in the centre of the dam consisted of steel sheet piles with a total weight of 2800 tons (metric). Fig. 12 shows a section through the cofferdam and the old and new sites for the Great Temple, together with diagrams of the varying Nile water level and the progress of work.

Protecting of temples and bulk excavation. The temples had once been carved deep into rather soft and fragile sandstone. The first step in dismantling the temples was to remove the overlying rock. The use of explosives was prohibited. In all some 150,000 cubic metres of rock were removed by bulldozers, rippers and pneumatic tools. The front façades of the temples had been protected in advance by sand filling. The temple chambers deep in the rock were supported by steel scaffolding. The procedure is shown in fig. 13.

Dismantling and strengthening of temple blocks. The last stage of the excavation of the rock, just above and around the façades and chambers of the temples, was carried out to a distance of 0.8 m from the temple surfaces. The rock sections that then formed the statues, walls and roofs of the temples, were cut into blocks of suitable sizes for lifting and transport, in accordance with a cutting scheme worked out in July 1964, by archaeological experts. These blocks, which were approximately 0.8 m thick and about 3 m high and with a length sometimes up to 5 m, were then transported to a storage site. Blocks from the walls and roofs usually had a maximum weight of about 20 tons, while more compact parts from columns, statues, etc. weighed up to 30 tons each.

The sandstone in the temple region is mostly coarse-grained, with low strength, and in some cases badly fractured. Therefore, before the weaker blocks could be moved, they had to be strengthened. This was mainly achieved by first drilling and inserting steel reinforcing bars into the blocks and then cementing the entire block together, using epoxy resin mortar. Other methods were also used, for instance concreting behind the blocks, but this was only done in special cases.

Cutting and lifting of blocks. Several different tools and methods for cutting the sandstone into blocks were tried out. Saws of various kinds were found most suitable for the purpose. The saws were, however, subjected to excessive wear and tear and had to be equipped with special teeth of hard metal. Motor-driven chain saws were used to cut through the back of the blocks to within 10 to 20 cm of the sculptured surface, and then the remainder of the cut was made from the front side, using hand saws specially designed for this work. The hand saws made a cut only 6 to 8 mm wide, which helped to minimize the effect on the sculptured surfaces. Other methods of cutting the sandstone blocks were used, such as line drilling with wedging, and wire-cutting. The wedging method was used to some extent on the roof blocks, wire-cutting very infrequently. The system of dividing the temple walls in blocks is shown in fig. 14. The total area of the executed saw cuts for the temple blocks only amounted to 7200 square metres.

The next stage of the operation was to lift and transport the 1042 blocks of sandstone into which the temples proper had been cut. Lifting was a problem requiring careful study with regard to the fragility of the sandstone and also to the fact that no lifting equipment was permitted to touch the delicate sculptured surfaces of the temples. The problem was overcome by drilling holes into the blocks, almost reaching their lower edge, and cementing-in steel lifting bolts with epoxy resin. With special lifting yokes the blocks could then be lifted by the big cranes which ranged over the entire working area. The principle of lifting wall blocks is shown in fig. 14. Once lifted from their original positions, the blocks were placed on sand beds on low loaders and moved to a storage area on the desert plateau above the old temple sites.

Preparations at the storage area. Before the temples were re-erected in their new positions, all blocks were carefully inspected at the storage area and restored by specialists from the Antiquities Department of the Egyptian Ministry of Culture. The blocks were also prepared for re-erection. Their rear sides, to which supporting concrete was to be cast, were provided with steel anchor bars, and the surfaces were made waterproof by impregnation with resin.

Re-erection. The temples were to be re-erected at a new site at the top of the same cliff into which they had originally been carved. This new site was first prepared by the excavation of sandstone, so as to form a suitable foundation for the temples proper as well as for the great domes that were to be constructed over the temples. Rather extensive excavation had also to be carried out in front of the temples, to form a suitable foreground. The material excavated had a volume of about 26,500 and 100,000 cubic metres respectively.

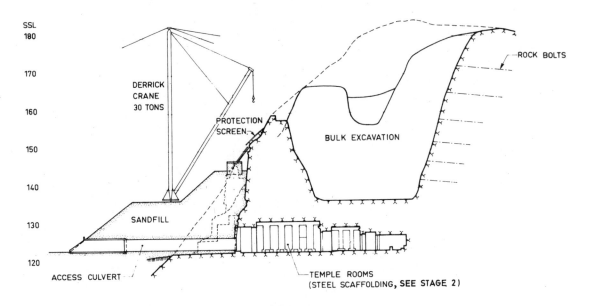

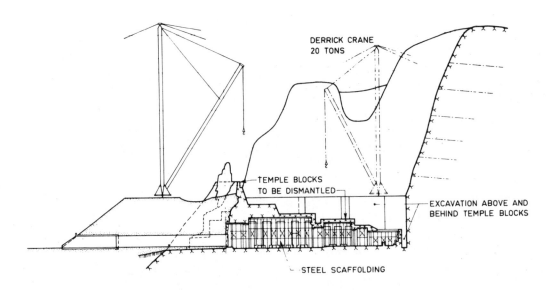

Fig. 13 Sections through the Great Temple, showing excavation and dismantling.

STAGE 1
VERTICAL SAWING

STAGE 2
HORIZONTAL SAWING

STAGE 3
LIFTING

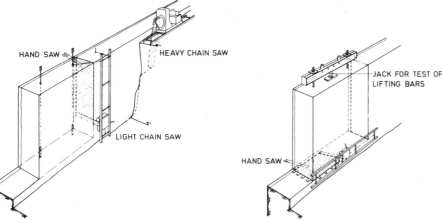
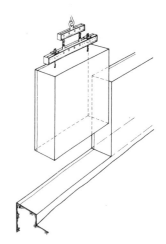

Fig. 14 Drawing showing the principle of cutting and lifting of wall blocks.

The positions of the temples were carefully set out at the new site, so that their positions relative to one another, and the directions in which they faced, were the same as they had been originally. The re-erection of the temples was then carried out in steps.

For the façades with their giant statues, supporting frameworks were first erected. The blocks were then placed in position against this framework and embedded in concrete. The temple rooms, on the other hand, were re-erected by placing the blocks in position and casting a supporting concrete structure behind and over them. Some idea of these supporting structures can be obtained from figs. 15 and 16.

Domes. Two concrete domes were then constructed, one above each temple. The two domes completely span the temples and carry the weight of the artificial hills which were finally built over and behind the temples. The dome which was built over the Great Temple is in itself a unique engineering feat. It has a span of 60 m, a height of 25 m, and width of 45 m, and carries a load ranging from 20 tons per square metre at the crown to 70 tons per square metre at the footing, all in all about 100,000 tons in one span.

The quantity of concrete in the Great Dome is about 8000 cubic metres and the quantity of reinforcement 600 tons. A plan section of the two domes can be seen in fig. 15 and a vertical section of the Great Dome in fig. 16.

Artificial hills. Above and behind the temples, and carried over these by the domes, artificial hills were built up from sandstone rock fill, in the steep vertical fronts supported by masonry walls. The latter were covered with several thousands of sandstone blocks taken from the surface of the original cliff and

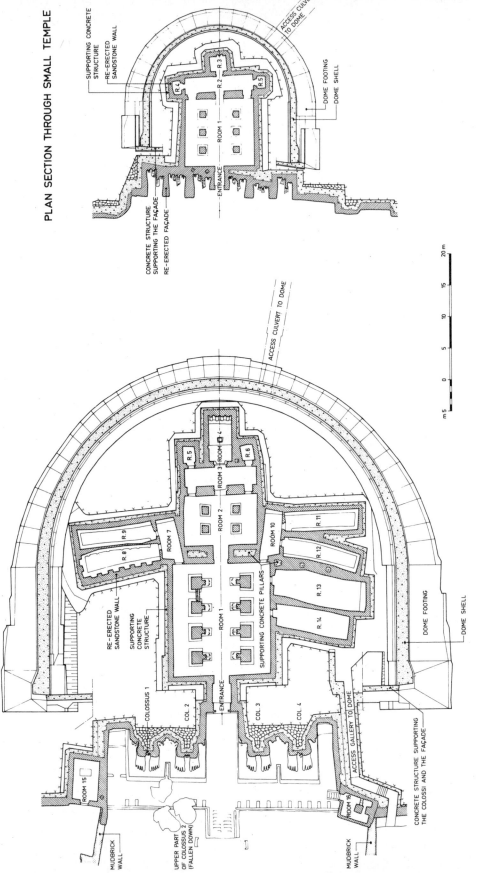

PLAN SECTION THROUGH SMALL TEMPLE

SUPPORTING CONCRETE STRUCTURE

RE-ERECTED SANDSTONE WALL

R.4

R.3

R.2

R.5

ROOM 1

ENTRANCE

DOME FOOTING

DOME SHELL

ACCESS CULVERT TO DOME

CONCRETE STRUCTURE SUPPORTING THE FAÇADE

RE-ERECTED FAÇADE

PLAN SECTION THROUGH GREAT TEMPLE

ACCESS CULVERT TO DOME

R.4

R.5

ROOM 3

ROOM 6

ROOM 2

R.8

R.9

ROOM 7

ROOM 10

R.11

R.12

R.13

R.14

ROOM 1

RE-ERECTED SANDSTONE WALL

SUPPORTING CONCRETE STRUCTURE

SUPPORTING CONCRETE PILLARS

COLOSSUS 1

COL. 2

ENTRANCE

COL. 3

COL. 4

DOME FOOTING

DOME SHELL

ACCESS GALLERY TO DOME

CONCRETE STRUCTURE SUPPORTING THE COLOSSI AND THE FAÇADE

ROOM 15

UPPER PART OF COLOSSUS 2 (FALLEN DOWN)

ROOM 16

MUDBRICK WALL

MUDBRICK WALL

20 m

15

10

5

0

m 5

Fig. 15 Horizontal section of Great and Small Temple, respectively.

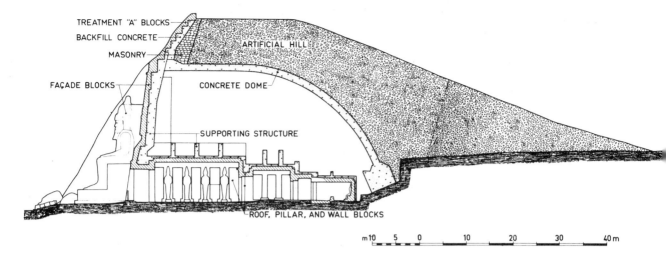

TREATMENT "A" BLOCKS
BACKFILL CONCRETE
MASONRY
FAÇADE BLOCKS
ARTIFICIAL HILL
CONCRETE DOME
SUPPORTING STRUCTURE
ROOF, PILLAR, AND WALL BLOCKS

m 10   5   0   10   20   30   40 m

Fig. 16 Section. The outer setting of the temples was given the form of hills with steep fronts and moderately sloping areas. The vertical section of the Great Temple, above, shows the general building-up of the hills by means of rock fill, supported by masonry walls along the steep fronts, and the domes carrying the rock fill and the wall above the temples proper.

elsewhere, to complete the picture of the original massive cliffs. The total volume of the artificial hills amounted to about 330,000 cubic metres.

The site. Transport to and from the site was another of the problems that had to be solved. The temples are located in sterile desert bounded on one side by the waters of the Nile. The nearest town is Aswan, some 300 km to the north, and the only land connection is across the desert by jeep or camel caravans. This is a difficult journey, so the main means of transportation to the site must be by air or by boat. All staff, mail and urgent material were transported by air in small four-seater aircraft, while the labourers, machinery, food and other items were brought in by boat up the Nile from Aswan.

Approximately 1700 workmen and 200 staff members were employed on the site, and when their families had joined the growing community, approximately 3000 people lived there. Naturally, no accommodation was available on the site when work started on the project. Then all the personnel had to live in tents, sheds or on houseboats. These living quarters were unenviable, especially during the summer season when the temperature could rise to around 45° to 50° C in the shade. The plans that had originally been made to build a small township on the site were delayed in the rush to complete the cofferdam on time, and it was almost $1\frac{1}{2}$ years before the community had developed and everyone had acceptable living quarters.

Besides houses and offices, the township had a mosque, a police station, a hotel, mess rooms, shops, a swimming pool, tennis court, etc., and on the whole, after the initial difficult period, the facilities matched those of any other civilized community. However, the desert was never far from the borders of the township and this limited the possibilities for sport and recreation. The isolation from the outside world was also oppressive and this resulted in a somewhat high turnover of personnel on the site.

From this short description of the work, it can be seen that not only the general concept of the salvage operation but also the design of some of the structures involved might be regarded as unique. Bearing in mind the exceptional environment of the site and other prevailing conditions, it can also be said that the successful carrying out of the works on site was a feat of engineering and planning.

The foregoing technical account omits, as one would expect, any mention of the tense situations which arose during the $4\frac{1}{2}$ years of the Abu Simbel salvage operation, which was completed in the autumn of 1968, 20 months ahead of schedule.

Foremost in the mind of everyone concerned was the race against all manner of delays to prevent the rising waters of the Nile reaching the temples; would the protective cofferdam be completed in time to avoid a catastrophe? The base of the smaller temple was at the level of 120.2 m above sea level (MASL), that is to say less than 1 m above the maximum level of the old reservoir, and that of the larger temple 4 m higher, so the safety margins were extremely small at the start. By the summer of 1964 the Nile would be barred by the High Dam already under construction, and the water level upstream would begin to rise, to reach 128 MASL in 1964 and 133 MASL by late 1965.

The completion of the cofferdam, an outstanding feat in its own right, with the associated extensive and complicated drainage system to take care of the water seepage unavoidable in all dam structures, was vital. Yet work on it had to await the signing of the contract which did not take place until 16 November 1963. Then the contractor had first to establish a working site with essential installations, together with lines of communication and delivery of materials, and all this in a blistering and trackless desert 300 km from the nearest supply base at Aswan.

So it was not until the following April that work started on the cofferdam itself. All other work had to give way before the extreme urgency of the dam building; reasonable living conditions – housing, comfort, proper medical arrangements, leisure facilities – in the scorching heat of the Nubian summer, had perforce to be postponed.

It was a razor's edge between success and catastrophe. In August of that year, the rising water, swollen by an exceptionally high flood, passed the critical level of 120 MASL. November 1964 saw another moment of crisis when the water rose to within 2 m of the crest of the cofferdam as it was at that time. Happily the dam and its drainage system stood up to the test and the danger passed.

The price of the long delay in the final choice of project was high, not only in money – expenditure on the cofferdam and drainage system absorbing one sixth of the total (about $7 million) – but also in human suffering; one of the leading experts never recovered fully from the effects of the appalling working conditions.

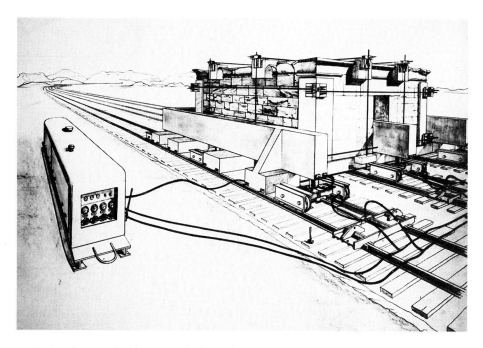

18 Project drawing for the removal of Amada temple on rails.

19 Amada temple on its new site.

20 Wadi es Sebua temple before removal.

21 Derr temple before removal.

22 Dendur temple re-erected in New York's Metropolitan Museum of Art.

23 Taffa temple rebuilt in Leiden Museum of Antiquities.

24 (Opposite, above) Dismantling Semna West temple from the roof down, under the direction of the architect F. Hinkel.

25 (Opposite, below) Semna West temple reconstructed in the garden of the new Sudan National Museum, Khartoum. Note the movable shelter to protect the temple from the annual rains.

26 Sudanese visitors to the Sudan National Museum, queueing to see the Nubian archaeological discoveries made during the Campaign.

27 Columns in the Museum gardens brought from Faras on the border with Egypt. The green hill (right) contains Djehuthotep's tomb chamber from Debeira.

28 Philae. Dismantled temple blocks in storage area.

29 Philae. View around 1900.

30 Philae. Rebuilding the outer court of the Isis temple on Agilkia Island. In the background the re-erected first pylon.

31 Trajan's kiosk re-erected on Agilkia Island.

32 Qasr Ibrim. Excavations in progress, 1974.

33 Qadan. Scene of a stone age massacre. Burials from around 10,000 B.C. with fatal arrows in position (indicated by pencils).

Another moment of drama came at the start of the dismantling operation. Exhaustive tests had been made to determine how best to remove the immense mass of the overlying rock and cut free the two temples from the mountain (blasting, of course, was ruled out), and the zones of weakness and stress forces within the mountain probed and measured, and counterbalanced by steel scaffolding and stress-relieving cuts along the corners between roof and walls. Would all those calculations and experiments in lifting blocks up to 30 tons' weight by means of inserted steel rods prove to be effective, or would the removal of the first roof block release pent-up stress forces and cause the temple to split apart? The effect can be illustrated by compressing three table-tennis balls in one hand, then brusquely removing one.

On 12 August 1965 everything was ready to go. The moment of truth had arrived. Would the experts prove to be right or would the Cassandra-like utterances of the cutting scheme's opponents be justified? The experts, engineers, archaeologists, representatives of the Joint Venture and of the VBB were assembled, some on the crest of the cofferdam fronting the temple, others on the mountain above, all tensely watching the operation. The noise of the heavy machines working elsewhere suddenly ceased and only the rumbling of a winch was heard.

The heavy block of stone attached to the winch starts to move. The cut around it, hardly visible before, opens more and more as the block eases away and is slowly moved to the waiting trailer which will carry it to the storage area. Everything goes to plan; the scaffolding and the stress-relieving cuts have stood the test; the dismantling can go forward according to schedule.

By July 1966, the last block had been transported from the original site to the storage area where the 807 blocks of the Great Temple and 235 blocks of the small temple were stored, and where they were repaired and consolidated before being brought to the re-erection site.

The re-erection was, of course, an operation necessitating meticulous accuracy, and each block had to be closely examined for cracks or weaknesses before being inserted into the immense three-dimensional jigsaw puzzle.

Here may be recalled the impressive ceremony in March 1967 when the crown of Ramses was put back in place, in the presence of the Executive Committee and mass-media representatives from across the world.

It was an unforgettable event, and a moment of triumph for all those who had fought for the cutting scheme. The only persons unmoved, at least visibly, were some Nubian workers clinging to the immense legs of the God-King, filling the joints of the blocks.

Of the two domes built above the temples, the larger will house an audio-visual museum intended to illustrate the successive phases of the Abu Simbel project. The construction of these domes involved hours of computer calculations, the use of special low-heat cement and complicated cooling arrangements to offset the extremely high ambient temperatures of the Abu Simbel area. They are a major feat of engineering, as Rex Keating noted:

"Pass through an inconspicuous stone doorway to one side of the façade of the reconstructed temple and you step straight from Ancient Egypt into the latter part of the 20th century. Soaring above your head to a height of 60 ft is an immense self-supporting dome. It is 200 ft across. There are bigger domes in existence but none, I'm told, which support a load of 70 tons to the square metre at the footings to 20 tons at the crown – which represents the distributed weight of the artificial hill above. Beneath the dome and dwarfed by it, a series of sharply angled planes of concrete rises and falls in a beautifully controlled pattern; encased in the concrete are the free-standing halls and chambers of the reconstructed temples. To right and left of these structures rise two large masses of living rock – raw and stark. They tell me the rock was left in place to spare the expense of cutting it away. Be that as it may, in this precise fabrication of grey surfaces it catches the breath. Let into the concrete are instruments to record and measure movements within the structure while at intervals projecting grills reveal the system by which air circulates inside the temple. All visitors to Abu Simbel should be taken to see this triumph of civil engineering, which is as impressive an achievement as the masterpiece it has been built to protect." ("The Stones Move", 1968.)

In the book "The World saves Abu Simbel" (p. 94), Georg Gerster, acknowledges "the clockwork precision of the work" but adds "Should one forget the fact that the archaeologists to a man and right up to the last minute strongly opposed the humpty-dumpty project as a 'solution of despair' because they regarded the dissection of the temples as an act of wanton destruction . . . all prognosis at the start of the work was far from favourable. Estimates by experts . . . are on record, according to which the loss of one out of every three blocks was to be expected".

That nothing of the kind occurred was due to the meticulous preliminary studies and experiments undertaken, to say nothing of VBB's long experience in tackling technical problems in civil engineering. Down to the smallest detail the work had been specified by the consultant engineers and followed to the letter by the contractors with the happy result which is now history.

TRIUMPH – THE INAUGURATION

The overall concept of the enterprise and many of the means used to carry it through were unique while the completion of the task in so short a time – $4\frac{1}{2}$ years and 20 months ahead of schedule – was an astonishing feat of planning and organization. For all those who had carried the burden of the project – planners, engineers, masons, labourers and, of course, the executing contractors – 22 September 1968 was a day of deep satisfaction.

It was a day of triumph for the Egyptian Government and the Egyptian authorities involved, triumph for Unesco and its officials and for the international community represented through the various committees and groups of experts who had worked for the project, and for the Member States and all private donors who had contributed in the name of international cultural solidarity. For Egyptologists, archaeologists and historians every-where it was also a day for rejoicing.

It was indeed a historic occasion and it was celebrated by some 500 guests brought to Abu Simbel to attend a solemn inauguration. Saved from destruction, the temples of Ramses II would, as an eighth wonder of the world, continue to fascinate visitors for generations to come. The events of that memorable day have been described by Saroite Okacha:

"On 22 September 1968, a joyful wind of victory was blowing across the Egyptian sky, the victory we had won over all the obstacles and difficulties with which we had been faced. Great was our pride to have been able to save from certain destruction some of the finest monuments of our ancient civilization and to have preserved the temples of Abu Simbel for eternity. To achieve this, hands had stretched across oceans in a gesture of staunch cooperation and faith in the value of culture and in the importance of artistic works. Men of different languages, races and creeds had joined together, inspired by their enthusiasm and the voice of conscience, in a gesture of dignity and humanity.

"On 22 September 1968, men of culture came to Egypt from all corners of the earth to share our joy at having preserved the temples of Abu Simbel for all mankind. The Minister of Culture had invited Mr. René Maheu, Director-General of Unesco, Mr. Vittorino Veronese, former Director-General, Prince Sadruddin Aga Khan, Mr. Bedrettin Tuncel, President of the General Conference in 1966, Mr. Attilio Dell'Oro Maini, Chairman of the Executive Board, Ambassador Paulo de Berrêdo Carneiro, Chairman of the Executive Committee for the international campaign to save the monuments of Nubia, and a large number of other leading figures from Unesco. The ministers responsible for relations with Unesco in the fifty states which had contributed to the preservation of Abu Simbel were likewise invited, as were the ambassadors of these countries currently serving in the United Arab Republic and the ambassadors of these states to the United Arab Republic, the Ministers of the United Arab Republic who, by virtue of their position, had participated directly in the campaign to safeguard Nubia, and a large number of eminent Egyptian figures, men of letters, scholars and artists.

"On that historic day, I summed up in my speech the various stages of this important project, the successful accomplishment of which was there for everyone to admire. On behalf of the Egyptian people and its government, I thanked all those who had helped us and paid tribute to the work of the specialists, technicians and engineers involved in the operation. Ambassador Paulo de Berrêdo Carneiro and Mr. René Maheu in turn expressed their satisfaction at this cultural and human success which had been brought about thanks to fruitful cooperation between the United Arab Republic and, through Unesco, the world community." (*Translated from the French*).

Governments, official and semi-official bodies and institutions, revenue from exhibitions and other fund-raising devices – all these provided the financial props which sustained the campaign, but beyond those were the private contributions, many of which were substantial. To give but two examples, well over $1 million was collected by the American Committee for the Salvage of Abu Simbel through the enthusiastic efforts of Joe Brew, Froelich Rainey, John Wilson, Edmondo Lassalle, Henry Fisher and Max McCullough. Mrs. de Witt Wallace, owner of the "Reader's Digest" alone gave $1 million to the project. The list of private donors who sacrificed moneys, large and small, would run into many pages.

Contributions reached Unesco from the humblest of people. One of the letters addressed to the Director-General was read out to the General Conference on the day after the Appeal. It was from a little eleven-year-old girl from Tournus (France) saying "I do not know what the beautiful temple of Abu Simbel is like, but I do know what Egypt must be like because we have just learned about it at school. I do not want all these beautiful temples to be lost. I have just broken my piggy-bank and I am sending you what was in it. I am also making a collection at my school". The Egyptian Government later invited the little girl to visit Egyptian Nubia with her mother.

Another letter received by Unesco was from a charwoman in Bordeaux whose husband had been killed during the war. She wrote: "I have made sacrifices all my life so that my daughter would be educated and cultivated. She is happily married, she has a job and children. And so I am sending you what three of my dinners a week would cost, for if I cannot hope to see these Nubian temples myself, I want my grandchildren to see them."

No greater compliment could have been paid to those who brought the Abu Simbel enterprise to its triumphant conclusion than the query of a journalist present at the inauguration: "Everything looks exactly as it was before! What have you done with the forty million dollars?"

AFTER THE SALVAGE

Sandstorms and Snakes. In their final report the VBB insisted on the absolute need for continued maintenance, since although the Abu Simbel temples were in fairly good condition on their re-discovery in the 19th century – the Great Temple had most of the time been very well protected by the dune sand which had more or less covered it – modern times had considerably changed the situation. The natural climatic conditions were still rather favourable, but the presence and activities of man now exercised such an influence in various ways that careful and continuous maintenance had become as necessary for the Abu Simbel temples as for practically everything created by man.

A detailed maintenance programme worked out by the VBB and now being followed takes into account all relevant factors such as temperature changes, wind and water erosion, changes in the composition of certain materials used, wear and tear, etc.

Measurements made regularly in the domes have proved that these structures are absolutely stable and display no signs of unforeseen changes. The stability of the temples seems to justify the statement of the VBB in their final report that every piece of stone sculptured in the rock more than 3200 years ago still exists, and they had reason to hope and believe that the temples will last for as long as man can conceive.

However, the two great artificial hills built over the reconstructed temples and their domes have of course changed the environment while the area fronting the temples gave rise to unforeseen problems.

Originally when the lifting scheme was analysed, the threat of wind erosion was feared. In this part of the Nile Valley, where the river threads its way through the arid vastnesses of the Eastern and Western deserts, the winds can be terrifyingly destructive; the air is thick with the whirling grains of quartz sand, and its eroding power is incredible.

Archaeologists who have worked in these parts of the Nile Valley well know that tomb superstructures in the cemeteries, even if constructed as solid stone rings or stone mastabas, not to speak of mudbrick buildings or silt tumuli, are often eroded down to the level of the soil. It is a phenomenon which can make archaeological survey extremely tricky since no trace is seen on the surface of even large cemeteries.

Thus with first-hand knowledge of the abrasive power of sand the archaeologists concerned had serious doubts as to how the soft sandstone temples would fare when removed to exposed surroundings high above the desert peneplain. However, the experts were insistent that the artificial hills to be built around the temples would protect them fully from the prevailing north or west winds. The prediction has proved correct.

It so happened that after the completion of the salvage work a fierce sandstorm did in fact damage the façade of the small temple, but the sand which caused the damage (since repaired) came not from the desert but from the carpet of sand lying in front of the temples and filling the artificial wadi between them. Once this was removed and replaced by lawns, there was no further trouble from sand.

What followed, however, is a good example of the unforeseen consequences of man's interference with a stabilized ecological system. The lawns had to be watered and the moisture attracted frogs and they in turn attracted snakes, hardly a tourist attraction! The new surroundings were also much to the liking of birds which moved in in such large numbers that soon the temples were smeared by their corrosive droppings.

The lawns were replaced by low growing vegetation and the bare rock exposed and now the problems seem to be well in hand, although requiring constant supervision. As for the birds, they seem to be abandoning the temples in favour of the development area connected with tourist expansion and a growing human population; the Toshka canal project (see below) should also prove an attraction to the feathered population of Abu Simbel.

The Temples as a tourism project. Before the Nubia Campaign, Abu Simbel's temples were not among the "musts" of the average tourist; they were distant from Aswan, transport was difficult and slow, and there were no other startling monuments in the vicinity. As for the Philae temples, they were under water for much of the year and so were most of the other temples and archaeological sites of Nubia. Wadi Halfa, the terminus of the paddle steamers to the Sudan, was a charming enough example of a small African town but no attraction for tourists *"en masse"*.

When the Nubia Campaign started, travel arrangements to Abu Simbel improved. The trip to Wadi Halfa with stops at Aniba and Abu Simbel became fashionable, and during the Campaign the possibility of visiting the temples in one day using the speedy hydrofoils introduced by the Egyptian authorities specifically for this traffic, increased the flow of visitors considerably. These trips became an important factor in furthering the promotional activities of the Campaign and in arousing interest in the unique salvage enterprises being undertaken in Lower Nubia.

After the completion of the High Dam there was no further development of the boat traffic and visitors were brought to Abu Simbel by aircraft from Aswan. Their stay was very short, barely enough for a rapid tour around the temples. The hotel, available since the heyday of the salvage operation, was underused; communications could not meet the demand.

Later the airstrip was enlarged to receive bigger aircraft, such as the Airbus, but a plane-load of tourists arriving by Airbus for an overnight stay at Abu Simbel could not have been accommodated in the existing hotel. So it is planned to enlarge the hotel as part of the scheme to transform the Abu Simbel area into a tourist resort. The remoteness of the place, the glistening expanse of the lake and the boundless horizons of the surrounding desert, all have their own special attraction, quite apart from the overwhelming majesty of the temples themselves.

Then there is the Toshka Canal project, an irrigation scheme involving the United Nations Development Programme (UNDP) which is intended to transform the high silt plain west of Abu Simbel into farming land.

So Abu Simbel will, quite apart from its tourist potential, become an element in the economic development of this part of Nubia. In order to secure the "integrity" of the ancient monuments for future generations, a suitable town plan has been prepared, and approved by presidential decree.

Abu Simbel itself will be the major attraction in a tourist project intended to embrace the whole of Nubia and the Egyptian part of the Nile Valley, which is now under consideration. The salvaged Nubian temples already grouped in several locations will, like Abu Simbel, become centres for development in a revitalized Nubia once the lake has settled to its definite level.

Kalabsha – A Race With Time

THE TEMPLE OF MANDULIS – THE NUBIAN SUN GOD

"Be benevolent, O Mandulis, Son of Zeus, and nod to me in acquiescence! Save me and my beloved wife and my good children! I call upon Thee constantly that my companions and the female slaves, free from disease and toil, may return to our country.

"How happy is the people which lives in the holy (town of) Talmis, loved by Mandulis, the Sun God, and which is under the sceptre of Isis, of beautiful hair and many names!"

This prayer was inscribed, together with a lengthy poem in Greek, by the Decurion Maximos in the courtyard of the temple of Kalabsha, some 50 km south of Aswan.

The temple was built in the usual style of Greco–Roman times, with screen walls between columns with richly decorated, so-called composite capitals, and with an almost overwhelming richness of texts and reliefs in the inner parts of the temple. These chambers were once famous for their well-preserved colours which were tragically lost when the temple was submerged for much of the year in the reservoir behind the first dam at Aswan, appearing above water only during the summer months. The outer parts of the temple, the quay and the monumental pylons guarding the entrance, were left unfinished and undecorated in roughly hewn stone.

Apart from the complex of temples on the island of Philae, Kalabsha was the biggest temple of Lower Nubia. It was erected in the reign of Augustus who in the year 30 A.D. became Pharaoh of Egypt – earlier buildings of Ptolemaic date being torn down. The new temple was begun perhaps in the 18 years of Cleopatra's reign.

To judge from the prayer of the Decurion Maximos and many other prayers and names scribbled or neatly incised on the walls, a large part of the pagan congregation came from the Roman garrison of the town of Talmis, a mixture of races drawn from different parts of the Roman Empire, not only Thebes in Upper Egypt, but also for example from northern Syria and even Spain. The inscriptions date mostly from the 2nd and 3rd centuries A.D. and they give an insight into garrison life on the Nubian outskirts of the Empire. Incidentally, these texts are supplemented by others in the quarries of Qertassi, not far from Kalabsha/Talmis.

Thus the decree of the strategos Aurelius Besarion (249 A.D.) bids the peasants of Talmis to keep their swine out of the temple and a famous somewhat later text of Silko, King of the Nobades, probably of the 6th century, celebrates his victory over the Blemmyes, second of the two principal tribes of Lower Nubia. This victory also probably implied the final triumph of

Christianity over the last followers of the old Pharaonic religion and could be related to the conversion of the temple of Isis on Philae into a church, when the last pagan worshippers of Lower Nubia had vanished from the political scene and no longer was there any insistence on the old privilege, accorded by a peace treaty with Rome, to have access to the pagan temples of Philae.

An echo of the victory of Christianity in Lower Nubia when the temple of Kalabsha was transformed into a church, is in two brief Coptic texts on the pylon: "I, the priest Paulos, have prayed here for the first time" and "I, the priest Paulos, have erected the cross for the first time in this place".

The decoration of the courtyard was never completed but among the few reliefs is one showing King Ptolemy IX offering a field to Isis, Mandulis and Horus, the principal gods of the temple, and Amenophis II of the Eighteenth Dynasty in front of the fertility god Min and Mandulis the Nubian god. These representations are not contemporary with the rulers depicted but were made in memory of their role as earlier temple builders.

The hypostyle hall with its beautiful columns was decorated in the reigns of the Emperors Trajan and Antoninus Pius, whereas the innermost rooms, once famous for their vivid colours, were finished in the reign of the Emperor Augustus. The motives are the usual ritual scenes, in which the Nubian god Dedun also appears as well as the celebrated and much-revered Imhotep who was the architect of the venerable Step Pyramid of King Djoser of the Third Dynasty at Saqqara and who in late times was deified as a god of healing, identified with Asklepius.

Behind the Holy of Holies, on the rear wall of the temple proper, the leading gods are, as usual, depicted in huge reliefs – $3\frac{1}{2}$ m high – on the one side representations of the King in front of Isis, Horus and Mandulis, and before Osiris, Isis and Mandulis on the other.

Hewn in the rock outside the temple was a small chapel of earlier date – from Ptolemaic times – and behind it a mammisi or "birth house".

THE GERMAN SALVAGE OPERATION

Following the appeal of the Director-General of Unesco a National Committee was organized in the Federal Republic of Germany and in the autumn 1960 ways and means of responding to the appeal were discussed. The German Ambassador in Cairo was subsequently able to transmit to the Egyptian Government an offer by his government to dismantle and re-erect on a safe site the temple of Kalabsha, all costs to be paid by the Federal Republic of Germany. This generous offer was gratefully accepted by the Egyptian Minister of Culture and National Guidance.

The reasons behind this offer have been explained by Stock and Siegler in their book "Kalabsha, der grösste Tempel Nubiens und das Abenteuer seiner Rettung". The decision in favour of Kalabsha was based not only on purely scientific considerations but on the cultural desirability of saving a significant monument; next to the temple complex on the island of Philae, Kalabsha was the largest of the Lower Nubian temples even if compared with the rock temples of Abu Simbel, which are smaller in area.

In making so considerable a contribution to the Campaign, the Federal Republic of Germany was carrying on a tradition of archaeological exploration and scholarship in Egypt which dated back more than a century, beginning with the famous expedition of Richard Lepsius (1843–48) and followed by extensive excavations at the pyramids, in Akhenaton's city of El Amarna and on many other important sites. Moreover, fundamental contributions to the study of the Egyptian language had been made by German scholars.

The temple of Kalabsha had been visited and partially documented by the architect Franz Christian Gau in 1819, and later studied and illustrated by many artists and scholars of the 19th century. As already mentioned, it was famous for its well-preserved colours and the celebrated French Egyptologist Gaston Maspero described it as the most beautiful Nubian temple of the late period. When the first Aswan dam was constructed the temple was consolidated by Barsanti, in 1907. He cleared away the later Coptic additions and made an anastylosis – reconstruction – of fallen architectural elements. In its new state it was published by H. Gauthier in the series "Temples immergés de la Nubie" (1911–14). Finally, the Documentation Centre had documented the temple in a series of excellent plans and sections together with copies of the texts, all of which was of fundamental importance in the planning of a salvage operation.

To move an ancient monument of such huge proportions, consisting of some 16,000 blocks, was unprecedented and there was no experience to draw on in assessing the needs for such an operation in relation to costs, materials, technique and personnel.

Estimates made by the Italian expert, Gazzola, had produced a figure of some 6 million D.M. for dismantling, transport and re-erection, but this was a preliminary calculation, intended only to give a very rough idea of the likely costs. The firm Hochtief AG, Essen, made an estimate based on the proposition that the temple could be moved westwards to the next possible site, but this proved impracticable for several reasons, among them the problem of traversing large stretches of mud-covered land.

The most favourable site proved to be a rocky height at Khor Ingi overlooking the High Dam. Another decision taken was to re-erect other monuments on this site: the rock temple of Ramses II at Beit el Wali near Kalabsha, and the small Greco–Roman temple or kiosk of Qertassi also from the same neighbourhood originally.

Kalabsha temple was entirely submerged for nine months of the year and only in July, August and September were the lower parts exposed above water. In August 1961 the firm Hochtief AG received a contract for the removal of the temple and had made all necessary preparations to start work in November when the upper parts of the edifice could still be reached from barges. The intention was to work from barges on the water and also from land when in the summer months the lower part of the building would become accessible.

However, in November the water started to rise, so the first season of work in 1961 was short, more of a pilot project to test the methods to be used. During the whole winter of 1961/62 the temple was under water and not until May 1962 was work resumed.

A flotilla of boats arrived at Kalabsha – two for living accommodation, one containing a workshop, plus some five motorized barges of 300–450 tons which could move under their own power to the new site. In addition there were four general-purpose craft and one speedboat for use in emergency. Five big cranes, capable of lifting up to 30 tons, were used to handle the 16,000 blocks; these had an average weight of about 1 ton, but some, like the architraves and ceiling blocks, approached 30 tons. In addition to the Egyptian and German technicians some 250 Egyptian workers were employed. An Australian architect, Mr. G.R.H. Wright, directed the work from the beginning. The abundant population of snakes, scorpions and spiders made it impossible for the workers to live in tents and other housing had to be provided. The pride of the mission was the ship *Souna*, originally the luxury *dahabiyah* of some pasha, but now adapted for the needs of management with cabins, photo laboratory and offices and a sheltered upper deck to provide some relief from the fierce heat of the Nubian summer.

During the first phase the dismantling was done from the barges and the work became a race with time, not as was the case at Abu Simbel against rising water, but against the receding river which fell about half a metre every day. Each layer of stone blocks had to be mapped and photographed before removal and the time schedule was so tight that the dismantling had to be completed in one summer.

Barsanti's repairs and reinforcement in concrete, made at the beginning of the century to strengthen the temple against the rise and fall of the water, produced problems since the fragmentary stones held in position by the concrete were very brittle and therefore difficult both to extract and handle. Some damage was inevitable and there were accidents, the gravest occurring during the night hours when the block with the inscription of King Silko, the most famous in the entire temple, slipped out of balance and fell with a crash into the barge below. It could easily have killed somebody and pierced the hull of the boat but fortunately other blocks cushioned the fall; it was possible to repair the stone but it was an irony that this, the only grave accident, should happen to the most precious of the temple's stones.

At the end of July the work continued on land, though still with problems caused by the receding water which made transport down to the river ever longer and more difficult. The pressure of work was tremendous, nevertheless the whole of the dismantling down to the foundations was finished on 1 October – a heroic achievement!

The re-erection of the dismantled temple encountered unforeseen difficulties. The reconstructed elements, executed by Barsanti in concrete, proved to be much more substantial than had been assumed before the dismantling; the roof beams of the inner rooms were all broken save one, and the heavy roof slabs proved impossible to handle in one piece for replacement.

The main question was how far the re-erected monument should be a reconstruction and to what extent it should be left as rebuilt and reinforced by Barsanti. It was a problem with both practical and ethical implications, and a matter of fundamental theoretical importance for the re-erection of all the Nubian temples. In the case of Kalabsha the solution, generally speaking, was a conservative one and no fundamental changes were made in the degree of reconstruction. The overriding principle was to insert the original pieces in such a way as to preserve and protect them against damage. However, one exception was made to this basic concept, if it can be regarded as an exception, and that was the roofing of the inner rooms of the sanctuary. It gave rise to intense and prolonged discussions between experts and the decision to roof the inner rooms with a modern construction, not even using the only preserved beam, was based on the following considerations:

(a) the roofs would add to the solidity of the construction
(b) the decorated walls would be better protected
(c) the subdued light harmonized better with the quality of the reliefs which were never intended to be exposed to strong sunlight. Originally they had been covered with stucco which hid the often somewhat inferior cutting, and were painted in brilliant colours. Now all these finer details were gone and the roughness of the cutting would give a false impression of the quality of the original work.
(d) a roofing of the inner rooms would re-establish the architectural rhythm of the temple, a rhythm which had religious implications with its transition from the bright sunlight of the courtyard through darker and darker rooms to end in the mysterious Holy of Holies to which practically no light penetrated and where the visitor could experience something of the religious awe inspired within the sanctuary.

The transfer of this great building to a new and secure site was a great success. It had importance also for the solution chosen for the salvage of a still bigger temple complex, the buildings on the island of Philae. The methods used, which had been proven in a number of other temples, encouraged those responsible for the Philae operation to follow similar lines which in the event proved equally successful.

THE ''WONDER STONES''

During the dismantling of the Augustean temple it was found that older blocks in a superior style and dating to Ptolemaic times had been re-used. They were called by the Germans "die Wundersteine", "the wonder stones", and amounted to about 100 pieces. Unfortunately not enough were found to make possible a reconstruction of the original buildings from which they came. It was therefore decided to organize one more mission to the site of Kalabsha in a last attempt to find additional blocks, towards the end of the summer of 1963. It was also important to excavate below the later temple in order to expose the groundplan of the earlier buildings. This mission, which was at work from the end of July to the end of August, labouring under great difficulties occasioned by the rising water, the extreme heat and the hordes of tormenting insects, proved fruitful; the groundplan of the earlier buildings was revealed, as was a smaller chapel with a landing quay, and a portico of imposing dimensions, plus some blocks ascribed to the Meroitic King Ergamenes.

Even before the international campaign was launched, "grants in return" had been promised to those who contributed to the salvage of Abu Simbel, while archaeological missions were to be recompensed with part of their finds. What could the Egyptian authorities do to express their gratitude to the Federal Republic of Germany for its major contribution to the Nubian Campaign in saving this great temple, using its own resources? They decided to keep the small, early Ptolemaic temple discovered by the German expedition in its final mission and to re-erect it at the southern end of Elephantine Island where it now adds to the beauty of one of the most charming spots in Aswan. The portico discovered was presented as a gift to the Federal Republic of Germany. Since 1973 it has become one of the main attractions in the Egyptian collection of West Berlin.

Temple on Rails

THE FRANCO–EGYPTIAN SALVAGE OF AMADA

France decided to join in the Nubia Campaign by contributing funds towards saving the temples of Abu Simbel and by providing technical and financial help for the removal of the temple of Amada. The architect Jean Trouvelot, French Inspector-General of Historic Monuments and Clerk of Works, has provided this description of a remarkable feat of civil engineering:

"Although this temple (Amada) was not big, measuring 25 m by 10 m, it was one of the most distinctive and best preserved examples of the art of the XVIIIth dynasty. It consisted of a naos (sanctuary) and a pronaos. The masonry walls of the naos were built without mortar and their inner face was covered with a coating of plaster which hid the joints. This was finely sculpted in light relief and painted. The pronaos, built a little later, had stone side walls and pillars with no painted plaster-work. On the side towards the river was a pylon of sun-dried bricks.

"As it stood near the Nile, the temple was going to vanish under the rising waters. To save it from inundation it had to be raised 60 m, and as the slope of the river bank was only very slight, the temple had to be moved 2 km. 600 m.

"Where the pronaos was concerned, it was possible to use the conventional method of dismantling the blocks of stone, carefully numbering them, and then re-erecting them on the new site. For the naos, however, this was out of the question. Whatever precautions might have been taken, the painted and sculpted plaster decoration would have flaked disastrously where the joints met. Plans therefore had to be made for moving the naos, at least, in one piece.

"Bearing in mind the small size of the temple, our first idea was to move the whole building by floating it, taking advantage of the rising waters. It was technically possible, but the lake created by the dam was rising so slowly that the temple would have had to remain on the water for several years, and this was very risky. In addition, at the end of the operation the temple would have had to be hoisted and slid to a point some metres above the highest water level.

"This idea was abandoned, and it was then planned to take advantage of the gentle slope and regularity of the ground (a topographical survey of which had just been made by the French Geographical Institute) to transport the temple in one piece on prestressed concrete runners. Unfortunately this delicate operation turned out much too expensive and also had to be abandoned.

"In February 1964, the firm of Sainrapt and Brice came up with a solution more in line with the moderate funds available. They proposed that, to avoid any damage to the interior decoration of the naos, it should be separated from the pronaos and moved on its own, in one piece, on flat trolleys fitted with jacks and running in rails. This firm had considerable experience with this method of transport, and it had been successfully employed at a variety of sites.

"The Governments of Egypt and France finally adopted this idea and provided extra finance to cover its cost. The work nevertheless had to be carried out quickly as the level of the Nile was already rising. The technical and financial studies were carried out in the record time of a few weeks and work began.

"There was no painted plaster over the joints in the masonry of the walls and columns of the pronaos, and the stones were thus dismantled with care by the Egyptian Antiquities Organization, numbered, and taken by lorry close to the new site for the temple (the work being directed by Taha-el-Shiltawi, head of the Engineering Office of the Egyptian Antiquities Organization).

"At the same time, preliminary work went ahead for the transport of the naos in one piece. The painted walls were first protected by cotton flock padding. The naos then had to be made firm and not liable to distortion, so the open joints between the stones were cleaned from the outside and injected with a special mortar. Concrete angle-pieces were placed on the corners of the building and prestressed by horizontal and vertical cables, and a series of concrete beams was put in place under the temple where the rock had been removed. These beams, carrying the 900 tons of the naos, were in turn supported by three principal beams resting on hydraulic jacks on flat, rail-borne trolleys. All the beams were made of concrete which was both reinforced and prestressed in order to avoid, either while loading or during transport, any give which might cause cracks in the stonework.

"One of the great difficulties of the move arose because the three jacks had irregular contours and had settled unevenly, something which unfortunately could not be avoided. To prevent any distortion, it was essential to maintain the same pressure at all times on each of the supports. To do this, the hydraulic jacks were interconnected, and as the pressure on the various jacks was thus automatically the same, they each exerted an equal and constant push on the beams. The naos and its supporting structure was thus in continuous floating suspension on the jacks. The move was made using 'pushing' jacks which exerted their backward thrust on the rails. It took the three months of January, February and March 1965 to complete the journey.

"Many difficulties were encountered in saving the temple of Amada. Firstly its total isolation in a completely empty Nubia meant that all communications and supplies had to come from Aswan, either via the Nile (190 km and 3 days sailing) or across the desert (220 km of bad tracks where vehicles frequently bogged down in the sand). During the hottest months, work became difficult and often technically more awkward, with the dehydration of the concrete. In fact, the operation almost failed as the waters were rising while the Aswan Dam was being built. The exceptionally high waters of the Nile in 1964, higher than forecast, combined with the delay in supplies for the site, rendered the situation critical in Autumn 1964. The water rose 40–50 cm a day and threatened to flood the foundations of the temple before its removal had begun. A protective bank was hastily thrown up and on 12 December the naos left its original site. It was just in the nick of time, because the waters of the Nile flooded the site the moment the pumps were stopped.

"To begin with, the temple was raised up a fairly steep slope from the level of its foundations to the natural ground level where the railway tracks had been laid. Only 150 m of rails had been supplied so these were taken up as progress was made and re-laid higher up. The 2 km 600 m journey was not all in a straight line as the track had to skirt uneven terrain which would have been difficult to cross.

"The temple arrived at its new site in March 1965. The new foundations had already been prepared in the rock, ready for the temple to be re-erected with exactly the same alignment as at the original site. The lower beams on which it had been carried were made fast on the foundations and buried in the sand. The upper beams were taken out and broken up.

"The ancient sandstone quarry which had supplied the stone for the temple was discovered nearby, with some half-extracted blocks of stone still there.

"In July 1966 began the methodical re-erection of the pronaos, the parts of which had been brought to the site by lorry. After the ground had been levelled, the surroundings of the temple were reproduced from detailed surveys of the original layout. The sun-dried bricks of the low walls were moulded by hand using mud from the banks of the Nile, obtained before the water rose. The temple surrounds, the terrace in front of the entrance and the beginnings of the two superimposed *dromoi*, which were with the temple at its original site, were thus faithfully reproduced in order to preserve all its religious, cultural and monumental significance.

"At the front of the temple of Amada there was originally a pylon, with its two side-pillars flanking the doorway. Some remains, built of sun-dried bricks, still existed at the beginning of the nineteenth century. Marks on the ground and on the walls, the only traces we found, gave the exact position and we decided to reproduce it. Studies of perspective drawings and a model led us to limit the reconstruction of the pylon to its lower part, leaving the upper part as a ruin since we did not know either its exact height or how it was topped. We tried simply to give it an architectural aspect sufficiently evocative for the visitor to have the feeling of an ancient temple once again in this new and very beautiful landscape of pale sand and red hills."

Achievements of the Egyptian Antiquities Organization

"HELP YOURSELF . . ." THE SALVAGE OF THE SMALLER TEMPLES

In international campaigns of the type first launched in Nubia the attitude of the "host countries" is fundamental. Its importance has already been acknowledged in the initial analysis of the role of Unesco and the responsibilities of Egypt and the Sudan. Both countries lived up to their obligations, and for Egyptian Nubia this was demonstrated by the active Egyptian participation in the big salvage operations of Abu Simbel and of Philae, and particularly in the rescue of the numerous smaller temples and monuments.

Already in 1960 Egypt had started to rescue the temples of Taffa, Debod and Qertassi, in 1961 Dakka and Maharraqa, and in 1962 Dendur; all this was done by the Egyptian authorities using their own financial and technical means, sometimes in collaboration with international experts.

A United States grant covered the costs of removing to safety in 1964 the temples of Wadi es-Sebua and Beit el Wali and the rock tomb of Pennut at Aniba, but the work of re-erection was done with Egyptian resources.

Encouraged by the success of these operations the last monument, the temple of Derr, was also saved in 1965 – a rescue operation of which the experts had at one time despaired.

Parts of the temple of Gerf Husein and of the chapel of Abu Oda were cut out of the rock, as well as the chapels of Qasr Ibrim together with a large number of rock inscriptions and drawings.

This is indeed an impressive list of achievements, especially if one considers the financial and technical implications, and the working conditions in isolated places lacking even elementary comfort and safety, yet little has been published on the subject, except in the case of temples given as "grants-in-return" to certain countries; these temples and their museological roles will be described later. Meanwhile here is now a brief account of the Egyptian rescue operations in Lower Nubia.

In the summer of 1960 the temples of Taffa, Debod and Qertassi were saved. The Ministry of Irrigation lowered the level of the water upstream of the Aswan Dam to 101 m above sea level, to make the removal of the monuments and the excavation of the sites possible. The temples of Taffa and Debod were given away as "grants-in-return" whereas the temple of Qertassi was re-erected by an Egyptian team near those of Kalabsha and Beit el Wali in the immediate neighbourhood of the High Dam.

In the following summer of 1961, the temples of Dendur, Dakka and Maharraqa were saved. The temple of Dakka needed special attention as it only appeared out of water during the inundation season when the water level was lowered upstream of the Aswan Dam. The period available for the rescue was thus very short to remove every stone and to investigate the site.

The temple of Derr was the last monument to be detached from the rocks in which it had been cut by Ramses II. To protect it from the rise of the water of the reservoir in 1965 a wall had to be built. The temple together with the tomb of Pennut were removed to form a group near the new site of the Amada temple.

Dakka and Maharraqa were re-erected at Wadi es-Sebua near the re-erected temple from that neighbourhood. Unfortunately it was not possible to save the temple of Gerf Husein and the chapel of Abu Oda. The former was hewn in bad rock and its salvage would have been very expensive. However, parts of the temple, including relief blocks and an Osirid statue of Ramses II were saved, as well as blocks from Abu Oda (a rock chapel from the time of King Horemheb *c.* 1325 B.C.), including the reliefs covered by Christian frescoes. These parts of different monuments will be exhibited in the Nubia Museum, in Aswan, for the establishment of which there is now an international campaign.

Several hundred rock inscriptions and rock drawings were also cut out and rescued, but all of them could not be saved. However, the chapels of Qasr Ibrim were rescued by an Egyptian team under the direction of Mr. A. Lutfi.

The costs of these operations were met by the High Dam Authorities. Three hundred thousand Egyptian pounds were allotted in 1959–61, as well as one million pounds for the safeguarding of these monuments. Their removal cost more than one million, and the excess was covered from Egyptian funds which partly depended on normal budgetary sources.

THE OPEN AIR MUSEUMS OF EGYPTIAN NUBIA

That the rescued temples of Nubia should not become forgotten monuments in a deserted stretch of the Nile Valley was a decision taken by the Egyptian authorities and one which was strongly endorsed by the Executive Committee. The result is the creation of what could best be described as a string of "cultural oases".

The northernmost, near the High Dam, is the new site of the temple of Kalabsha, and the charming little Greco–Roman kiosk of Qertassi, offering splendid views over the lake. Behind the free-standing temples the small rock temple of Beit el Wali has been inserted in the hillside; the unusually refined reliefs describing the triumphs of Ramses II in the north and in the south with their many absorbing details seem always to fascinate visitors.

One hundred and ten kilometres further south in the neighbourhood of Wadi es-Sebua is the next group. The main attraction here is the temple of Wadi es-Sebua, re-erected on a higher level. This magnificent building of Ramses II, with its forecourt and rows of sphinxes, its impressive pylon and its inner parts decorated with reliefs, was in Christian times converted into a church; the old reigning gods were replaced by a fresco representing the Apostle Peter, so that Ramses II is seen offering to the saint instead of to pagan divinities. Surmounting a slope is the small re-erected temple of Dakka; built by the Meroitic king Ergamenes, his contemporary Ptolemaios IV of Egypt (222–204 B.C.) had added a forecourt and the Roman emperors a pylon and the sanctuary. The third monument in the group is the undecorated Roman temple of Maharraqa from the town of Hierasykaminos once at the southern frontier of the Roman Empire, some 50 km north of its new site.

In one of the most beautiful parts of Lower Nubia, 45 km upstream from Wadi es-Sebua, is the third group of monuments. Here at Amada is the site to which the temple of Amada was transported on rails, as described elsewhere. Here too is the rock temple of Ramses II from Derr with its well-preserved colours exposed during the salvage operation, and finally the small rock tomb of Pennut, who had been a Nubian official of Ramses VI (c. 1150 B.C.) at Miam Aniba, the capital of Lower Nubia during the New Kingdom.

These three splendid sites with their variety of arresting monuments are but the prelude to the wonder evoked by the reconstructed temples of Abu Simbel, the culmination of an unforgettable journey through Lower Nubia.

TEMPLES AS AMBASSADORS

Already in October 1959 at an international meeting of experts the Egyptian Minister of Culture, Dr. Saroite Okacha, had confirmed his government's undertaking to award certain Nubian temples to Member States which had made the greatest contributions to the Campaign. The monuments selected to be what Dr. Okacha called "new ambassadors extraordinary" were the temples of Debod, Taffa, Dendur, Derr, and Ellesiya. However, Derr could not be rescued in its entirety; later the Kalabsha portico was included among these gifts.

The Egyptian Government had specified that the monuments should be allocated to museums or scientific centres open to the public and that steps should be taken to ensure their permanent safety and to create an environment appropriate to their archaeological character. The costs of dismantling, transporting and reconstructing the monuments should be borne by the receiver. Thus preservation facilities, atmospheric conditions, appropriate setting, and accessibility for scholars and the public had to be given due consideration.

These requirements posed special problems, especially in overcoming the divergence of interests between the preservation, public accessibility and installation of the monuments in modern surroundings.

The problems were solved in different ways by the receiving museums, the famous Egyptian galleries of the Metropolitan Museum of Art, New York (Dendur), Leiden (Taffa), Turin (Ellesiya) and West Berlin (Kalabsha portico). While these monuments could be housed indoors, a similar solution was not feasible for the Debod temple which needed a wide area to contain its sanctuary and two gateways, all at a distance from one another. It was re-erected in a beautiful outdoor setting in a park in Madrid with some risk for its protection and preservation but with maximum accessibility for the public.

The temples that are exhibited in well climatized museums are better protected and have attracted high numbers of visitors. To mention only one instance: in the year following its opening to the public the Dendur temple in New York was seen by a record total of 1,152,000 persons.

THE TEMPLE OF DENDUR IN NEW YORK

The Temple of Dendur was originally sited on the west bank of the Nile, some 80 km south of Aswan. Though ostensibly built by the Roman emperor Augustus to honour two deceased sons of a local Nubian chieftain and ally, the real recipient of the offerings was the goddess Isis of Philae, whose clergy staffed the temple.

The small, three-roomed temple was built against a cliff in which a small speos had been already hewn. This small room, which could not be removed, may have been the original burial place of the two brothers mentioned above, Pedesi and Pihor.

In May of 1968 the blocks of the temple of Dendur saved by Egypt in 1962 and stored on Elephantine Island were inspected, crated, and in June they were taken by barges down the Nile to Alexandria, where they passed through final customs and were loaded on to the Norwegian freighter, the S.S. *Concordia Star*, bound for New York.

A simple enormous vitrine-like enclosure was intended to protect the temple in the Metropolitan Museum and, at the same time, to expose it to natural light as much as possible. However, as plans for the entire north wing of the museum were changed for financial considerations, the projected enclosure for the temple grew markedly in size and complexity. And in the end it was to be provided with natural light from the long north wall, and diffused light from the grid ceiling. In addition, the south side of the enclosure was to have three different levels, screened for gallery and office use.

In an attempt to provide more focus for the temple complex, there was a preliminary suggestion to place each of the two elements of the complex (the temple and the gateway) on its own pedestal, rather like individual pieces of monumental sculpture. This and other suggestions were ultimately rejected in favour of a reconstruction of as much as was known of the original Nubian setting. The materials used in the approximation were to be permanent and easy to maintain. They would also be clearly differentiated from the original portions of the temple complex. Gray granite was selected to represent the reconstructed areas of the complex and the major topographical features: red granite designated the public areas.

Besides focusing more attention on the temple by giving its setting more substance, the additional elements introduced into the modern setting had other purposes: they provided the viewer with an idea of the original setting of the temple of Dendur; and they could be adapted to protect it, without using traditional barriers such as guardrails. This last element became very important since from the beginning it had been known that due to the smallness of the rooms and the fragility of the sandstone visitors could not be allowed into the temple itself. After much discussion on the present state of the art of stone consolidation, it was decided only to de-salt the masonry blocks of which the temple was constituted; and not to proceed with a programme of impregnation, which would have markedly changed the colour and texture of the stone and possibly caused other problems in the future.

In the meantime, however, lights have been installed in the pronaos, the only completely decorated room in the temple, to facilitate public viewing from the temple's façade and side doors and photographs depicting the interior of the temple and details of its decoration have been incorporated into the educational material located on the south wall of the enclosure.

If there is no doubt that the temple looks its best at night, when the stark contours of the enclosure have become blurred and indistinct, this is, after all, in keeping with the opinion of Amelia Edwards who visited the Temple in 1874 and confided the following, much-quoted passage to her journal:

"At Dendoor . . . we visit a tiny temple on the western bank. It stands out above the river . . . and consists of a single pylon, a portico, two little chambers and a sanctuary. The whole thing is like an exquisite toy, so covered with sculptures, so smooth, so new looking, so admirably built. Seeing them half by sunlight, half by dusk . . . the rosy half-light of an Egyptian afterglow covers a multitude of sins, and steeps the whole in an atmosphere of romance."

(*Cathleen Keller*, Assistant Curator, Department of Egyptian Art).

THE TEMPLE OF TAFFA IN LEIDEN

In July 1960 a team of Egyptian and Polish architects dismantled the Temple of Taffa stone by stone, a complicated task because the walls had collapsed inwards after being struck by a ship. The blocks with which the temple had been built were numbered and, until it could be built elsewhere, they were laid out on the south tip of Elephantine, an island in the Nile opposite Aswan, together with the blocks from three other temples which had been saved. Taffa was the first part of the Nubian rescue Campaign.

Before the 657 blocks could be shipped to the Netherlands they had to be packed in plastic and then crated for the sea-journey; the packing occupied the summer and autumn of 1970 and on 12 October the blocks were loaded on to large flat Nile boats in 644 sealed cases. Exactly one month later the convoy with its cargo of 250 tonnes left Aswan on its 1300 km journey down the Nile to Alexandria. Before the end of the year this unusual cargo was lowered into the hold of *De Sinon*, a ship owned by the Royal Netherlands Steamship Company and under the control of the shipping company Hudig and Veder. The temple of Taffa arrived in Rotterdam on 18 January 1971 and on the same day it was transported to a warehouse in Leiden for storage.

However, Egypt had parted with the temple on two conditions: it had to be rebuilt in a heated, enclosed space, as the Nubian sandstone would suffer if it was exposed to the Dutch climate. Admission to the temple, since it was a gift from the Egyptian to the Dutch people, had to be free. The Egyptians also expressed a wish for the temple to be housed in the National Museum of Antiquities in Leiden. The temple would be a natural addition to the museum's Egyptian collection, one of the best in the world, and moreover the museum is the main link for a number of scientific and cultural connections between Egypt and the Netherlands.

The plans for rebuilding the temple were ready in 1970 but it was not until six years later that work would begin on this great project centred around the temple. In the meantime the plan had been radically altered, thanks to technical advances and as a result of new ideas on the shape of the hall in which the temple would be housed. Finally, in April 1977, the first piles were driven into the ground for the foundation of the terrace on which the temple would stand and for the pillars which would carry the colossal acoustic ceiling and the roof.

In the ensuing months the courtyard of the museum was altered according to plans drawn up by Haak, a Delft architect, to become a majestic gallery with the largest capacity for any building of its kind in the Netherlands. By the end of 1977 the roof was completed, the ceiling put in and limestone wall panels for the new hall had been mounted on the courtyard walls. During the winter months of 1978 hundreds of blocks from the temple were either brought to the site or laid out in the store behind the museum. Arranging the blocks according to layer and preparations for rebuilding, which included casting a concrete platform for the temple, were carried out following the recommendations of Hassan el-Ashiery, an Egyptian architect and Egyptologist. The rebuilding itself was carried out by the museum, a project which in all respects was unique for the Netherlands. The temple was restored in the summer of 1978, immediately after it had been rebuilt. A method was chosen whereby the missing and damaged parts of the buildings, notably where the outline was disturbed, were filled in level with the original surface of the stone but only in those cases where there was certainty about the structure. The museum renovators also took advantage of the opportunity to use modern methods and the latest materials to replace the 1908 "restoration" which had been carried out in the space of one month using just cement, but which nevertheless saved the temple.

For almost 2000 years the temple of Taffa, the charming Isis sanctuary on the banks of the Nile in Nubia, has been associated with water; not only the fertile Nile flood but also the turbulent currents of the Nile cataract. It was this very high water which, for the benefit of future generations, would have put an abrupt end to the temple's existence in 1960 if our generation had not taken action. The preservation of the temple means that more chapters will be added to the history of Taffa.

(*Dr. Hans D. Schneider*, Director, Rijksmuseum van Oudheden, Leiden).

THE TEMPLE OF DEBOD IN MADRID

The temple of Debod was built in the 3rd century B.C. when the Ptolemies reigned in Egypt, and Egyptianized kings of Meroë ruled the upper part of the Nile Valley.

The central hall of the original part of the temple was decorated by Azekheramun with reliefs of a high quality, representing him, the Meroite from the Sudan, offering to a whole pantheon of 24 Egyptian divinities. In the sanctuary, behind this hall, there is a granite naos of Ptolemy XIII Neos Dionysos (according to Porter & Moss, Topographical Bibliography; according to Almagro, however, Ptolemy XIV and the famous Queen Cleopatra); a similar naos of Ptolemy VII Euergetes II was destroyed between 1821 and 1827. The forecourt, in front of the hall of Azekheramun, was decorated by Emperor Augustus or Tiberius.

This small temple or rather chapel was originally surrounded by walls of sundried bricks with three large gates of stone, of which the third has collapsed and disappeared sometime during this century. The second gate was an addition to the temple of Azekheramun, according to a Greek inscription, in the name of Ptolemy VI Philometor and Cleopatra II between 172 and 170 B.C. Here no longer Amun, but Isis takes the first place – Debod is now a station on the journey of the goddess around the northern part of Lower Nubia to give blessing to the land.

The temple of Debod was the first to be dismantled by the Egyptian Government in 1960 and the blocks were brought to the island of Elephantine and stored there.

In 1968 it was given as a gift-in-return from the Egyptian Government to Spain in recognition for contributions to the Nubia Campaign, specifically to the salvage of Abu Simbel. This was done in accordance with a recommendation of the Executive Committee at a session in Madrid.

The blocks were brought from Elephantine to Spain, and now there was the problem of how and where to re-erect the temple.

The architectural structure of the monument – a chapel with two gates in front and at some distance from it – gives it a form, 40 m by 10 m, which is awkward or even impossible to place indoors in a museum.

So the basic preservation requirements concerning the gifts-in-return, that the monuments should be given to museums and that steps should be taken to ensure their permanent safety, were indeed difficult to meet.

There were some discussions whether the temple should not be re-erected rather in a part of Spain with a desert-like climate where it would not be exposed to such great variations of humidity and temperature as in Madrid.

This alternative was, however, turned down and a site was selected in a park in the central part of Madrid, a hill not far from the Royal Palace and with a wonderful vista over the surroundings.

The temple was rebuilt on a concrete basement and a large pond was constructed in front of the temple proper, with the gates placed on a platform in the middle of the lake, mirrored in the water. On the platform the central road up to the temple as well as the alignment of the original adobe walls were marked with different types of stone.

The setting is a complete success and the palm trees planted in this part of the park give one somehow a feeling of Egypt.

So, despite the risks involved for its safety in the long run, this temple has also become a monument recalling to the inhabitants of the capital of Spain and to innumerable visitors the international solidarity between the Member States of Unesco and the brilliant success of the Nubia Campaign.

A NARROW ESCAPE – THE SALVAGE OF THE SPEOS OF ELLESIYA

At Ellesiya, some 200 km south of Aswan, is the small temple which Tuthmosis III cut in a rock-face around 1450 B.C. and dedicated to the Nubian god Horus of Miam (Aniba) and his consort the goddess Satis. The reliefs depicted the King making offerings and performing ritual acts to minor deities accompanying the principal gods of the chapel, deities such as Horus of Buhen, Hathor of Ibshek, and the deified Middle Kingdom King Sesostris III. Although somewhat eroded by the action of the water, the reliefs were still well enough preserved to give an impression of the great classical Egyptian art of the

Eighteenth Dynasty. Such was the artistic and historic interest of this speos that every effort had to be made to save as much of it as possible.

In May 1962 Italy had been asked to try to rescue one of the Nubian temples and following an inspection tour of Nubia by Egyptian officials and a mission from Turin it was decided that the salvage of the temple of Ellesiya should be an Italian contribution to the salvage of Nubian monuments.

Following consideration of various tenders the mission from Turin was told in August 1964 that the Egyptian Antiquities Organization would be prepared to carry out the salvage using their own personnel and technical resources, an offer which was accepted by the Italian authorities. In January 1965 the project was officially approved by the Egyptian Government, Egypt undertaking to salvage Ellesiya on Italy's behalf, and in April the Province and City of Turin agreed to bear the cost of the scheme.

Time was now running short (the reservoir would start to fill in September and the speos was only 110 m above sea level) and the Egyptian Government declared its intention to bring the speos to safety, if necessary paying the costs out of Egyptian funds, in which case Italy would not of course receive the monument as a gift.

Originally it had been intended to keep the temple in Nubia even though regarded as a gift to Italy, but later it was decided it should be moved to Turin. Unesco had backed this alternative on the grounds that, if left in Nubia, it could not compete with the much more imposing monuments, such as Abu Simbel and Kalabsha. Few visitors would have seen it, whereas in the Egyptian Museum of Turin, housing one of the world's outstanding Egyptian collections, it would be a central exhibit, complementing the many other Egyptian pieces of art, not least a remarkable statue of Tuthmosis III, the king who was responsible for constructing the speos of Ellesiya. It would, moreover, be of considerable interest to the many students and scholars who visit the Turin collection annually.

The Egyptian Government accepted these arguments and ceded the monument to the Egyptian Museum of Turin, the city which had provided the financial backing.

Turin's Superintendent of Egyptology, Professor Silvio Curto had been called in to attend the salvage operation. Owing to the abnormally high Nile of the summer of 1965, like that of 1964, it turned into a hazardous adventure and some planned precautions had to be abandoned in a desperate attempt to save whatever was possible, be it only a few square metres of the decorated walls.

The expedition, consisting of a flotilla of boats and barges, arrived at Ellesiya on 13 July 1965, only to find the monument inaccessible because of the muddy waters which still covered the space in front of the speos. Slowly the Nile receded, so that on 15 July the entrance was almost out of the water and the grotto could be entered by boat. On the following day the sanctuary was free of water, but two days later the situation became critical. The experts forecast that the Nile would stay low for a very short time only. Even in the best of conditions the monument was difficult to reach because of the marshy land which fronted it, covered with water too shallow for ordinary boats but too deep for an approach on foot; in a single day the marshy terrain could become impassable. To reach the monument from behind the steep rock into which it was cut was impossible.

Silvio Curto has described the salvage operation though he omits mention of the conditions of work in the full blast of the Nubian summer, with temperatures seldom below 45° or 50° C in the shade, usually non-existent, handicapped by slippery mud and blisteringly hot sandstone; in short a torturing experience for all concerned.

"In this desperate situation the official of the Service in charge of the work came up with a brilliant expedient. On the surface of the remaining water he had a big iron barge of shallow draught pushed forward by his men with immense effort, shoving it along with poles. To this floating platform, parked at the façade of the temple to the right of the entrance, he brought, with several boat trips, the necessarily light equipment for the work, provisions and the workers, some 50 men who installed themselves there and on a rock shelf only a few square metres in extent to the left of the entrance. On the 19th the barge was stranded on the ground, isolated from the rest of the world. Working from this platform, using some cranes and rock saws, an electric generator and flashlights, in 20 days of frenzied work non-stop for 24 hours a day, these workers cut out with perfection all the inscriptions of the façade, the reliefs and even the upper half of the inner socle. They loaded the blocks on to the barge one by one to the number of 66, the blocks averaging one cubic metre in size and weighing a ton, though some were bigger. Five days later the Nile began to rise, and soon the barge was afloat and could be tugged to Wadi es-Sebua where its precious load was unloaded in safety." (*Translated from the Italian*).

In January 1966 the blocks were brought to the harbour at the High Dam and from there transported in crates to Alexandria, loaded on the MS "Esperia" and brought to Italy.

In the Turin museum the temple was rebuilt in a perfect museological setting. The roof was constructed in light metal, isolated from the stone blocks of the walls by a slot through which the reliefs of the walls could be lighted. The well-known firm of car builders and airplane constructors, Pininfarina, not only put their skilled workers at the disposal of the Museum but also paid these and other expenses.

In September 1970 the re-erected monument, rescued from destruction in Nubia, was inaugurated, to bear witness to the grandeur of Pharaonic art, to international solidarity and to Italy's adherence to its great cultural traditions.

The Monuments of Sudanese Nubia

THE TASK

The most impressive monuments of Sudanese Nubia were of a nature which
could not be rescued from the waters of the High Dam Lake; built of sun-dried
bricks, the impossibility of removal seemed obvious, a conclusion confirmed
by investigation. However, the perishability of the building material did not
detract from their historical and cultural value. The chain of Middle Kingdom
fortresses, dating from the first centuries of the second millennium B.C. were
masterpieces of military architecture which embodied certain defence devices
not found elsewhere before the period of the Crusades. These immense and
intriguing monuments could be no more than examined and documented by
the archaeologists; removal of even the most interesting architectural details
was out of the question. So these unique constructions will survive only
through the plans, the publications and the finds made in them.

The same applies to the numerous churches – notably the wonder of Faras,
the cathedral decorated with more than a hundred beautiful and well-dated
frescoes, and the whole series of other churches containing a wealth of wall
paintings and architectural detail, all reflecting a creative Nubian art in a vivid
cultural interrelation with the Near East. Here again, although the buildings
themselves could not be rescued, the frescoes were removed from the walls,
sometimes in one layer painted over another, reinforced and brought to safety
for display in museums, mainly in Khartoum and Warsaw.

Sudanese Nubia was, however, not entirely void of stone monuments to be
salvaged. The rescue operations are of interest not only by virtue of the historic
value of the monuments, but also because of the ingenious and simple yet
effective means which were used to save them.

These monuments were: the remains of a temple of Ramses II at Aksha, near
the Egyptian border, the rock tomb of Djehutihotep, a Nubian prince who
ruled the district of Debeira (at that time called Teh-khet) in the reign of Queen
Hatshepsut and Tuthmosis III (*c.* 1490 B.C.) – a tomb decorated with striking
paintings in purely Egyptian style – the contemporary temple in the huge
Middle and New Kingdom fortress of Buhen, at the point where the placid Nile
was transformed into the turbulent Second Cataract and, finally, the two
temples of approximately the same date in the Middle Kingdom border
fortresses at Semna East and West, set in the heart of that wild landscape of
broken waters known as the *Batn el-Hajar*, or Belly of Stones.

No special international campaign was needed to finance the salvage
operations. The Sudan was aided by several Member States, who covered the
costs of dismantling and removal to the National Museum in Khartoum, which
had been built with Unesco support. Financially, France took care of the temple
of Aksha, the United Kingdom of Buhen, the Netherlands of Semna East and
Belgium of Semna West.

The success of these operations was due almost exclusively to the ingenuity of one man, the German architect Friedrich W. Hinkel, who had been put at the disposal of the Sudanese authorities by the Academy of Science of the German Democratic Republic. In two books – "Tempel ziehen um" (1966) and "Auszug aus Nubien" (1978) – he has described not only the thrilling removal of the monuments and their re-erection in the National Museum in Khartoum, but also the tragic exodus from Nubia of his friends and collaborators among the Nubian population.

Hinkel was ably supported by the Sudanese authorities, specifically Sayyid Thabit Hassan Thabit, Commissioner for Archaeology, and his representative in the Wadi Halfa district, Sayyid Nigmeddin Mohammed Sharif who later succeeded Thabit as Commissioner for Archaeology. Nigmeddin Sharif is himself a Nubian, and it should never be forgotten that it was through the faithful service and dedicated skill of the Nubians themselves, not least the local workers, that the monuments were saved and the history and culture of their land properly explored, and all this at a time when they themselves were fighting for the future of their families involved in the emigration to Khashm el-Girba, far from their own "Blessed Country".

THE SALVAGE

On Christmas Day 1962, four gentlemen were walking from shop to shop in the bazaar streets of the little town of Wadi Halfa. They were Friedrich Hinkel, Dr. Plenderleith, Director of the International Conservation Centre in Rome, and his two assistants, Dr. Mora and Dr. Toraka. They were not looking for Christmas gifts; their shopping expedition was connected with the dismantling of the Buhen temple. The chemicals essential for the consolidation of the very brittle sandstone had been dispatched to Wadi Halfa during the preceding summer but they had never arrived – a not unusual situation in the Sudan with its single harbour to handle all export and import movements, and connected with other parts of the country with a single-line railway. It was a situation that no efforts on the part of the Sudanese authorities, in giving top priority to the Nubian Campaign, could overcome.

The experts on the spot were of course in a quandary, so to avoid further delay something had to be improvised. Hence the visit to Wadi Halfa, to a strange kind of market where one could perhaps find the latest transistor model but not a safety pin. A thorough search provided a solution – shellac in quantities sufficient for their needs. A 4–8% solution of shellac in alcohol was an old and well-tried recipe for treating brittle sandstone.

Three weeks later the consolidation of the Buhen temple had been completed. A similar method was applied at the tomb of Djehutihotep at Debeira and at the temple of Aksha. The blocks with colouring on them had to be bandaged with fine cotton cloth and for this purpose the 6 -m-long veils or shawls worn by the Sudanese women proved to be just what was needed and were obtainable in the local market.

For the dismantling of the Buhen temple no suitable cranes or derricks were available, the only large crane being a floating affair in Wadi Halfa harbour made in the year 1902, so it was decided to fall back on the method used by the Ancient Egyptians, only in the reverse order. The temple was filled with sand up to the lower joints of the top layer of masonry and the stones of this layer were then lifted or pushed on to a sledge made from mahogany, a hard wood which in the Sudan is much cheaper than imported soft timber. A similar construction was put on top of the block and the two sledges, bolstered with cotton wool, were held firmly together with screwed iron bars at each of the four corners. When the top layer of blocks had been removed the sand was shovelled away down to the next level of joints and the same procedure repeated until the underlying soil or rock was reached.

This method of packing the blocks gave them effective protection despite the somewhat rough handling inevitable during the transport of each block, when some 30 workers dragged it down a causeway of mahogany planks to the boats waiting to carry the blocks across the river. The 59 cases weighing in all some 600 tons were loaded on to 28 railway wagons and taken to Khartoum, 926 km to the south. All the blocks arrived undamaged and the total costs "f.o.b." Khartoum amounted to no more than 25,150 Sudanese pounds (about $50,000).

At the same time the decorated wall of the temple of Aksha, the only one selected to be rescued, was dismantled. It was a delicate operation because groundwater humidity and salt incrustations had cemented the joints.

The tomb of Djehutihotep at Debeira was cut from the rock in which it had been hewn. It consisted of a smallish room with a statue chamber behind, where the deceased and his family are seen sculptured in the round. The first room was decorated with interesting scenes from the life of the Egyptianized Nubian ruler of Debeira under Queen Hatshepsut. The paintings are in the style of the Theban capital and show gardening activities with light-brown and black men watering a rich variety of trees, a festival with Nubian musicians and dancers, the Prince enjoying a meal and hunting in the desert in his chariot – in short, representations of all the pleasurable pursuits of a noble lord of his time.

Having broken down the rock around the tomb, the workers cut the painted rock into blocks with a very thin saw – the same procedure as that followed at Abu Simbel though in miniature, so to speak – the Nubians demonstrating their skill by making saw cuts of only a few millimetres in width. Hinkel had to supervise the work on three sites at the same time, check the unloading in Khartoum and make the measurements necessary for the proper re-erection of the monuments. And these activities continued throughout the spring sandstorms and the blistering heat at the beginning of summer.

In the next season, 1963/64, it was the turn of the temples of Semna East and West, although they would not be threatened by inundation until 1968/69. In the meantime, a number of particularly interesting rock inscriptions and rock drawings were rescued. A rock inscription of the utmost historical significance, from above Buhen, was also saved; it recorded the victory of an Egyptian Early Dynastic king, possibly Djer, over his Nubian enemies, and is the oldest Egyptian inscription found in Sudanese Nubia.

In January 1964 all the necessary material and equipment had arrived on site at Semna and work could start. The "road" from Wadi Halfa to Semna, some 60 km, was no more than the remains of a long-disused railway bed dating from Kitchener's River War, and the last kilometres only a track through a stony valley down to the Nile, ending on a soft sandy plain which necessitated the construction of a plank causeway for the transporting lorries.

At Semna the Nile breaks through a granite barrier into a very narrow channel where the current is immensely strong. This passage and the rocks surrounding it made Semna the natural border for defence against enemies from the south, and is the reason for the siting of the two Middle Kingdom fortresses built one on each of the hills bordering the channel.

The problem was how to transport the blocks from Semna West across a stretch of racing water, where a boat going adrift would be smashed to pieces in the next torrent downstream. While several experts were debating the method, Hinkel solved it. He constructed a pontoon with a platform of mahogany planks, supported on empty oil drums collected as surplus material in Wadi Halfa. This "ferry" was secured to a wire hawser stretched from bank to bank and a dozen Nubians dragged it across the river, some 300 m wide at this point, using wooden levers. The 16-mm-thick cable had been carried across the river by a man in a rowing boat at great risk. He first brought a thin rope and to this the hawser was secured and firmly anchored from bank to bank.

On the west bank, a causeway of mahogany planks 500 m long was built. The causeway itself was laid on a bed built of Middle Kingdom mud-bricks from the fortress, 4000-year-old bricks which would have been destroyed anyhow by the rising waters. The dismantling used the same method as that at Buhen, by filling the temple up to the top level with sand and rubble and packing the detached blocks securely between mahogany sledge frames. They were then dragged by teams of Nubian workers singing in rhythm to the beat of a "chorus master" down the sloping causeway to the river bank, then on to the "ferry" already described and to the second causeway of planks laid across the sandy plain, to continue the journey by lorry along a pot-holed track to Wadi Halfa, thence by rail to Khartoum. All 146 blocks, totalling 130 tons, arrived without loss or damage.

While this operation was going on, certain financing problems for the salvage of the temple in the fortress of Semna East (sometimes wrongly called Kumma) were solved. Since the railway station of Wadi Halfa would soon be under water, it was decided to start immediately the work of salvaging the temple. After some weeks, labouring under conditions of extreme heat, absence of wind, more snakes than usual, increasing repairs to worn out equipment, and ever more difficulties in getting food and necessities from a more or less abandoned Wadi Halfa, the 480 blocks totalling 185 tons were on their way to Khartoum. The foundations of the temple were found to contain a number of extremely well-preserved, beautifully decorated blocks from the original temple constructed by Queen Hatshepsut and Tuthmosis III; these stones had been re-used by their successor Amenophis II who built the temple that was dismantled.

With the completion of these successful operations in the Sudanese section of Lower Nubia Hinkel and his Sudanese colleagues could, with some pride, report: "Mission accomplished" and turn to the problems of the re-erection of the monuments in Khartoum.

GEMS OF THE NATIONAL MUSEUM IN KHARTOUM

When the Nubia Campaign started the Panel of Experts for Sudanese Nubia discussed at some length whether the temples should only be removed to a higher level and allowed to remain in Nubia, or whether they should be removed to Khartoum. There a new National Museum was under construction with the support of Unesco, largely to house antiquities from northern Sudan and, specifically, the finds and monuments of Lower Nubia. Some experts thought it wrong to remove, for example, the Semna temples from their strikingly beautiful surroundings. Others were in agreement with the wishes of the Sudanese authorities to bring the monuments to the capital where they could be protected and where they would be easily accessible to visitors from the Sudan and from abroad.

The environment of the temples may have been beautiful in our eyes but not so for the Ancient Egyptian architect. When built, a temple was surrounded with a wall some 12 m high, the obvious purpose being to isolate the holy place. This was more or less the general rule for temples in Egypt. Moreover, an appreciation for this type of desert landscape is a recent phenomenon. The first modern travellers in Nubia expressed no feelings of admiration for the *Batn el Hajar* and were only too happy when they had passed it in safety. According to their texts the Ancient Egyptians shared those feelings of relief. An additional reason for removing the temples to Khartoum was that they risked being vandalized or even destroyed if left unprotected in a remote and deserted land.

So for good reasons the decision was taken to bring the Nubian monuments to safety in Khartoum instead of leaving them in an evacuated country. It was a decision, however, which raised problems. The museum building, completed during the Nubia campaign, was designed for the display of normal-size even large objects, but not to house entire temples. On the other hand the climate of Khartoum was unkind to masonry of poor quality; some architectural fragments placed in the garden of the old museum had been reduced by the summer rains to shapeless lumps of stone. Whereas rain is practically non-existent in the Wadi Halfa region, with an average of 2.1 mm in July and practically zero during the rest of the year, Khartoum has an average precipitation of 64.9 mm in July and 77.4 mm in August; moreover, the rains are often torrential.

As usual, Hinkel came up with a solution. In the garden fronting the museum building a 200-m-long canal was dug, a kind of "pseudo-Nile", its banks planted with trees, bushes and flowers. Along this curving surface of water the monuments have been re-erected in their proper geographical order and in their original orientation. Visitors first pass a separate entrance hall and then either cross a bridge over the "Nile" through an alley of sphinxes to the main building, or they can follow a winding road along the "Nile". On the "West Bank" there are first five large granite columns from the cathedral of Faras, then the wall from the temple of Aksha with its famous list of conquered peoples, then the Buhen temple, a selection of rock inscriptions, and, finally, the small temple of Semna West. A turn around the end of the "Nile" brings the visitor to the temple of Semna East, opposite its Semna West counterpart, and further "north" is an artificial rock structure in which the tomb of Djehutihotep from Debeira has been inserted.

The quality of the soil required very strong foundations and the buildings were insulated from humidity and rising water by the use of lead foil. Protection against the heavy rains of summer was secured by the erection of glass and steel structures mounted on rails, enabling them to be moved back from the temples during the dry season and hidden by trees and bushes. In the rainy season they are moved forward to cover the monuments, becoming in effect a light and airy hall with ventilation openings in the roof to avoid over-heating. In this way the monuments are, so to speak, placed both outdoors and yet indoors.

The work of re-erection began in December 1964 with the placing of the big columns from Faras. The rebuilding of the temples and the construction and installation of protective structures was a long and difficult task demanding a high degree of precision; it lasted not less than 28 months but the result was a complete success. The monuments from Nubia are now the highlights and gems of the new National Museum.

This museum is a great attraction. Even during a very hot festival day in September recently, Sudanese visitors from all parts of their immense country and of all social classes could be seen crowding the garden and the museum, while a long queue waited patiently in front of the entrance hall in the pitiless sun. The Sudanese now have a truly National Museum which reflects faithfully their immensely long cultural history.

The Final Triumph – The Salvage of Philae

THE PEARL OF EGYPT

During the 19th century Philae became the most cherished and admired goal for travellers in Egypt and many are the watercolours depicting this romantic place with its temples, palm trees and beautiful flowers. Many also are the enthusiastic descriptions, from the "Description de l'Egypte" to Pierre Loti's elegiac "La Mort de Philae".

Robert Curzon, who visited Philae in 1834, wrote in his book *Visits to the Monasteries of the Levant*: "Every part of Egypt is interesting and curious, but the only place to which the epithet beautiful can be correctly applied is the island of Philae. . . . Excepting the Pyramids, nothing in Egypt struck me so much as when, on a bright moonlight night, I first entered the court of the great temple of Philae. The colours of the paintings on the walls are as vivid in many places as they were the day they were finished." It was, however, not Philae alone which commanded Curzon's admiration but also its setting "in the midst of a thousand islands, some of bare rock, some covered with palms and bushes, which interrupt the course of the river and give rise to those eddies, whirlpools and streams of foaming water which are called the cataracts of the Nile but which may be more properly designated as rapids". A description of Philae is given in Annex VI.

In a discussion of the salvage operations on Philae the question was raised whether one should not "clean" the walls of all kinds of texts and figures scribbled all over the place. From an aesthetic point of view the question was understandable, from a historical viewpoint it would have been a catastrophe.

Thanks to these scribblings the temples come to life. The ordinary sculptured texts belonging to the decorations are eloquent, as in all Greco–Roman temples in Egypt, giving us a wealth of information about myths and rituals, about pious offerings and donations by the rulers of the country, and also for example, as at the entrance to the pronaos of the temple of Isis, instructions to the custodians as to whom they should not permit to enter, being intimidated "neither by important personages, nor by ordinary people" – not only donkeys, dogs and goats, but also all strangers.

But to this treasure of information the scribbled graffiti, or carefully cut, more official secondary inscriptions, give an additional dimension – personal, social and political.

We find a richness of languages and scripts. Egyptian hieroglyphs and Demotic texts are of course numerous, as are Greek and Latin – the languages of the foreign rulers of the country – when Philae was one of the "musts" of a tourist traffic very similar to that of our times. And from the Christian period there are Coptic texts relating to the churches installed in the pagan temples.

Colour plates

XXIII

XXIV

XXV

XXVI

XXVIII

XXVII

XXIX

XXX

XXXI

XXXII

XXXIII

XXXIV

XXXV

XXXVI

XXXVII

XXXVIII

XXXIX

XL

XLII

XLIII

Colour plates

The Meroitic graffiti from the 1st century A.D. tell us about delegations and even priests holding permanent office on Philae, far away from their home town of Meroë, the capital of the Meroitic kingdom in the Sudan and Lower Nubia. As a rule they use their own Meroitic script and language, which we can read but only understand in rough outline, but sometimes they would use Demotic or hieroglyphs. So one Meroitic delegate scribbled in Demotic on the gateway: "I have come to Egypt, having sung a song of triumph over this desert thanks to the care and protection of Isis, the great goddess, because she heard our prayer and brought us safely to Egypt . . .". He is in fear of the dangerous way back home, exceptionally not on the Nile but through the desert, and continues: "Oh my lady, you who distribute lands to the gods, see to me that I be brought back to Meroë, the beautiful city of your beloved son (King Teqridamane) and keep me in good health in this fierce desert with the goods for which I have come, to bring them to your beloved son King Teqridamane . . . and the tributes which the King, my father, gave me, saying: 'Bring them to Isis!' I brought them."

So all these texts and pictures testify to a religious importance, and a popularity of Isis which had both advantages and disadvantages, as we learn from a text of the 2nd century B.C. graven on the obelisk brought to England:

". . . persons passing Philae, governors, epistates, thebarchoi, royal scribes, military officers, all other officials, the troops accompanying them and the rest of their suite, force us to pay for their stay against our will, and owing to this abuse the sanctuary is impoverished and we risk not to have the prescribed means for the sacrifices and libations made for you and your sons."

So the popularity of Isis had its disadvantages to the priests, and presumably temptations also which, according to a papyrus in Berlin, at least one priest was unable to resist; he committed a series of sacrilegious acts by disturbing the solemn mourning rites over the dead Osiris in his tomb in a grove on Biga, the god who triumphed over death at the New Year's festival. The accused, a certain Nespameti, is addressed:

"You know exactly what you have done. You have drunk wine in the house of the garden trees, which refresh King Osiris Wennofre. You have committed an outrageous act against Isis, because you have drunk the wine of the night, when the divine Ladies (the goddesses Isis and Nephtyhs) were mourning. You have called on your wife: 'Tefnet – there is no divinity like you!' The mourning wives were standing with their bosoms uncovered, but you brought singers and spent a happy time revelling. You woke the Soul of Osiris from his sleep and you opened the bottle of wine sacred to the New Year (rites), drinking together with the Blemmyes" (the Nubian barbarians).

SALVAGE PROJECTS

The first serious threat to Philae in modern times was through the construction of the first dam at Aswan begun in 1898 and completed in 1902, and heightened twice, in 1907–12 and 1929–34. As a consequence the Philae temples were under water except during the summer months, from July to October.

At the time proposals to preserve the monuments were discussed, either to move them to the island of Biga or of Elephantine – alternatives which were rejected – or to keep them in their original location, strengthening the foundations and consolidating the superstructures. Captain Henry Lyons made a careful investigation and carried out the consolidation operation most efficiently. Thanks to his excellent work, and since then regular maintenance each summer, the monuments survived for 70 years without serious damage. But the vividly coloured paint was washed off and the Christian town with its churches destroyed by the annual submersion. Before long the palms and bushes, one of the charms of the island, had also disappeared and only the buildings, bespeckled with silt and aquatic incrustations survived as sad reminders of a magic isle which Pierre Loti had named the "Pearl of Egypt".

With the building of the High Dam there was a radical change in the conditions of Philae. Situated between the old and the new dams, the island lay in a subsidiary reservoir which had a double purpose: to provide a regular flow of water to drive the turbines installed at the western end of the old dam for generating electricity, and to store water at night for release in the daytime for irrigation. The first of these purposes required the level of the reservoir to be maintained at a height which would always leave Philae submerged with even its highest monuments only partly visible, while the second involved fluctuations of several metres in the level of the water every 24 hours. These conditions would within a short time inevitably result in a total collapse of the buildings. The effects of storm and waves in the river were well-known and had once, in the fifties, caused a partial collapse of the famous kiosk of Trajan, damage which was later repaired. Obviously drastic action was called for if the monuments were to be saved.

As in the case of Abu Simbel, long discussions ensued on various proposals to rescue Philae, and again the fundamental question was that of the so-called "integrity of the monuments". Could this be respected only by leaving them in their original location and environment? The debates were, however, less complicated than those concerning Abu Simbel.

Among the methods for saving the monuments, discussed in Cairo in October 1959 at an international meeting of experts, were, in the words of I.E.S. Edwards, the British Egyptologist who played an important role in the rescue operations:

"1. To leave the monuments *in situ* and erect a dam around the island. A practical objection to the plan was that there would be a constant seepage of ground-water, which would have necessitated constant pumping. Aesthetically the plan would have been a failure, because the island, which had previously dominated its environment, would have lain at a lower level than the water which would have surrounded it.

"2. Dismantling the monuments to ground-level, superimposing additional courses of foundations on the old, thereby increasing their height by about 8 m, and re-building the monuments on the newly elevated foundations, to the level of which the surface of the island would also have been raised. This plan was discarded owing to doubts whether the original foundations could support the additional weight involved.

"3. More promising, both practically and aesthetically, seemed to be a third scheme, conceived by the Egyptian engineer Othman Rustem, namely to enclose Philae and its surrounding waters inside a bow-shaped barrier. It necessitated the construction of three fairly short dams, the first extending from the east bank of the river to the island of Biga, the second from Biga to Agilkia and the third from Agilkia back to the east bank. This plan had the advantage of leaving the monuments undisturbed and their setting as little changed as possible. The island would lie in the middle of a lake which would be fed by the seepage of ground water, but its level would remain constant as a result of the discharge of surplus water through pumping or through a long conduit ending at a point north of the original Aswan dam. It was this solution which was favoured at the meeting in 1959 and experts were sent to Egypt by the Netherlands Government to produce an estimate for putting it into effect. Their conclusion was that it would be premature to try to estimate costs before completion of the High Dam in 1968.

"4. The fourth plan to be considered was the most radical of all. It involved dismantling all the monuments and re-building them in the same relative positions on the island of Agilkia (sometimes spelt Agelika), lying about a quarter of a mile (about 400 m) north-west of Philae. Before the original Aswan dam was built, Agilkia was not an island; it was simply the name of the region at the north-eastern extremity of the island of Biga. When the water began to rise behind the dam, it cut off the whole of the northern tip of Biga and divided it into two islands, Agilkia being the eastern and Saliba the western. (It was this plan which was finally adopted, but before it could be put into effect much preparatory work had to be done, both at Philae and at Agilkia.)"

CHOICE OF PROJECT

When the international Consultative Committee of the United Arab Republic for safeguarding the sites and monuments of Nubia met, at its first session in May/June 1960, it recommended a solution along the lines of the third scheme: to leave Philae as an island in an artificial lake kept at a constant level by a system of dams. The Netherlands Government assumed responsibility for further preliminary studies through the firm Nedeco and a technical and financial report was submitted to the Consultative Committee at its second session in January 1961. This was accepted as technically sound and it was noted that operations could not start before completion of the High Dam, expected in 1968. The cost would be about $6 million.

In a message to Congress, on 7 April 1961, President John F. Kennedy declared: "The United States, one of the newest of civilizations, has long had a deep regard for the study of past cultures, and a concern for the preservation of man's greatest achievements of art and thoughts; we have also had a special interest in the civilization of ancient Egypt from which many of our own cultural traditions have sprung – and a deep friendship for the people who live in the Valley of the Nile. In keeping with this tradition, and this friendship, I recommend that we now join with other nations through Unesco in preventing what would otherwise be an irreparable loss to science and the cultural history of mankind."

Referring to Philae he continued:

"There would be no more effective expression of our interest in preserving the cultural monuments of the Nile Valley than an American offer to finance the preservation of these temples. I am directing that the Egyptian pound equivalent of six million dollars be set aside for this purpose". And he concluded: "In making these funds available, the United States will be participating in an international effort which has captured the imagination and sympathy of people throughout the world. By thus contributing to the preservation of past civilizations, we will strengthen and enrich our own."

Thus the danger to Philae seemed to be averted – so that it would be "possible when the time comes" (as expressed by Unesco's Acting Director-General, René Maheu) "to safeguard that magnificent group, in accordance with the plan drawn up thanks to the generosity of the Government of the Netherlands".

As a consequence no further action was taken until 1965, when the Executive Committee asked for a technical and financial report to permit a reasonable time for preparations and financing before the actual works began, at the latest, it was thought, early in 1967 because of technical imperatives arising from the level of water between the two dams. Further analysis of the problems should be referred to a Group of Experts to be chosen by the Egyptian Government and the Director-General of Unesco. On this occasion, 24–5 September 1965, the United States representative emphasized the necessity to clarify all financial and technical uncertainties before an appropriation request could be initiated in accordance with the message of the late President Kennedy.

In March 1966 the Executive Committee learned from the report of the Group of Experts that the cost estimates now amounted to $8.7 million (of which 65% was in hard currency) and that the Egyptian Government had undertaken to supply any sums needed above the total of international aid, provided the United States contributed $6 million.

This decision by the Egyptian Government, taken in conjunction with its many other efforts in the Nubian Campaign, was a good platform for the international appeal which the Executive Committee recommended the Director-General to issue to the Member States before the next session of the General Conference of Unesco. At the same meeting, the representative of the United States insisted that no request could be submitted to Congress until (a) a rescue method satisfactory from both the financial and technical viewpoints had been found, and (b) Unesco had launched an appeal for international aid. He also pointed out some uncertainties concerning the Nedeco dam project.

One year later, in March 1967, the International Group of Experts again analysed the Nedeco project and still found it feasible, with some modifications. But the costs were now estimated to be considerably higher. If for some reason the Nedeco project could not be implemented directly, the Group advised that other schemes ought to be investigated as soon as possible. The Executive Committee, though still adhering to the notion of preservation *in situ*, decided that another project, including financial estimates, should be prepared and the Group of Experts enlarged to include archaeologists, landscape artists and financial consultants. It was this enlarged Group which would be asked to recommend which project should be accepted.

The Egyptian authorities had become increasingly doubtful about the Nedeco scheme; the study of the dam project for Abu Simbel had brought to light two major problems – the detrimental effects of capillary water and the necessity to evacuate water seeping from the dykes by pumping or through a tunnel. It was considered by several Egyptian experts that the scheme did not guarantee the safety of the temples in the long run and under all conditions. The experience gained in the dismantling and re-erection of the temple of Kalabsha and the smaller temples suggested a similar solution for the Philae temples. Accepted as a possibility, the proposal was discussed with VBB Consulting Engineers and they suggested Agilkia island as a new site for the Philae temples. It was this alternative which had been brought to the attention of Unesco and which was now referred to the enlarged Group of Experts.

The group met at Aswan in April 1968 to study a revised report by Nedeco, and the "excellent study of a scheme to remove the monuments and re-erect them on Agilkia Island made by the Consortium of the Consulting Engineers and Architects of Cairo". The technical and financial experts found both schemes feasible, but the cost estimates favoured the removal project, the Nedeco scheme being estimated at $14.8 million and the removal project at $12.3 million. Of critical importance was the difference between the sums needed in hard currency – $8.5 million for the Nedeco plan and $5 million for the removal scheme.

The archaeologists and landscaping experts advocated, with one opponent in each category, a preservation *in situ* despite the higher costs. The main argument for the preservation *in situ* was the same as that for the dyke project for Abu Simbel which has already been described in relation to the "integrity of the monuments" viewpoint. The fact that the island had not been excavated with modern methods was also used as an argument. At the same time it was stated – correctly as subsequent events were to prove – that the dismantling would probably yield important information about earlier occupations of Philae.

The group recommended to the Egyptian Government that it adopt the dyke scheme, but added that should the financial problem not be solved the removal scheme should be adopted. After due consideration of the arguments in favour of the removal scheme, it was this alternative which was chosen by the Egyptian Government. The reasons were, according to the official declaration, largely financial, but also there was the desire to preserve the temples "from any future harmful effects" and "to give an adequate guarantee that these temples will be permanently preserved".

FINANCING

The choice of project by the Egyptian Government was communicated to the Executive Committee on 9 May 1968, and at its next session the Committee authorized the Director-General to launch an appeal for the preservation of Philae during the 15th session of the General Conference of Unesco.

In his appeal which was made on 6 November 1968 the Director-General, René Maheu, presented the plans drawn up for the preservation of Philae and explained that to enable the operations to be carried out Unesco must before the end of 1972 collect at least $6 million. In 1966 the Egyptian Government had undertaken to give any sums needed in excess of the international aid, provided $6 million had been contributed from abroad.

The appeal went on to state:

"It is inconceivable that the Member States of Unesco, which have given such abundant proof of their generosity, should fail, so near the goal, to make the final effort necessary to save this wonderful group of monuments, justly called 'Pearl of Egypt', from disappearing beneath the waters. Such a failure would be . . . incomprehensible to our own and future generations. . . . May the intellectual and moral solidarity of mankind which it is Unesco's mission to promote be further strengthened on this occasion in the saving of this precious treasure, thus vindicating the worth of the human spirit and advancing the cause of peace!"

Following the appeal, a plan for the financing of the project was drawn up. Personal contacts with the representative of the United Nations Development Programme (UNDP) in Cairo and negotiations with the representatives of the World Food Programme led to an agreement in 1969 to supply provisions for the workers amounting to the value of some $2.5 million. This sum, taken with the $1.7 million, all that had so far been pledged by Member States, still fell short of the necessary $6 million.

In 1970 the Director-General was able to present a more optimistic report because of further developments, among others a substantial contribution from the Federal Republic of Germany. The deadline to raise the necessary $6 million could be set later, since the work could start only after some delay and would take nearly five years to complete. So to enable the Director-General to conclude an agreement, similar to that relating to Abu Simbel back in 1963, it was necessary to raise not more than $1.9 million in foreign currency for the period 1970–72. In December 1970 Egypt had declared her willingness to utilize, for immediate financial needs, the hard currency funds that were held in trust by Unesco and to sign a contract with the firm concerned.

So everything was well prepared for a meeting of the donor states which was held in Cairo on 19 December 1970 when the agreements concerning the preservation of the Philae monuments were signed between Egypt and Unesco and with contributing Member States.

The promotion campaign of Unesco again proved its effectiveness and international solidarity its strength once a financially and technically sound scheme was launched. The pledges and contributions increased steadily with a notable increase brought about in 1974 by two important and encouraging events. The first was the Tutankhamun exhibition in London which was an outstanding success, yielding a net income of not less than $1.6 million and which also showed that here was a source of revenue that could (and did in the future) contribute substantial sums.

The other event was the active participation in the campaign by the United States of America. For some time the USA had not been represented among the contributing Member States. It is true that President Kennedy had already in 1961 earmarked $6 million for the salvage, at that time estimated to be the whole cost of the operation, but in the meantime the USA had contributed $12 million to the salvage of Abu Simbel and the late President Kennedy's successors had regarded that preliminary message to Congress as more or less overruled. So in the statement of 31 January 1973 the USA was still not numbered amongst the donors.

At the 21st session of the Executive Committee held in Aswan on 21–2 March 1973, the USA representative informed the Executive Committee that the Executive Branch of the US Government had included in the budget for the Smithsonian Institution a request for the equivalent of $4 million in Egyptian pounds as a contribution to the Philae project. After members of the Senate had been shown the Unesco film on Philae, which was very well received, the request was submitted to the appropriate Sub-Committee, and at the next meeting of the Executive Committee (November 1973) the confirmation of the first million dollars was announced. The United States Government had acted in the spirit of the message of President John F. Kennedy. Moreover, theirs was a gesture which made for smoother relations between the two countries.

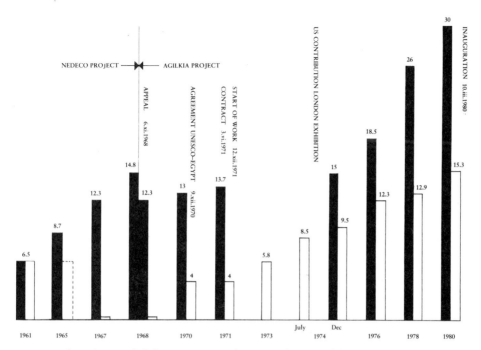

Fig. 17 The salvage of Philae. Diagram of estimated costs of different projects (black) in relation to international contributions pledged or paid (white). The $6 million of 1961 represent President Kennedy's pledge, later replaced by payments to Abu Simbel. Only the adoption of a less-expensive, realistic project starts to attract more important contributions, increased especially from 1974 onwards. Inflation and unforeseen complications cause a doubling of the costs in six years (1974–80) and an increase in the deficit to be covered by the Egyptian government (December 1974 c. $5.5 million; 1980 c. $14.7 million). (Cf. Abu Simbel, fig. 11, above.)

The final total of the international contributions, not less than $15.3 million, was an impressive demonstration of cooperation between the Unesco Member States. On the other hand without Egypt's very substantial financial contribution – about an equal amount – the salvage of Philae would not have been possible. President Anwar el-Sadat's declaration to the meeting of contributing Member States on 19 December 1970 that Egypt would contribute one-third of the expenses entailed had been greatly exceeded.

A final point concerning financing should perhaps be made. Because of delays, for example in preparing the new site on the island of Agilkia and the resultant impossibility for Condotte Mazzi to start the re-erection programme in accordance with the timetable, the total cost of the project rose and already in 1976 the contractors had submitted higher claims for payment of certain items, increases due to inflation and price escalation. These claims caused prolonged and difficult discussions and it was not until 6 March 1980 that an agreement was reached with the Italian firm and, some months later, with the Egyptian company.

According to the Chairman of the Executive Committee, Professor Paulo E. de Berrêdo Carneiro, who took an active part in the negotiations, this was a demonstration of how difficult it is in complicated operations such as the salvage of Philae, to take into account all possible contingencies when drawing up the contracts. Time must also be allowed for comprehensive studies and experiments concerning methods and techniques to be used, and of course those responsible must ascertain that the contractors have the expertise and equipment necessary to complete the work satisfactorily within the contractual period.

In the case of the Philae operation there were delays due to shortcomings in these respects. Nevertheless, to bring the project to its successful completion despite unforeseen obstacles, not least among them problems arising from the 1973 war, was a memorable feat by all standards.

THE SALVAGE OPERATIONS

To preserve the international character of the project the contract was awarded, in June 1971, to a Joint Venture consisting of the Egyptian High Dam Company for Civil Works and the Italian Condotte Mazzi Estero S.P.A. The Egyptian Company would be responsible for constructing a cofferdam around the island, for freeing the monuments of water and for preparing and landscaping the new site on Agilkia Island. The Italian firm would take care of dismantling, transporting and re-erecting the monuments.

This solution and division of the work was reached only after complicated discussions and negotiations with the firms concerned, Unesco supporting the idea of a Joint Venture which would presumably be an asset in promoting the international Campaign. Finally President Anwar el-Sadat asked his deputy to intervene to solve the problem.

The Consulting Engineers chosen were Dr. William Selim Hanna, and his colleagues Dr. E. El-Ramly and Mr. M. Shawqi, Directors of the Consortium of the Consulting Engineers and Architects of Cairo who performed their duties with energy and skill. It was indeed sad that Dr. Hanna did not live to see the triumphant inauguration of the monuments for the rescue of which he had struggled so hard and with such devotion.

At the end of 1972, Dr. Ahmed Kadry was appointed first General Director then Under-Secretary of State for the preservation of the Nubian Monuments and for six years, until March 1978, a period full of difficulties and unforeseen complications, Dr. Kadry demonstrated his considerable resourcefulness. He also assisted Dr. Gamal el-Din Mokhtar, President of the Egyptian Antiquities Organization and permanent representative after Mr. El-Sawi on the Executive Committee. To these two and, after March 1978, to Dr. Shehata Adam, who replaced Professor Mokhtar as President of the Egyptian Antiquities Organization, much is owed for the final triumph of the Nubia Campaign.

The comprehensive account of the salvage operations which follows has been contributed by I.E.S. Edwards:

"It was not feasible to dismantle the buildings of Philae during the short period each year when they stood clear of the water. . . . The only practical course was to construct a temporary cofferdam around the island and to pump out the water, so that the dismantling of the monuments could be carried out on dry land without interruption from start to finish.

"In fact, three monuments were left outside the dam: the gateway of Diocletian, the small temple of Augustus and the ruined temple of Harendotes. The reason for their exclusion was that the water at the northern end of Philae, where all three were situated, was deeper than at the southern end and an extension of the dam to embrace them would have doubled its cost. Eventually the gateway and the temple of Augustus were rescued by divers of the Egyptian Navy and the British Royal Navy, working together for two periods of six months in the winters of 1976–7 and 1977–8. Nothing could be done to save what had survived of the temple of Harendotes while the temporary dam was in position because a vast amount of silt had accumulated against it, covering the temple. The multinational Committee of Archaeologists and Landscape Architects appointed by Unesco and the Egyptian Ministry of Culture to advise on the removal of the monuments recommended that the remains of this temple, and also blocks which had been detached from it and had been embodied in the walls of a nearby Coptic church, should be recovered when the temporary dam had been dismantled and the accumulation of silt had been washed away.

"The building of the cofferdam was undertaken by the Egyptian engineering firm, the High Dam Company for Civil Works. Work began in August 1972 and ended in May 1974. The dam, which had a peripheral length of 752 m, was a box-like construction filled with sand. Its walls, which were 12 m apart, were made of 3115 steel sheet-piles driven into the silt bed of the river. Each pile was 17 m in length, the total weight of steel in the walls amounting to 4562 tons. Approximately a million cubic metres of sand went into the dam. It was sand of a particular texture, of which the nearest source of supply lay at a distance of about 8 km from Philae, in the desert east of Shellal. Some of the sand was brought to the dam by truck and barge, but most of it was mixed with water near the source and the resultant slurry was pumped through a pipe-line from the desert to the dam, where, on being exposed to the warm air, the water evaporated leaving behind the dry sand.

"With the dam completed, the task of pumping the water from the island began on 21 May 1974 and continued until the following autumn. Outside the dam the water-level fluctuated from about 111.5 m above sea-level to about 108 m, while the level inside was reduced to 105 m, leaving the surface of the island dry. In order to maintain that level it was still necessary to pump out ground-water, at first at a rate of 1000 cubic metres an hour, but, although seepage continued to the end, the amount diminished progressively in the course of time.

"The last of the preparatory operations at Philae consisted in the removal of the vast accumulations of silt from the surface of the ground and the removal of incrustations of silt from the monuments. Once the monuments had been cleaned, the Institut Géographique de France was able to resume, after a lapse of fourteen years, its photogrammetric recording of the reliefs and inscriptions. This important precursor to the dismantling of the monuments covered about 95% of the inscribed and decorated surfaces and required about 600 photogrammetric records.

"On 9 September 1975 engineers working for the Italian firm, Condotte Mazzi Estero, lifted out the first blocks from the monuments, using mammoth cranes and other modern equipment. Each stone, when lifted from its bed, was first marked with an indication of its position in the building; it was then conveyed by truck to a quay at the south-east corner of the island, transported by barge to the east bank and finally stored in a specially constructed enclosure at Shellal. Detailed records of every building, layer by layer as it was dismantled, were kept by the contractors and stones which required repair or conservation were given the appropriate treatment under the direction of the late Dr. Zaki Iskander, a former Director of the Research Laboratory of the Cairo Museum. By March 1977 all the buildings had been dismantled and 37,363 blocks had been transferred to the storage enclosure. A further 900 blocks were recovered by the divers when dismantling the gateway of Diocletian and 313 blocks were similarly recovered from the temple of Augustus. Thirty-nine divers of the British Royal Navy were employed in the operation and 20 divers of the Egyptian Navy. Some columns and architraves which had been taken to the Cairo Museum, probably when the original Aswan Dam was built, were brought back to be incorporated in the rebuilt temple at Agilkia.

"The engineering difficulties involved in the transfer of the monuments were not confined to Philae; even tougher problems attended the preparation of Agilkia. When work began it was a rugged granite island, its highest peak rising to 150 m above sea-level. Before the monuments could be re-erected there, it was necessary to lower the whole surface of the island to 116 m above sea-level (about 13 m higher than Philae) and to use the surplus rock thus obtained for enlarging the island to the north-east and the south-east, so that the size and shape of the island conformed approximately with those of Philae. Ideally the area of the extensions would have amounted to 13,000 square metres, but the material available was not sufficient to enable the whole of the reconstruction to be carried out. Even so, some 270,000 cubic metres of rock were blasted by dynamite and moved to the required places, the whole operation occupying five years and ending early in 1977.

"On 29 March 1977 the first stone, at the base of the First Pylon of the temple of Isis, was laid by Unesco's Assistant Director-General for Culture and

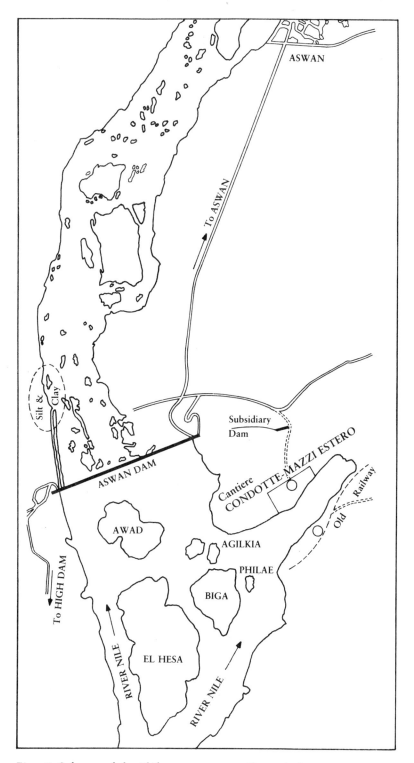

Fig. 18 Salvage of the Philae monuments. General plan.

Communication, Mr. Makaminan Makagiansar, the President of the Egyptian Antiquities Organization, Dr. Gamal el-Din Mokhtar, and the Governor of Aswan. The rebuilding of the monuments by Condotte Mazzi Estero occupied a further two years, followed by a further year for landscaping, building approaches from the river and other preparations.

"In order to speed up the completion of the works and to economize the costs the original plans had been modified in two important respects. It had been agreed to reconstruct on the Agilkia island the big granite hillock south of the kiosk of Trajan and to place such installations as electric transformer, toilets, etc., inside this artificial rock structure. The project was abandoned and there was thus an empty, open and flat area south of the kiosk. A garden has been planned and has been partly planted, so that modern amenities and installations can be hidden here among bushes and trees. A greater loss was the abandoning of the Osiris chapel on Biga Island opposite Philae, a temple complex intimately connected with the Isis cult on Philae. It was planned to dismantle and re-erect it on the Saliba island opposite Agilkia. The original orientation and distance between the Osiris chapel and the Isis temple could not have been restored by this removal operation and a drastic re-shaping of the beautiful island of Saliba would have been necessary. So the Osiris chapel was left on Biga. It is to be hoped that it can be recovered later, just as the Harendotes temple on Philae, as already mentioned.

"It was only to be expected that a side-benefit of dismantling the monuments would be some addition to our knowledge of the history of Philae, and so it proved to be, but it also left several problems unanswered and brought to light others which had not previously been detected. Egyptologists, in general, had supposed that nothing of importance stood at Philae in the time of Herodotus (c. 450 B.C.) because he made no mention of the island, although he was only about 8 km from it when he visited Elephantine. In support of this view, it could be argued that the oldest standing monuments dated from the time of Nectanebes I, the first king of the XXXth Dynasty (380–363 B.C.). Some blocks showing the name of Amasis II of the XXVIth Dynasty (570–526 B.C.) were already known to be embodied in the Second Pylon and in the columns of the hypostyle hall of the temple of Isis, but their presence could be explained on the supposition that they were re-used blocks which had been brought to Philae from a temple of Amasis II which had stood elsewhere. When, however, the floor blocks of the hypostyle hall were lifted, the outline of the walls of the temple of Amasis II were clearly visible. Here therefore was one building which certainly antedated Herodotus. In all, some 310 blocks from the temple were discovered and the relative positions which they had occupied in the walls of the temple could, in some cases, be determined. When the blocks had been used

Fig. 19 *Plan of Philae Island showing position of cofferdam. Main monuments (south to north):* N = *Nectanebo temple;* D = *outer court with porticos;* I = *Isis temple with two pylons (P.SP);* T = *Trajan's kiosk;* HA = *Hathor temple;* AU = *Augustus' temple;* DG = *Diocletian's gateway.*

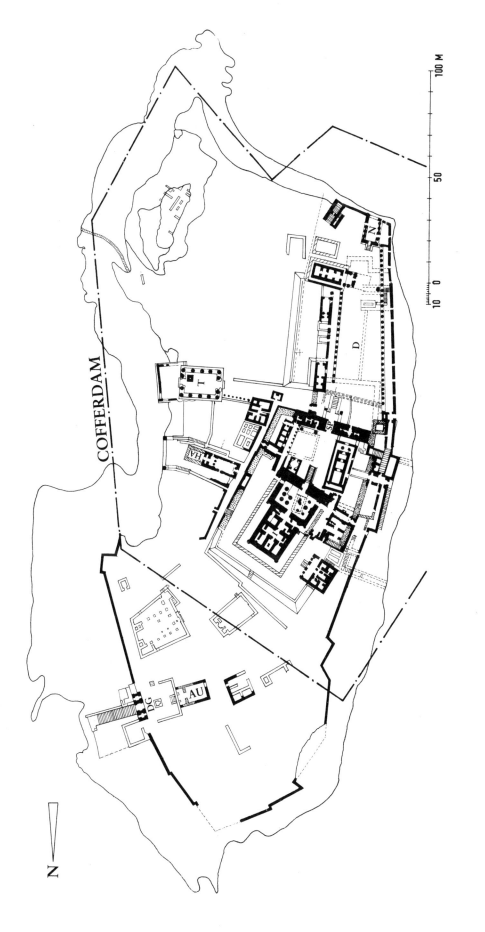

COFFERDAM

N

100 M

50

10

0

N

T

D

SP

HA

DG

AU

simply as filling material in the core of the Second Pylon, they were removed and new blocks were substituted for them when the Pylon was rebuilt. In some instances, when two adjacent sides of a block were carved with reliefs or inscriptions – one side for the Amasis temple and the other for the temple of Isis – it was not possible to saw the block into two pieces and thereby to separate them. Such blocks were carefully recorded by the Antiquities Organization and were restored to the temple of Isis when it was re-erected.

"Another building which also antedated Herodotus was found on the western edge of Philae; it was a small kiosk of Psammetichus II (595–589 B.C.) the second predecessor of Amasis II. All that remained of the building was its stone floor and parts of the eight short columns which had once supported its roof. While these two buildings have as yet done no more than prove that sanctuaries were built at Philae before the time of Nectanebes I, it would be surprising if, with closer study of their inscriptions and architectural features, they were not to yield information of value to philologists and art historians. An interesting discovery made by Dr. Haeny, Director of the Swiss Archaeological Institute in Cairo, was that the so-called porch of Nectanebes I stood on terraces which had not been constructed in the time of that king or in the time of Ptolemy II, Philadelphus. The latter king had, however, carved an inscription on the outer west wall of the temple, saying that he had erected the building 'anew', but apparently it was somewhere else. Similar terraces were found on the south and west sides of the island, built in order to extend it in those directions for additional buildings and probably to accommodate the large crowds who attended the festivals. This discovery showed that the temple must have been moved twice, once by Philadelphus to a position which cannot be precisely determined and later by another king to the position which it occupied on Philae.

"Hopes were entertained that blocks from older monuments would be found, having been re-used in the foundation courses of the various buildings. In the event, out of 5986 foundation-blocks lifted and examined only 44 proved to be inscribed or decorated and all of them were situated in the four uppermost courses. A complete clearance of the foundation courses could not be undertaken because the water-level inside the cofferdam could not be reduced below 101 m, owing to seepage of water. Although there is no certainty that re-used blocks would not have been found at a greater depth, the fact that those which were discovered were all situated in the four highest courses suggests that the lower courses were composed of new blocks.

"Besides the blocks already mentioned, some 2200 inscribed or decorated blocks were recovered from the silt at Philae. These were blocks which had fallen from the buildings and as many as possible were restored to their proper places when the buildings were re-erected on Agilkia. Further work remains to be done on the temple of Hathor, from which about 300 blocks had fallen, and the ruined temple of Harendotes, as has already been explained.

34 Prehistoric rock carving (prob. 5000–3000 B.C.; the subpluvial period). Elephant with later graffiti and hieroglyphic texts.

35 Rock carvings of cattle (3rd or early 2nd millennium B.C.). Abka in the Second Cataract region.

36 The earliest known text from Nubia, at Gebel Sheikh Suleiman near the Second
Cataract. This rock inscription by King Djer(?) of Egypt's First Dynasty records a victory
over the Nubians (*c.* 3000 B.C.). Extreme left, the royal name preceded by a prisoner and
two signs for conquered townships. To the right slain enemies and a ship. *Inset* showing
detail of rock inscription.

37 A-Group objects.

38 Clay figurines found in a female's tomb of the A-Group period (*c.* 3000 B.C.) near Wadi Halfa.

39 Buhen: artist's reconstruction of the Pharaonic fortress showing the advanced military architecture of *c*. 2000 B.C. The fortress guarded the northern end of the Second Cataract.

40 The fortress of Buhen opposite Wadi Halfa, showing bastions, arrow slits, ramparts and inner dry ditch.

41 Slipway for ships bypassing the cataract, showing indentations of sleepers and heels (Middle Kingdom).

42 The Middle Kingdom fortress of Mirgissa (The Pharaonic Iqen) in the Second Cataract region. From the central fortress with its double defence lines runs a fortified spur northwards and parallel to the river. On the sandy plain near the river a sizeable garrison town was excavated.

43 Burnt clay female head of C-Group culture (1900–1500 B.C.) in Leipzig Museum.

44 The Prince of Teh-khet Amenemhet, brother of Djehuti-hotep, offers to his father and mother (left) and receives offering from his wife Hatshepsut (right). Upper part of stela found in the tomb of Amenemhet, Debeira West.

45 Faras Cathedral. Removing fresco from mud wall.

46 Portrait of a typical Nubian. Second Cataract area.

47 Nubians at their favourite game of quarterstaff. Second Cataract area.

48 Saving their own history. Nubians at archaeological excavations on Meinarti island.

"The transfer of the buildings from Philae to Agilkia must surely be considered one of the great achievements in the salvage of ancient monuments. The two islands are situated so close together that the physical setting of the monuments is virtually the same. The monuments are now visible throughout the year, not merely for three months each summer. The silt and vegetable incrustations which had adhered to the stonework were carefully removed, so that the surfaces of the buildings are as clean as they were before they were first submerged, and probably cleaner than for many centuries. They are also more complete. What they have lost by the move is some of the emotional appeal which came from the sensation of treading the very ground on which the ancient worshippers had walked.

Another probable loss will be in the quantity and type of vegetation which will grow on Agilkia. At Philae, where the vegetation contributed so much to the physical charm and the natural setting of the monuments, a layer of silt, in some places deep as the height of the buildings, enabled palm-trees and other vegetation to flourish without artificial irrigation, in spite of the great heat of the summer months. Agilkia consists of solid rock, which had the practical advantage that, when the monuments were being built there, it was only necessary to lay one foundation course on a floor of ferroconcrete, but it remains to be seen whether, even with pits sunk in the rock and filled with silt, combined with regular irrigation, it would be possible to grow palm-trees. A better chance of success may exist along the eastern and northern fringes of the island, where the surplus rock was dumped and the roots of the trees can reach moisture which has penetrated through the rubble from the Nile. When this problem has been solved and when the temples of Hathor and Harendotes have received further attention, it can truly be said that everything possible has been done to provide posterity with a faithful replica of the Pearl of Egypt."

THE INAUGURATION

On 10 March 1980 the inauguration ceremony was performed with all due solemnity. It was a celebration not only of the completion of the preservation of the Philae monuments, but which also crowned the success of the International Campaign to Save the Sites and Monuments of Nubia. More than 500 people were invited and the ceremony took place between the two colonnades which lead up to the first pylon of the Isis temple.

In the darkness, well before sunrise, the Cairo Symphony Orchestra, under the wondering eyes of the Nubians, in full evening dress and with their instruments, had filled the Nubian boats to be carried to the re-erected Philae. With them went guests to hear the morning prayer and see the temples first red then golden in the light of the rising sun.

Later the guests of honour arrived, Mrs. Jihan el-Sadat, the First Lady of Egypt, Mr. Mansour Mahmoud Hassan, Minister of Information and Culture, Mr. Amadou-Mahtar M'Bow, Unesco's Director-General, and Professor

Paulo E. de Berrêdo Carneiro, Chairman of the Executive Committee. Representatives of the diplomatic corps and of the Egyptian and foreign authorities and organizations involved were also amongst the guests.

After the orchestra had performed, Mr. Mansour Hassan delivered a message from President Anwar el-Sadat, followed by addresses by the Director-General of Unesco, Professor Carneiro and Dr. Shehata. Mrs. Jihan el-Sadat presented the decorations offered by the Egyptian President to Mr. Amadou-Mahtar M'Bow, Director-General of Unesco, to Professor Carneiro, and to the late Mr. René Maheu, former Director-General of Unesco.

It was indeed a day of victory, and one fully in keeping with the message of President Anwar el-Sadat:

"The success we are celebrating today gives us concrete evidence that when people work together for a good cause they can achieve miracles.

"We have joined hands in saving an ancient civilization, so let us join hands to save the future of all peoples by strengthening peace."

4 The Archaeological Campaign

An Overwhelming Task

The drama of Abu Simbel was, undoubtedly, the draw which concentrated attention on Nubia. Here was a country virtually unknown to the world outside, apart from a handful of specialists, and at first even they did not appreciate the magnitude of the other major task to be undertaken: the archaeological salvage of Nubia. During a period of about five years, the greater part of the area to be inundated had to be surveyed and investigated by teams of archaeologists and other specialists, that is to say a 350-km stretch of the Nile Valley from the High Dam in Egypt to the beginning of the Second Cataract in the Sudan, plus another 150 km further south.

In Egypt, the amount of necessary salvage work could be pretty well estimated, thanks to the extensive previous surveys. There were some cemeteries that had not been investigated in the earlier campaigns, but the principal need was to excavate a number of habitation and fortress sites that had been by-passed in earlier work. These could be allotted more or less on an individual basis to the different expeditions which volunteered to work in Egyptian Nubia.

In the Sudan, the size of the salvage task was very poorly known at the start of the Campaign, though it was generally assumed to be large. A preliminary reconnaissance had revealed the existence of about two dozen conspicuous and important sites between Faras and Gemai, but there were known to be many other, smaller sites. Some of these could actually be identified on aerial photos. It was in order to make an inventory of sites, and to assess the size of the archaeological challenge, that the Unesco Archaeological Survey of Sudanese Nubia was originally organized. This survey, which was active in the field between 1960 and 1970, revealed the presence of more than 1000 archaeological sites between Faras and Dal. They were of all different sizes, and covered every period of prehistory and history from the Middle Palaeolithic to the Mahdiya in the 19th century. The inventory included habitations, towns and villages, fortifications, temples and churches, workshop sites, epigraphic sites, and mortuary sites.

Here indeed was an overwhelming undertaking, and one which had to be completed in what seemed at the outset an impossibly short time. Fortunately, the international appeal had such an effect that in the event no territory of an equal size has ever witnessed such a concentration of archaeologists and other specialists from far and wide as did Nubia in the decade beginning with 1960.

Finding solutions to the difficulties which always arise in archaeological campaigns of any size is never easy even under normal conditions, but in Nubia conditions were far from normal; the logistic, scientific and strategic problems which arose sometimes seemed insurmountable, and always there was the harshness of the climate to contend with.

The demographic situations in Egypt and in Sudanese Nubia were very different; whereas Egyptian Nubia was more or less abandoned when the last heightening of the Aswan dam inundated the entire flood plain, Sudanese Nubia had been relatively unaffected.

The 300-km length of Egyptian Nubia held no town or commercial centre of any size. Aniba was the most important administrative location, but to call it the "capital" would be a misuse of the word for a small group of houses, primary school, secondary school, a health dispensary, a police station and a few offices; there were no real shops or other amenities. The rest of Egyptian Nubia was largely drained of human resources, most of the men working elsewhere, so that labourers when needed usually had to be imported. Access by boat was both meagre and erratic while communication by telephone or telegraph was something of a lottery, although it improved as the Campaign advanced. The situation eased after work started in Abu Simbel in 1964, but by then the archaeological operations had been more or less completed.

Every expedition had perforce to bring along all that was needed in the field – a houseboat for the scientists, tents for the workers, food, materials, medicines, petrol, and so on. And last, but certainly not the least, the trained overseers known as *Quftis*, from the town of Quft in Upper Egypt where there is a long family tradition in archaeological "digging", dating from the days of Sir Flinders Petrie who was the first archaeologist to introduce into the Nile Valley the principles and methods of scientific field excavation.

The Egyptian authorities, who themselves took an active part in the archaeological work, assisted the foreign missions in various ways, granting Customs facilities and making available houseboats and pontoons.

A first and essential element was the provision of up-to-date topographical data for locating sites, so accordingly the Egyptian Government prepared a new detailed map in 1:10,000, an older American map in 1:20,000 made for the High Dam studies being neither then available nor regarded as adequate for the needs of site location. The production of the new map was entrusted to the French Institut Géographique National in collaboration with the Egyptian Military Survey Department, and it was financed with a contribution from Brazil.

From a scientific viewpoint Egyptian Nubia offered a considerable advantage in the findings of the earlier archaeological explorations, so that it was usually possible to assess in advance the scope of the work to be undertaken, although as is always the case in field archaeology, closer investigation and excavation brought surprises and revealed an unexpectedly high number of additional sites. On the other hand, apart from the bigger, untouched sites and centres such as Qasr Ibrim and Gebel Adda, revolutionary discoveries were hardly to be expected.

The logistic problems encountered in Sudanese Nubia have already been discussed in connection with the salvage of the monuments. The market in the small town of Wadi Halfa was an uncertain source of supply so most of the material and outfits required had to be imported either through Egypt with ensuing Customs difficulties or through Port Sudan, the only and inadequate harbour, and thence to Nubia via a railway of limited capacity. The Sudanese authorities granted priority rights to the Nubia Campaign but there were limits to what they were able to do. However, the commodious Nubian houses were available to the expeditions, increasingly so as the evacuation of the population proceeded, and practically all parts of the reservoir area could be reached by boat or by desert-type vehicles which proved invaluable in carrying out the preliminary surveys.

Until the evacuation, government offices such as Public Works, the hospital, and the local office of the Antiquities Service rendered considerable assistance to the foreign missions, which was greatly appreciated. The District Commissioner, Hassan Dafallah, the local representative of the Antiquities Service, Sayyid Nigmeddin Sharif, together with the Unesco experts Drs. W.Y. Adams, Hans-Åke Nordström and others were always available for advice and assistance.

Scientifically, Sudanese Nubia provided all the excitement of anticipation that goes with the exploration of unknown territory, and it was Sudanese Nubia which yielded the richest harvest in sensational discoveries and fundamentally new knowledge.

Strategy

ATTITUDE AND GENERAL ROLE OF UNESCO

Many archaeologists have expressed surprise that Unesco and its responsible committees did not do more to organize the purely archaeological aspect of the Campaign. In fact, to start with, the odds were not at all in favour of archaeology and scientific research. During the first phase of the Campaign it was even seriously discussed in the Action Committee whether the archaeological work actually belonged at all to the Unesco Campaign, which should rather concentrate on the salvage of monuments. It was necessary for those who were interested in that part of the salvage problem to fight for its acknowledgement and time and again during the Campaign to underline that Unesco should fulfil its responsibility regarding the purely archaeological aspects of the salvage programme. Especially for the Sudan the odds were such that without prompt and effective international assistance the losses would have been immense and irreparable.

Typical of the general attitude with which Unesco started is the recommendation in one of the first working papers, in regard to the purely archaeological work in Egyptian Nubia: "Governments and competent institutions will doubtless wish to organize at their own expense expeditions which will be of great scientific interest. Unesco will not collect funds for the financing of such expeditions, but will act merely as intermediary between their organizers and the Government of the United Arab Republic." And concerning the similar problem in the Sudan it merely states (ibid.): "As in the case of the United Arab Republic, governments and institutions may organize missions at their own expense."

This attitude towards the archaeological excavations and survey missions was confirmed by the 11th session of the General Conference, which resolved that such operations "should be paid for by the institutions organizing them".

The various committees which came to be set up were primarily intended for fund-raising and for the allocation and control of the disbursement of those funds. That Unesco as an organization appeared less active in the development of the archaeological investigations was thus a consequence of the nature of the Campaign itself. However, it would be wrong to suggest that the Organization distanced itself from the archaeological ingredient; indeed, as time passed Unesco became increasingly involved in this aspect of the Campaign in ways that have already been described.

CO-ORDINATION AND AIMS

The possibility, and desirability, of solving all survey and excavation problems by means of a single enterprise, in short a large international expedition covering the whole inundation area and proceeding systematically from one end of the area to the other, was discussed more than once at the outset of the Campaign. The benefits, it was said, would be a uniformity of standards, a comparability of results over a wide area and a certainty that the whole territory was properly explored. The experience of the earlier archaeological surveys of Nubia, organized in this way, bore out this view.

Disadvantages were however evident. Even if the standards of such an expedition were high, individual interests and special problems could more easily be neglected or become too dominant. Also it would be difficult to reconcile the national feelings and to co-ordinate the work since two sovereign states, Egypt and Sudan, were involved. It would have meant that Unesco would have found itself shouldering more political and administrative responsibility than was practically feasible. Consequently the work was organized separately in the Egyptian and Sudanese areas and the situation developed differently in the two parts of Nubia. An exception was the

Combined Prehistoric Expedition which by special arrangement worked over the whole of the threatened area.

EGYPTIAN NUBIA

The way things evolved in Egypt has been described by Louis A. Christophe who was engaged by Unesco as liaison officer and coordinator for the archaeological campaign in Egypt. According to him it was the under-mentioned circumstances and considerations which dictated the solution adopted, that is to say not one joint expedition but an arrangement involving several missions from different countries and institutions, independently financed and freely managed in accordance with certain stipulated minimum standards.

"Firstly, there was the tradition and presence in Cairo of established missions with their institutes, which until recently had practically never worked together.

"Secondly, it should not be forgotten that there was the well-organized Egyptian Department of Antiquities, responsible for supervising the archae-ological operations.

"Thirdly, neither at the big meeting of experts in October 1959 nor at the meetings of the Consultative Committee, set up by the Egyptian Government, did any of the archaeologists suggest that the work should be carried out as a single operation.

"Fourthly, the archaeologists had difficulty in securing government funds (with the exception of the Americans) for their excavations. Would the states have agreed to pay money into a joint fund? And if so, how would the funds, work and equipment have been distributed?

"Fifth and finally, how would the person to lead this international enterprise have been chosen?

"My conclusion clearly is that the Nubian campaign in Egypt was carried out in the best possible way. In addition, it provided useful experience. Should a similar occasion arise, other methods might possibly be envisaged, provided that there would be time to reach an agreement, collect funds, and so on. There again, the state needing help would have to agree to delegate its responsibilities to an international organization." (*Translated from the French*).

This latter problem had already been discussed at the start of the Campaign, and the Egyptian Government and Unesco agreed that Egypt could not relinquish its responsibility towards its own heritage by ceding it to an international organization.

Mr. Christophe had been recruited by Unesco on 1 September 1960 as local liaison officer, and the Egyptian Government went so far as to grant extra-territorial rights to his office in the Documentation Centre in Cairo, where the new maps of Nubia and other relevant data were kept for consultation by the heads of missions. Christophe was also Secretary of the Consultative Committee where offers to take responsibility for a concessional area were registered and, more or less automatically, granted, always assuming the applicant was an archaeologist of standing with adequate personnel and financial resources at his disposal. Thereafter the Egyptian Government gave support to the approved missions in every possible way. Louis Christophe was thus the intermediary between his colleagues the archaeologists and the Egyptian authorities, while at the same time performing similar functions in connection with the rescue of the monuments, which perforce took up much more of his time.

The early surveys of Egyptian Nubia had made it possible to divide the territory into sections or concession areas, each as a rule including at least one well-known site of high priority. The concessionaire, having chosen one such section, became responsible not only for the proper exploration of the outstanding site or sites, but for the entire area of his concession.

At its first meeting (May–June 1960) the Consultative Committee had adopted a number of recommendations concerning the organization of the archaeological field work aiming at a total survey and excavation of all the sites in Egyptian Nubia. A sondage expedition, prehistoric expeditions and an epigraphic expedition were planned, the object being a complete archaeological map of Egyptian Nubia. At the same time excavations should start on the sites of high priority allotted to foreign missions. The work of these missions would fall within the Antiquities laws (cf. A. Khater, "Le Régime Juridique des Fouilles et des Antiquités en Egypte". Le Caire, 1960), and they were recommended to work according to the principles drawn up for the sondage expedition. Other co-ordinating principles were laid down by a special sub-committee. The Committee also made recommendations regarding the logistic problems of the Campaign.

At the second session (January 1961) the Consultative Committee adopted another series of recommendations pertaining to the logistic aspects and to co-ordinating principles of the archaeological operation. These principles concerned mostly the documentation of the results (topographical maps, use of the metre instead of the foot as a standard measurement, etc.); the role of the Documentation Centre in furnishing the missions with the topographical material and other information was stressed as was the duty of the expeditions to report their results to the Centre.

Thus from the very beginning the archaeological work was, at least in principle, well co-ordinated both as regards methods and aims. In practice there were inevitably shortcomings, some of which the Committee dealt with at its third session (January–February 1962).

That the aim was total excavation and not a sample according to certain guiding principles or to solve certain problems, appears in different statements, such as those quoted above and, for example, the wish of the Sub-Committee "that directors of excavations should not move on to a new site until they have completely exhausted the concession originally allocated to them. Investigations should be made to the east and west of the allocated area to include all the ground that will eventually be covered by the waters of the reservoir."

SUDANESE NUBIA

While it was possible to complete the archaeological field work in Egyptian Nubia quite early in the Campaign, in the Sudan it was otherwise.

The sector to the north of the Second Cataract, from the northern frontier towards Egypt at Faras and down to Gamai (62 km), which was inundated first, was fully investigated in the first four years of the Campaign, and after the winter of 1963/64 could be regarded as dealt with. The eastern shore had been completely excavated by the Scandinavian Joint Expedition (and a few sites by other missions) and the western shore was handled by a number of foreign missions, concentrating on some of the more important sites, and by the three archaeologists put at the disposal of the Antiquities Service of the Sudan, which paid the excavation costs.

As in Egyptian Nubia, the Panel of Experts for Sudanese Nubia had at its first meeting worked out the principles of survey and excavation, the standards to be observed by the missions, the co-ordination of the work, the logistic details etc.; the roles of the Unesco officials and of the Antiquities Service had also been clarified in a discussion, which showed that the Sudanese authorities were anxious to do everything possible to facilitate the work of the missions and the co-ordination of their programmes, but desirous, as a matter of course, to retain the final right of decision and the legal responsibilities.

On the whole this part of the programme functioned well; the aims were attained and collaboration between the missions and the Antiquities Service was effective. There were, of course, unavoidable shortcomings. Thus it was regrettable that the Polish expedition was unable to excavate the lower levels at Faras because a gallery of marvellous Christian frescoes found in the upper levels absorbed all the resources of the Expedition until the inundation put an end to the work. However the outstandingly successful salvage of the frescoes made up for the loss.

Throughout the Campaign, Dr. W.Y. Adams was the Unesco expert put at the disposal of the Sudan Antiquities Service. Like Louis Christophe in Egypt, Adams came to play an increasingly important part in the archaeological campaign, especially in his dual role of co-ordinator of the missions and their practical and scientific adviser. What follows is his description of the situation in that part of Nubia south of the Egyptian border:

"The principal complication in the Sudan arose from the fact that there had been no previous systematic survey, and so there was no 'baseline' of previously accomplished work or of accumulated knowledge from which the campaign could be developed. Resources were clearly not sufficient to permit the excavation of all of the threatened sites, and therefore some basis of selection among them was needed. On the other hand there was not sufficient time to carry out a preliminary inventory before sites were selected for further investigation. It was necessary instead to develop an excavation programme which would combine survey with selected excavation, and which would at the same time help to co-ordinate the efforts of a number of different national and international expeditions. To a considerable extent this was successfully achieved.

"A further complication in the Sudan was posed by the presence of some enormously large sites – particularly the famous Second Cataract Forts, not all of which had been adequately investigated by the Harvard–Boston Expedition in the '30s. There were in addition the great *koms* or mounds at Faras and Meinarti, and several very large medieval villages such as those at Debeira West and Abkanarti. In general it was felt that each of these sites should engage the full attention of a single expedition, which would have no other responsibilities than to investigate the one site that was granted to it. Unesco and the Sudan Antiquities Service were exceptionally successful in attracting expeditions to work on these very large sites, with the result that no really major site in the Sudan was neglected.

"If there were special complications, there were also special advantages in the archaeological campaign in the Sudan. One of these was the existence of a co-ordinating centre, Wadi Halfa, within the threatened area, and of a good system of overland transport radiating out from Wadi Halfa. This made it possible for the Sudan Antiquities Service to maintain a much closer and more continuous communication with the different expeditions than was possible in Egypt, and to maintain a considerable degree of co-ordination of effort among the different groups. Importantly, it also enabled the various national expeditions to remain in close communication with one another, to discuss and share their results, and sometimes to assist one another in special tasks.

"A further advantage in the Sudan was the existence of a good set of topographic maps and of aerial photos of the whole threatened area. These were made freely available to the expeditions by the Sudan Antiquities Service.

"The Sudan Antiquities Service could not offer to participants in the Nubian Campaign the prospect of later rich pickings in other parts of the country. The Antiquities Service therefore decided to allow foreign concessionaires to confine themselves to sites of their own choosing, and, concurrently, to organize from its own resources a survey similar to the earlier surveys in Egyptian Nubia. The purposes of the survey were, first, to find and define remains worthy of excavation by foreign expeditions, and second, to supplement the work of the foreign expeditions by excavating anything not claimed by them.

"The Survey of Sudanese Nubia, organized at the beginning of 1960 with assistance from Unesco, ultimately explored the full length of the Nile Valley between the Egyptian border and the head of the proposed reservoir (about

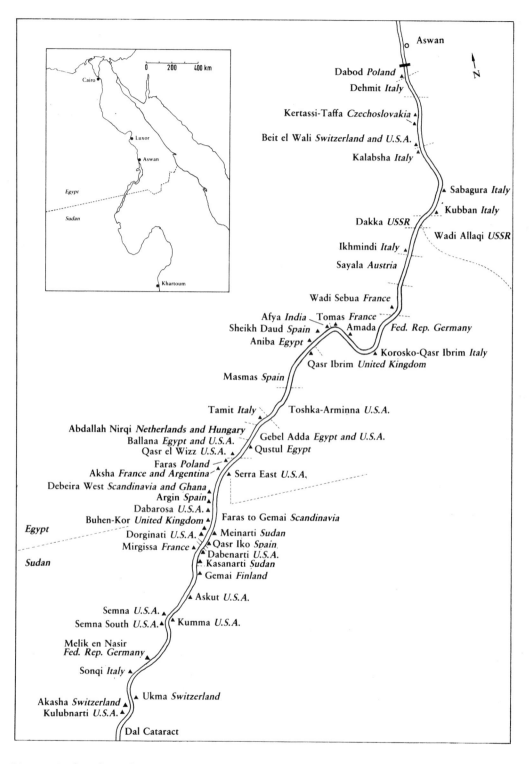

Fig. 20 Archaeological concessions granted to various foreign expeditions.

160 km), discovered over 1000 sites, and carried out some excavation in more than one third of them. In the wake of the survey party, or in some cases before it, some 18 concessions were eventually taken up by foreign expeditions. Although their territory covered less than a quarter of the threatened area of Sudanese Nubia, they included most of the monumental sites and many of the largest cemeteries. There were in addition surveys other than that of the Antiquities Service. The large Scandinavian Joint Expedition made an exhaustive exploration of the East Bank from Faras to Gamai and excavated practically all important sites there, except for the fortress of Serra East, the church of Qasr Ico, and the small township of Abkanarti (the first ceded to Chicago Oriental Institute, the two others to a Spanish mission). The Scandinavians also documented a great number of rock-drawings in their concession area. Other specialized surveys were devoted to rock inscriptions and pictures outside the Scandinavian concession area (a German Democratic Republic mission) and to the investigation of Stone Age remains (the Combined Prehistoric Expedition and the Colorado mission).

"Because the Survey of Sudanese Nubia had the responsibility to excavate what was left behind by other missions, a close co-ordination with their work was necessary so as to be in a position to supplement it. Thus a central archive was maintained in Wadi Halfa, in which the results of each expedition's work were recorded as they progressed. In its own work, the Antiquities Service survey sought to concentrate on those periods and types of remains which were not receiving attention from other expeditions, thereby assuring that at the conclusion of the Nubian campaign the various parts would add up to some sort of connected whole."

International Response

When Egypt requested the assistance of Unesco for the Campaign the Government stated its readiness "to cede at least half the proceeds of their finds to parties which have carried out excavations in Nubia in the threatened area, on the understanding that certain items which are unique or essential for completing the collections most representative of the civilization, history or art of Nubia shall . . . be assigned to the museums of the United Arab Republic". The Government also proposed to authorize excavations outside the threatened area, in Lower, Middle and Upper Egyptian sites, not at present forming part of recognized concessions. Assignment of these finds would be as in the case of excavations carried out in the threatened area of Nubia. The proposed sites would include the Royal Necropolis of Saqqara. Moreover, as already described, a number of temples would be ceded as gifts-in-return for services rendered. At the same time Egypt discouraged excavations elsewhere, other than in Nubia, until the Campaign objectives had been attained.

Since Egyptian Nubia had already been explored and as many sites had been destroyed or disturbed by the inundation the chances of making really valuable finds, or at least exhibits of museological interest, seemed slight. Consequently the promise to grant concessions in Egypt itself and on rich sites was undoubtedly a considerable lure, probably more so than the promise of half of the Nubian finds. This offer of Egyptian sites was especially attractive to those who had had such concessions in Egypt prior to the Nubian Campaign, and to that special group with Archaeological Institutes located in Egypt or with long-established traditions of field excavation there. They would certainly want to return to Egypt to continue work on their concessions. This was also an incentive to museums with little interest in Nubia but always hoping for more "showy" pieces from Egypt.

Another attraction of Egyptian Nubia resulted from the world-wide promotion campaign of Unesco, especially in relation to the rescue of Abu Simbel. Moreover, the composition of the Consultative Committee as well as the activities of the Documentation Centre entailed connections with many foreign institutes, which again increased the attraction of Egyptian Nubia.

The Sudanese Government, in its request, had pointed out that, under Sudanese law, an excavator was entitled to half the finds, excluding unique objects of historical value. Unlike Egypt, however, the Sudan could not offer any monuments to be ceded as grants-in-return because of their scarcity. Nevertheless the Sudanese authorities were to show great generosity in the division of the finds – the famous frescoes discovered by the Polish expedition at Faras are an example. In practice the division meant that the Sudan kept only types of objects not well represented in the Sudanese museums and ceded the great majority of finds to the excavators.

As in Egypt the Sudan Antiquities Service adopted a nominal policy of not granting concessions in other parts of the country, and advised expeditions already excavating elsewhere in the Sudan (for example, the Germans – GDR – at Mussawwarat and the French at Sai) to suspend operations pending the completion of the Nubian Campaign. Most of the expeditions which subsequently came to Sudanese Nubia had no previous experience of it and no plans for future work in other areas of the country. In contrast to Egypt, there were no archaeological "gold mines" of the kind likely to attract people with museum connections. In fact none of the expeditions was sponsored exclusively by a museum and most not at all. The decisive incentives were of another nature according to Professor Adams:

"I would say that the incentives of professional responsibility, national responsibility, and scientific contribution all played a part in contributing to the success of the Unesco Campaign in the Sudan. Egyptologists were, in the beginning, the only archaeologists with a sense of prior commitment to Nubia and it was primarily they who responded out of a sense of professional responsibility. I think this would best characterize the motivations of the British expedition at Buhen, the Franco–Argentine expedition at Aksha, the French expedition at Mirgissa, the Chicago Oriental Institute work at Serra,

Dorginarti, and Semna South, and the Scandinavian Joint Expedition. I think a sense of national responsibility to assist a fellow Member State of Unesco was perhaps most specifically responsible for the coming of the Spanish, Ghana, Yugoslav, Humboldt University, Heidelberg, and Swiss expeditions. An interest in the scientific possibilities and results for their own sake was probably the primary motivation for most of the American expeditions (New Mexico, Colorado, University of California, Los Angeles [UCLA] and Kentucky) and for the Finnish and Italian expeditions.

"I do not know to what extent Unesco made a conscious effort to appeal to these different motivations, and to address its message accordingly. I myself was motivated almost exclusively by the possibilities of scientific and scholarly achievement, and this was my 'pitch' on the two occasions (1960 and 1962) when Unesco commissioned me to contact institutions and to attempt to recruit expeditions from the United States. Under the circumstances it is perhaps not surprising that I had my best success with my fellow American anthropologists; I had considerable responsibility for the recruiting of the New Mexico (later Combined Prehistoric), Colorado and UCLA expeditions. I had, on the other hand, no part in recruiting the Oriental Institute expedition, and my contacts with the Metropolitan Museum, the Brooklyn Museum, the Boston Museum, and with the Egyptologists at Yale, Harvard and Pennsylvania were all unsuccessful. However, various other appeals at Unesco certainly were successful in reaching both the Egyptologists and the concerned Member States, and I feel that in the end the number of responding expeditions in the Sudan was adequate to the task we had in hand."

In both Egyptian Nubia and Sudanese Nubia the two States themselves made important contributions to the archaeological exploration of their respective territories. In Egyptian Nubia the Antiquities Service carried out excavations at the Pharaonic temple of Wadi es-Sebua and investigated X-Group tombs at Ballana. Cairo University was responsible for several successful campaigns at Aniba under Professor Abu Bakr, a leading Egyptologist, active both in the Consultative Committee and in other groups of experts. The finds from Aniba, which in the New Kingdom was the political centre of Lower Nubia, covered all periods but were of special interest in relation to the C-Group, Meroitic and X-Group cultures. Alexandria University made a survey and excavations at the Late Nubian centre, Gebel Adda. There can be no doubt that the role of the Sudan Antiquities Service – and its field work as described earlier in the chapter – was of decisive importance for the success of the campaign in Sudanese Nubia.

Such national efforts could not of course have carried through such an immense task within the critically short time available; fortunately the appeals for international assistance resulted in an impressive response from a very large number of Member States, so that in all, some 40 missions were sent to Nubia from many parts of the world.

From Africa an expedition came from Ghana and explored the mediaeval town of Debeira, to obtain the maximum amount of information on domestic aspects of mediaeval Nubian life. Professor P.L. Shinnie, one-time Commissioner for Archaeology in the Sudan, was now head of the Department of Archaeology at the University of Ghana and because of his special interest and competence it seemed highly desirable that the University of Ghana should play a part in the international effort. Ghana's contribution would have a special significance in demonstrating that at least one African country was concerned with the attempt to acquire as much knowledge of the African past as possible before the waters washed away any remaining traces of early history for ever. The President of the country at that time, Dr. Kwame Nkrumah, decided that Ghana as an African country should contribute and directed that suitable funds be made available.

From Asia the Archaeological Survey of India under Professor B.B. Lal explored A-Group and C-Group cemeteries in the district of Afyeh.

Latin America was represented by a Franco–Argentine expedition to the site of the Ramesside temple of Aksha, and North America by eight missions from the United States and Canadian participation in the work of the American Research Centre in Egypt. The National Museum of Canada and the Yale Prehistoric expedition also explored the area at Kom Ombo where the Nubians were to be re-settled and which would be destroyed, from an archaeological point of view, by agricultural development. The field-work of the United States missions was mostly financed through a special grant in Egyptian pounds, but they had to meet their own dollar requirements.

Whereas the prehistorians organized a Combined Prehistoric Expedition under Professor Wendorf of the Southern Methodist University, Dallas, together with Polish, Belgian and French colleagues, the other institutions (Chicago Oriental Institute, Pennsylvania–Yale Expedition, University of Colorado, University of California, Brown University, University of Kentucky, and American Research Centre in Egypt) devoted their investigations to their individual interests. This bears out the doubts raised earlier in the Campaign as to whether the best solution for Nubia could have been a single expedition; if missions from the same country and sharing the same grant could not or would not be co-ordinated, how would it have been possible to do so between independent Member States?

The Scandinavian Joint Expedition to Sudanese Nubia followed a line which amalgamated the financial and personal resources of four countries – Denmark, Finland, Norway and Sweden – through a governmental agreement. This action followed a traditional pattern among the Scandinavian states who, especially in matters relating to the United Nations, as a rule collaborate closely and tend to act as a unit. There is little doubt that co-ordination was a more efficient solution than four smaller, separate missions would have been, the more so since of the four countries two had no Egyptological expertise or experience of work in the Nile Valley.

Other missions from Europe came from Austria, Czechoslovakia, Finland (a separate expedition), France, Federal Republic of Germany, German Democratic Republic, Hungary, Italy (Milan, Rome and Turin), Netherlands, Poland, Spain, Switzerland, the United Kingdom and the USSR.

Expeditions to Nubia fell into two main categories: those devoted to survey and recording, and those which undertook the systematic excavation of one or more previously selected sites. Some survey expeditions confined themselves to particular kinds of remains as for example the Combined Prehistoric Expedition with its programme to explore the full range of pre-history of the Nile Valley, or the German Democratic Republic team with its survey of rock pictures and rock drawings in the whole of Nubia (apart from the Scandinavian concession area).

Other survey expeditions such as the Unesco–Sudan Antiquities Survey and the sondage expedition in Egyptian Nubia led by Professor Harry Smith of the Egypt Exploration Society in London explored large areas to locate and assess all manner of sites, a task which necessitated partial excavation of each one in order to ascertain its nature, size and date(s). The Egypt Exploration Society's sondage expedition was charged with ensuring that no important sites were overlooked and which should be assigned to other missions for more detailed investigation. The Sudan survey had a similar brief.

The Scandinavian Joint Expedition to Sudanese Nubia began with a survey of the 60 km between Faras and Gemai but then took over the responsibility to excavate all sites, except a few of the larger ones (the Serra fortress, the Qasr Ico church and the Abkanarti village) because the special conditions there necessitated more or less total excavation for a proper assessment.

In principle the expeditions to Egyptian Nubia should have followed the same procedure, according to the instructions of the Consultative Committee, but the resources of the missions did not always suffice to cover all sites except the most spectacular.

In the Sudan some expeditions undertook the excavation of a variety of sites within a single specified and, as a rule, more restricted area (Argin by Spain, Gezina Dabarosa by Colorado, Murshid by Finland, and Ukma by Switzerland). Other missions confined themselves mainly to one or two monumental pharaonic sites (the environment of a temple, or a fortress etc.) or to a mediaeval town, village or church with its surrounding area.

The backgrounds, interests, and professional competence of the field workers reflected the nature of the sites or missions they chose to work in. The prehistory and general survey expeditions were manned by experienced field archaeologists, most of them with extensive experience in other parts of the world. Many had never before worked in the Nile Valley, nevertheless they were able to introduce new methods and new approaches to the problems. Trained epigraphists were of course needed on those missions engaged on epigraphic recording, while the expeditions excavating the pharaonic fortresses were all led and organized by Egyptologists with architects and archaeologists as assistants. Excavations in mediaeval villages and churches were mostly directed by scholars with a special interest in mediaeval Nubia, or in the mediaeval period in general.

Differences of background and interest cut entirely across national boundaries. Egyptologists, mediaevalists, prehistorians, epigraphers and physical anthropologists from many countries participated in the campaign, and individual expeditions often included personnel of several nationalities.

Regarding the technical methods to be used in survey or excavation work no instructions seem to have been generally adopted, and the expeditions had a free choice which as a rule resulted in the old-fashioned but long-established employment of Qufti foremen for the finer work, and numerous Nubian workers using hoes and baskets. The Lerici Foundation made some experiments with geophysical methods at Aniba to test the possibility of locating hidden structures, but these sophisticated methods were used only in very rare cases (for example, by the French mission to Mirgissa in the Sudan). Since it was impossible to obtain spares locally and as it was often hopeless to make such delicate devices function in camps exposed to sandstorms and the all-pervasive dust, the use of simple manual methods was usually deemed advisable. In Sudanese Nubia the aims of the excavations were similar and the methods used by most of the missions varied very little.

In both countries, however, it was sometimes noticeable, especially in the attitude towards plundered or damaged sites, that the possibility of finding objects which could be good items for exhibition influenced the work so that, for example, the ecological aspects were neglected. There were no rules concerning the examination and classification of pottery sherds scientifically, and sherds or even collections of broken vases were sometimes left behind, more or less undocumented, because as artefacts they were commonplace and the aspects of quantitative archaeology held little or no interest for some of the archaeologists. Also human remains – skeletal, mummified, etc. – were sometimes re-buried for lack of anthropological specialists or pressure of time.

These shortcomings were however offset by the positive effects of the scientific collaboration which developed between expeditions of different nationalities and between experts of varying backgrounds and schooling. It was a collaboration supported by the co-ordinating national offices in Egypt and the Sudan which arranged an interchange of services between missions, offering basic resources and technical assistance, and receiving, often on a personal, unofficial level, expertise from the staff of the missions.

"International collaboration was reflected in many ways and at different levels of operation," wrote Professor Adams. "At the highest and most official level, the Scandinavian Joint Expedition, the Franco–Argentine Mission, and the Combined Prehistoric Expedition were all formally sponsored by more than one nation, as were the excavations at Khor Dehmit and Beit el-Wali in Egypt. The British expedition to Qasr Ibrim is not formally designated as an international mission, but it received regular contributed assistance from the

United States Smithsonian Institution and the University of Kentucky, and has also received assistance in the past from the Polish Centre for Mediterranean Archaeology, the National Museum of Leyden, and the French Centre National pour la Recherche Scientifique. Still more informally, many expeditions have included personnel from different countries, as for example the Qasr Ibrim expedition, the Leyden excavations at Abdallah Nirqi, the American excavation at Gebel Adda, and most of the excavations of the Chicago Oriental Institute in the Sudan.

"There were also many instances of inter-institutional collaboration. The Pennsylvania-Yale Expedition to Toshka and Arminna was a joint venture of two American universities, and the excavations at Qasr Ibrim as well as those of the Spanish missions brought together individual scholars whose services were contributed by a number of different host institutions.

"From the standpoint of lasting scientific progress, interdisciplinary collaboration and cross-fertilization were probably the most important and most lasting of all the accomplishments of the Nubian Campaign. Not only the survey expeditions but also many of the excavation teams brought together prehistorians, culture historians, philologists, physical anthropologists, and ancillary specialists from a variety of backgrounds, and with previous experience in many parts of Europe, Africa, Asia, and North and South America. From this conjunction of interests and outlooks there arose a new perspective on Nubia, its peoples, and its history which is no longer dominated by the peculiar perspective of Egyptology.

"At the practical level of operations, the success of the Nubian campaign can be measured not only in the quantity but also in the quality of field archaeology. The Campaign brought in specialists trained in the rigorous standards of European and North American archaeology, and in the use of such recently developed ancillary techniques as radiocarbon dating, palynology, neutron activation, and a host of others. The contribution of these 'outsiders' has helped bring the methodological and technical standard of archaeology in the Nile Valley up nearer to the levels that prevail in less archaeologically favoured areas, where meaningful results can be obtained only by scrupulously careful excavation and recording procedures."

A BALANCE AND AN EVALUATION

In Egyptian Nubia the whole area was soon divided among a series of foreign missions with what seemed to be full coverage and satisfactory guarantees to achieve the aim of a total archaeological investigation. Already at its 5th session (October 1963) the Executive Committee had been told that, with regard to documentation and excavations in Egyptian Nubia, "practically all the aims of the international solidarity campaign have already been achieved" and in a progress report covering the period 1 July to 31 December 1963 the work of the missions was described with the following comment: "All these missions have cleared their concessions systematically. . . . The waters may now cover everything, for no archaeological clue will have been overlooked."

That this aim was not always attained, in some cases depended on a misinterpretation of the report of the Sondage Expedition, which was ably conducted by Professor Harry Smith and which ended in November 1961. In his report (Preliminary Reports of the Egypt Exploration Society's Nubian Survey, Cairo 1962) Professor Smith has described his instructions and the premises of his results. Those who knew the peculiar conditions of Nubia – especially the fact that wind erosion and recent deposits of silt and sand can make all surface traces even of large sites disappear entirely – were aware that the methods which a rapid sondage expedition would have to use could as a rule reveal perhaps less than 50% of the sites which might be found with other more leisurely methods. Moreover, the instructions were not to traverse on foot areas where nothing of interest could be seen on the aerial photographs; thereby a large number of wind-eroded sites were undoubtedly not noticed (for instance, in the concession of the Scandinavian Joint Expedition the majority of the hundreds of sites excavated were not visible on the aerial photographs examined prior to excavation). The Sondage Expedition was also to report on sites considered to merit further exploration, but here, too, much evidence may have been lost – at least some of the sites which were excavated despite recommendation to the contrary, yielded important results, and some plundered sites often turned out to be of great scientific importance.

In some cases it seems as if the expeditions interpreted a "total investigation" of their concession as excavation only of the sites reported by the Sondage Expedition and sometimes this Expedition was unjustly blamed if unreported sites were found. In such cases the concession area cannot, of course, be regarded as completely investigated. In other cases, the mission concerned never intended to make a complete investigation despite the recommendations or instructions of the responsible authorities, yet failed to so report in time for other missions to take over.

Moreover, it is always difficult to balance the task of an exhaustive investigation against financial and personal resources which may easily be spent before the mission is accomplished. In some cases such miscalculations or an unexpected wealth of finds resulted in lacunae in the overall investigation.

To the south of Gemai at the Second Cataract the terrain was extremely rocky and difficult to traverse, and its productive resources were limited. The one through road in the area was many kilometres to the east of the Nile, and there was no overland transport at all on the west bank. Travel on the river itself was impeded by numerous rapids. Villages were small and widely scattered, and few supplies were available. There were known to be a number of important archaeological sites in the area, but, except for the previously investigated Second Cataract Forts, most of them dated from the later mediaeval period.

The group of experts meeting in Wadi Halfa in December 1963 recommended a rapid reconnaissance of the area, and a large-scale survey expedition to investigate this remaining part of the reservoir flood areas. The reconnaissance directed by the Unesco expert from Canada, Anthony Mills, started immediately and very soon revealed a great number of important sites that should be excavated. However, the large-scale expedition was never organized despite the recommendations of another expert meeting held in Venice in April 1966 and the decision of the Executive Committee to continue to put personnel at the disposal of the Antiquities Service. The Venice meeting tried to compress the programme by adopting priorities instead of the initial aim of total excavation, and also gave priority to some of the more important sites which later could be allocated to foreign missions. The burden of the work was shouldered by the existing survey expedition of the Antiquities Service with the aid of international experts put at its disposal.

In the end, the anticipated problems in the southern part of Sudanese Nubia did not entirely materialize. Supply and transport proved to be less difficult than expected, as local spur tracks were found which gave access to most points along the riverbank. The Antiquities Service survey expedition located some outstanding and well preserved archaeological sites; these in their turn attracted expeditions from several European countries and the United States.

The task of investigating 500 km of the Nile Valley in so short a time, an area full of innumerable sites of varying size – many extensive and rich – was indeed overwhelming, the more so as the logistic problems were considerable and the climate one of the world's harshest. The astonishing thing is that so much was accomplished and so little overlooked or neglected. So it is no exaggeration to state that this archaeological campaign covering as it did so huge an area is the most successful yet carried to completion. For an authoritative opinion one again may turn to Professor Adams, an outstanding international expert on salvage archaeology and one of those who were most intensively engaged in finding solutions to the many problems which emerged in Nubia.

In his view the success of the archaeological salvage campaign in Nubia has to be measured in many different ways and at different levels. At the most practical and immediate level – that of salvaging material and of salvaging knowledge from destruction – far more and far better archaeology was done in Nubia between 1960 and 1970 than had ever previously been done anywhere in the Nile Valley, or in most other parts of the world for that matter. Although the sites that were actually dug did not constitute more than one-third of the total volume that was destroyed, this represents a much fuller archaeological sample than we have from almost any other part of the world. It is, moreover, a scientifically valid sample, based on the deliberate inclusion of all different kinds of sites, large and small, from all periods of history and pre-history. There are still gaps in our knowledge of Nubian history and pre-history, but they are gaps due to vagaries in the archaeological record itself, not to the neglect of the archaeologists.

The advantages of having an adequate and reliable archaeological sample cannot be stressed too strongly. In most places, Adams points out, we know what was in the sites that we have dug, but we have only the sketchiest idea what is in the sites that we have not dug, because our sample is much too small to allow safe generalizations. Nubia, by contrast, is one of the very few places we can argue convincingly from negative evidence. If (for example) there are very few sites from the last millennium B.C., we can be fairly certain that it is because there was very little settlement during that period, not merely because we have not found or have not looked for the sites.

Better archaeology is reflected not only in excavation and recording techniques, but also and perhaps more importantly in the choice of what to dig and what not to dig. Earlier archaeological surveys of Nubia concentrated exclusively on cemetery sites, ignoring fortresses, villages, churches, workshops, and all kinds of other cultural debris which helps to round out our picture of human life and activity. This deficiency was largely overcome in the campaign of 1960–70, with the result that our picture of ancient and mediaeval Nubia is not only a fuller one but a much more rounded and balanced one. We finally have learned something about how the ancient Nubians lived, as well as about how they died.

Archaeology, however, is a means and not an end. More and better excavation techniques can only be justified if they contribute to our ultimate goal of enlarging human understanding of the past. Here again we can count the Nubian campaign as a major success. Through the combination of different backgrounds, different viewpoints, and a better approach to archaeology, we now see the country in its own fascinating light. It is particularly gratifying that the newly developing field of Nubian Studies, or "Nubiology", has not allowed itself to be confined within either temporal or topical limits, but rather has taken a unitary approach to all aspects of Nubian culture and history from the earliest times to the ethnographic present.

A Rich Harvest and its Consequences

To describe the results of the work done by the forty or so expeditions which explored some 500 km of the Nile Valley is not possible in a book where the main theme is rather the mechanisms which led to the success of the Campaign. The scientific findings are by no means fully published and the majority of the missions are still analysing their results, yet already it is clear that the cultural history of Nubia is being rewritten in the light of the fresh discoveries made there and new knowledge which touches on all periods and aspects of Nubian history. (See Bibliographical Notes and especially W.Y. Adams *Nubia. Corridor to Africa* and the Unesco Bibliography by L.A. Christophe.)

The thorough exploration of the reservoir area in Nubia yielded an overwhelming mass of new data and materials (the analysis of the human remains found by the Scandinavian Joint Expedition alone is based on some

35,000 measurements), of objects in daily use in ancient times such as thousands of pottery vessels, and pieces of art of great beauty, all contributing to a better understanding of Nubian culture through the millennia.

In describing now a very limited selection of the sensational discoveries, it must be stressed that in no way do they do justice to the range and quantity of those made, but they do at least convey some impression of their character and significance.

A STONE AGE MASSACRE – THE FIRST HUMAN REMAINS

The first traces of human life in the Nile Valley go back hundreds of millennia before our time and consist of primitive stone tools used by our hominid forebears long before the appearance of *homo sapiens*. However, in contrast to the findings in Kenya and Tanzania, skeletal or other human remains found in Nubia or Egypt proper date from rather late in pre-history.

The earliest remains are the traces of what seems to have been a human tragedy. Just north of Wadi Halfa, in the Scandinavian concession, 58 skeletons were found covered by a thin layer of sand and stones. The excavation, conducted by members of the Combined Prehistoric Expedition, revealed arrowheads among the bones, which indicated that here was a group of persons all killed in battle or massacred.

An analysis of the bodies and their ages taken in conjunction with what can be deduced from food remains and other finds in settlements dating from the same period, around 10,000 B.C. makes it possible to reconstruct their living conditions in some detail – in particular how they hunted the big game which came down to the valley to drink before retiring into the savannah areas which today are desert. Fish and migratory birds also contributed to their diet.

Subsequent research, which will be described later, has placed these first finds into a wider context which reveals an entirely new picture of the pre-history of Nubia, and the whole of the Nile Valley with its neighbouring areas.

AN EARLY NUBIAN STATE ANTEDATING EARLY DYNASTIC EGYPT?

Around 3000 B.C. the typical civilization of Lower Nubia is the so-called A-Group, known since the first survey of Nubia by Reisner for its wonderful handicrafts, especially ceramics, mixed with luxury goods imported from Egypt. Here the finds of the Chicago Oriental Institute expedition were sensational.

Near Qustul, just north of the Sudanese frontier, large and very rich tombs, excelling everything known so far, indicated the presence of a political centre ruled by a dominant chief or king. According to Bruce Williams the richness of the tombs in combination with certain pictures on objects indicate the presence of an Egyptian-type kingship belonging to rulers who first led Nubia to a political unity and cultural distinction, well before the First Dynasty of Egypt created the earliest known state of any size. These tombs, probably antedating Egypt's First Dynasty, would give evidence of a Nubian development towards a centralized state contemporary with or even preceding the same development in Egypt. This interpretation is not proved beyond doubt, but if correct, this, possibly Nubian, kingdom never approached the organizing ability and power of the first rulers in Egypt where rapid cultural and political evolution led to the first great state in the history of mankind, being marooned in a backwater of political and social development.

AN OLD KINGDOM TOWN

Before the end of the Second Egyptian Dynasty (*c.* 2650 B.C.) the A-Group people disappeared from Lower Nubia, either overwhelmed by the Egyptians or having deliberately moved out of this part of the Nile Valley possibly because of climatic changes.

It seems to be a recurrent pattern in Nubian history that the Egyptian apogees often correspond to a cultural or political vacuum in Nubia. This was the case during the Old Kingdom, the Pyramid Age, when Egyptian civilization reached one of its highest peaks and Egypt was the biggest and wealthiest state of its time.

No finds in Lower Nubia indicate the existence of a Nubian culture contemporaneous with the pyramid builders of the Fourth and Fifth Dynasties. For several centuries Nubia appears to have been, at least from the archaeological point of view, a vacuum, which remains an enigma despite all the intensive exploration. However, at least some light has emerged through new evidence. It was the quite unexpected discovery by Professor W.B. Emery of a fortified town just north of the Middle Kingdom fortress of Buhen opposite the modern town of Wadi Halfa. Texts on objects found dated it to the Fourth and Fifth Dynasties and the pottery indicated that the inhabitants were Egyptians. Remains of kilns for copper smelting seem to show that this was an Egyptian settlement for the exploitation of Nubian raw materials, copper in particular. It is a parallel in some ways, to the earlier discovery of diorite quarries northwest of Abu Simbel, far out in the desert, where the stone for the famous statues of King Chephren was quarried.

It would have been interesting to locate the source of the copper ore; Emery searched the surrounding desert but failed to trace the mine which the Egyptians must have worked some 45 centuries ago.

THE FORTRESS OF MIRGISSA

The Middle Kingdom Egyptian fortresses had been partly explored in the '30s, but the more thorough investigations made during the Campaign yielded many splendid and interesting objects both from the fortresses and the adjacent cemeteries, while the architectural analysis revealed refinements in military architecture and techniques hitherto unknown before Crusader times.

Analysis of the fortresses and the contemporary Nubian and Egyptian cemeteries and settlements has provided a remarkably comprehensive picture that makes it possible to follow the state of relations between the rulers from Egypt and the Nubian population, ranging from a military occupation to a period of Nubian independence under indigenous rulers – presumably from Kerma in the Dongola province – and to the period of more or less peaceful co-existence following the Egyptian conquest of Nubia in the New Kingdom.

The most fascinating results from the fortresses came from the excavations in Buhen by Professor Emery and from Professor Vercoutter's excavations at Mirgissa. Rex Keating has described his impressions from the latter site in the following way: "It had become obvious that Mirgissa was something very different from the other fortresses of the Second Cataract, much more in fact than a stronghold. Vercoutter had his own ideas on the subject and felt that proof of them would be found, if anywhere, in the upper fort. However, prudence demanded a concentration of work on the sandy plain below since this would go under water several years before the lake reached the cliff top and the upper fort.

"Not until the beginning of 1964 were trial diggings made in the upper fort in an attempt to determine when the fort had been built. The logical starting point was the north-west corner where Lyons had unearthed the two stelae of Senusret III, but instead of chronological evidence what turned up was an Eighteenth Dynasty shrine dedicated to the goddess Hathor. It was poorly constructed of mud brick but in it were scores of small objects: amulets, beads, scarabs, basketry, broken pots and vases, fertility cult figures and stones of unusual shapes. The statue or stela of the goddess was missing but they did find four other small wooden stelae and these revealed that the inhabitants of Mirgissa during the New Kingdom worshipped a triad: Senusret I (or III), the falcon god Montu and the humanized form of Hathor. Further clearance revealed more votive objects, some bearing the name of Amenhotep III of the Eighteenth Dynasty, and another small wooden stela which had been miraculously overlooked by the termites. This tablet is about the most important single object discovered at Mirgissa. It bore a text, 'Hathor, Lady of Ikn'. No more than that, but it confirmed what Vercoutter had long believed, that Mirgissa was nothing less than the long-sought Egyptian entrepot in Nubia. Several texts mention Ikn, notably the proclamation of Senusret III found at Semna which states that Ikn is the only place within the military zone of the Cataract district where Kushites are permitted to bring their produce for trade with the Egyptians.

"With this discovery the elaborate fortifications in the plain bordering the river, the garrison town and the 'outer' town all fell into place, as did the location of the site. Mirgissa, at the southern end of the most hazardous of the

Second Cataract rapids, was ideally suited to protect traffic to and from Egypt both by river and by land; from its fortifications high on the cliff sentries could survey the desert for miles around, as well as the river, while below the upper fort a smooth stretch of water offered a natural harbour. In short Mirgissa was ideal for commerce of the kind favoured by the Pharaohs of 1900 B.C. Egyptologists had long disputed the whereabouts of Ikn and now one small wooden tablet had closed the argument for good.

"Upstream of Mirgissa on the island fort of Uronarti, Senusret III left an inscription, found by Wheeler, which describes how bad the water was 'because of the time of the year' – that is to say, the winter months of low water – and that his army had been forced to drag their ships through the rapids. This 'dragging' of ships sounds improbable but is mentioned in a number of texts. The French mission actually found a slipway which had been used for dragging ships and a remarkable example of the engineering prowess of the Egypt of 1900 B.C. it proved to be, and unique in Egyptian archaeology. It took the form of a roadway laid with wooden poles rather like the sleepers of a railroad, each pole being slightly curved, with the lowest section in the middle, thus forming a shallow cradle. The whole roadway had been embedded in Nile silt. The poles had long since been eaten by termites but the dry mud had faithfully retained their imprints just as it retained the impressions of grooves made by the keels of the ships and the actual footprints of sailors who had pulled the vessels along the slippery surface some 40 centuries ago. When I saw the slipway the sand was already drifting over it but still I was able to follow its course due north for 3 km after which it lost itself in the dunes. The dangerous rapids nearby can be navigated in reasonable safety only during the period of high water between the end of July and November, and the slipway had been constructed to outflank them and make navigation possible throughout most of the year." (*Rex Keating*, "Nubian Rescue", pp. 88–90, 94–5).

Nubia under Egyptian rule during the New Kingdom (1550–1080 B.C.) provides a fascinating chapter of history as illustrated by the new finds during the Campaign. From this period there is now overwhelming evidence of all kinds, archaeological and textual, and much is also known about the individual actors in the drama – a recent doctoral thesis used some 800 textual and pictorial documents for a description of the administrative machinery of the time.

Experts disagree, however, in the interpretation of the archaeological evidence in the form of tombs which in every respect seem to be those of Egyptians, but which may equally well be the tombs of an Egyptianized Nubian population. Some authorities advocate the theory of a Nubian exodus, leaving the country to Egyptian immigrants, others maintain that the Nubians stayed on and adopted the civilization of their Egyptian overlords.

That the Egyptians did not exterminate the Nubian population or drive them out is quite clear from evidence derived from the tombs of Nubian princes which came to light during the Campaign. The two oldest, dating from the reigns of Queen Hatshepsut and Tuthmosis III (*c.* 1490 B.C.), were investigated by the Scandinavian Joint Expedition in the northernmost part of Sudanese Nubia, in the district of Debeira. They belonged to two brothers, Thoth-hotep and Amenemhet, born of Nubian parents to judge by their names. They bear the titles of Egyptian officials but also that of "Great Ones of (district) Teh-khet", which is the denomination of a foreign ruler according to Egyptian usage. The tomb of Thoth-hotep is decorated with fascinating paintings in exactly the same style as that of the contemporary tombs in the Egyptian capital, Thebes, but the motives are Nubian with representations of gardening in Nubia, a banquet with Nubian musicians, and so on. The tomb of the younger brother, Amenemhet, was also entirely Egyptian in style containing objects of good Egyptian craftsmanship, among other things a stela with the conventionalized autobiography of the tomb's owner.

A third tomb also belonged to a Nubian Prince. His name was Heqa-nefer, "Great One of Miam (Aniba)"; he was already known from his portrait in the Theban tomb of Huy, the contemporary Viceroy of Nubia, in the reign of King Tutankhamun. This portrait shows a dark-skinned man, dressed as an Egyptian but with exotic additions to his garments, while his face is quite un-Egyptian. One of the sensations of the Campaign was when Professor K. Simpson from Boston found the tomb of this very Nubian Prince, proving him to be a historical personage and not just a conventional figure in Egyptian iconography.

The titles of these Nubian Princes show that they were all educated at the Egyptian court alongside the Egyptian Princes, that they then pursued the customary career of an Egyptian official and were finally sent to rule their countrymen in their home district in Nubia.

THE WONDER OF FARAS

The Late Nubian era, that is to say from the first millennium A.D., yielded a wealth of finds.

The Meroitic period of the first centuries was represented in one way or another in most concession areas. It was a culturally rich epoch in Nubia, where at Maharraqa a cemetery excavated by an Italian expedition marks the northern limit of the Meroitic realm. New texts in their still poorly understood language will perhaps one day solve the many outstanding riddles, but in the meantime Meroitic settlements and objects of daily use have provided a better insight in the way of life of this versatile people and their subjects in Lower Nubia.

The ensuing period is characterized by the so-called X-Group – also styled the "Ballana phase" after the immensely rich royal tombs excavated by W.B. Emery during the last survey of Nubia which preceded the Nubian Campaign of the '60s. Here again a wealth of new finds has thrown fresh light on the nature and development of this culture. An impressive handicraft, which earlier investigations had largely neglected because of the problems of conservation, is represented by the textiles. An exhibition in the Art Institute of Chicago of the textiles found by the Chicago Oriental Institute at Qustul demonstrated what modern techniques can do to rescue and conserve such fragile material, which showed an extraordinary variety of weaving techniques and fascinating patterns in brilliant colours. It is a craft which can stand comparison with the finest the world can show.

All these Late Nubian discoveries, indeed all finds from Nubia, were, however, overshadowed by what the Polish Expedition uncovered at Faras, on the west bank just south of the Sudanese border. In the great mound of Faras the British Egyptologist F. Ll.Griffith had made significant discoveries shortly before the First World War. The site was then left untouched until the Polish Expedition moved in and quickly found a large number of blocks from a Thuthmosid temple and other valuable finds dating from Christian times, among them the tomb of a bishop. On top of the mound a farmer had installed his family and animals. There was an unforgettable moment when trenching exposed a corner of a fresco showing angels in heaven. It turned out to be the upper part of a magnificent large-scale Nativity scene inside a cathedral whose walls were decorated with more than 120 well-dated frescoes, mostly in excellent condition. The cathedral itself had been buried under the walls of an Arab citadel.

The Polish archaeologist, Kazimierz Michalowski, who participated in all the phases of the Nubian Campaign, described the discovery as follows:

"Today Faras lies some forty metres beneath the waters, but in the 7th century it was the capital of northern Nubia. During three years of excavations the Polish expedition succeeded in resuscitating a hitherto unknown chapter of the history of early Christian Nubia and a large part of its art.

"Among the most famous works discovered are a head of St Anne with a finger to her lips in the sign for silence, the black bishop Petros under the protection of the Apostle Peter, the olive-skinned bishop Marianos, the dark-complexioned Queen-Mother Martha, and a vast Nativity scene which includes the shepherds and the Three Wise Men.

"It would be impossible to list all the objects such as the splendid 11th-century glass chalice found during the excavations which covered not only the great church but also a whole complex of buildings including an eparch's palace, two monasteries and a second church.

"The excavations at Faras were a race against time. In the course of four seasons, each lasting five to six months, the expedition succeeded in salvaging the most important objects, not only the frescoes of the church which were taken down and packed in cases, but also the bronzes, the ceramics, the inscriptions and tombs of the bishops complete with their skeletons. The list of their names which was found on the walls of the church constitutes one of the original documents of Christianity in Nubia. Hardly had the expedition finished nailing up the cases for removal when the Nile water reached the level of the hill on which the excavations had taken place. Some months later, the tops of a few palm trees emerging from the lake were all that remained to mark the spot where Faras had once stood."

Half of the wonderful Faras frescoes were taken to the new National Museum in Khartoum, where today they are among the most outstanding exhibits. The other half was generously given to Poland as a token of gratitude for the splendid work done by the Poles in the Sudan, and they are now exhibited to full advantage in the National Museum in Warsaw.

The Nubian campaign also brought a harvest of many more frescoes of the Christian period, for example from Sonqi and Sheikh Abd el Qadir in the Sudan, and in Egypt from the church of Abdallah Nirqi, and the Pharaonic temples of Wadi es-Sebua and Abu Oda. The latter were removed to safety by Yugoslav experts, a difficult and delicate task, and will be exhibited in the planned Nubia Museum in Aswan.

QASR IBRIM

The other outstanding Late Nubian site is the great fortress site of Qasr Ibrim in the centre of Egyptian Nubia. It was the most important political and administrative centre after the heyday of Faras but competed with Faras in importance from Roman times onwards. It is situated on a high rock, beyond reach of the water and as a consequence the finds are extraordinarily well preserved, even the most delicate materials needing little conservation. Qasr Ibrim has yielded a wealth of written sources on papyrus, parchment and paper, with texts in all the languages used in Nubia during the later period: Meroitic, Greek, Coptic, Old Nubian and Arabic. Once they are published these texts will undoubtedly reveal many details of Nubian history from the Roman occupation of around 22 B.C. down to the time when a Bosnian garrison was installed there by Soliman the Magnificent in 1528, and on to modern times. The texts, sometimes bilingual, will also give important clues to a fuller understanding of the two still imperfectly known languages – Meroitic and Old Nubian.

In the north crypt of the stone-built cathedral, a magnificent edifice on the highest part of the rock, the untouched burial of the Nubian bishop Timothy was found together with his commissary letters of the year 1372 A.D., which took the form of two scrolls $4\frac{1}{2}$ m long. At one time, Timothy was thought to be the last bishop of Nubia, but a leather scroll in Old Nubian of the year 1464 indicated that a Nubian king Joel was then reigning in Gebel Adda and that a bishop Merki resided in Qasr Ibrim.

The beginning of Christianity in Nubia is well illustrated by Qasr Ibrim texts. A letter of the 5th or 6th (?) century A.D. describes some affairs of King Silko, the Nubian ruler previously only known through the famous text in bad Greek, inscribed in the temple of Kalabsha.

The Egypt Exploration Society was not able to complete a programme of excavation at Qasr Ibrim prior to the filling of the High Dam Lake, however, because of its elevated situation most of the fortress area is above the maximum lake level.

Because of their great historical importance, the excavations at Qasr Ibrim have continued intermittently from 1963 and are expected to continue for at least a decade to come. Under the present programme of operations there is a four-month season of excavation in every alternate year. The filling of Lake Nasser and the inevitable destruction of fields and villages have imposed some logistical difficulties on the operation at Qasr Ibrim. It is now necessary to bring in all personnel, labourers and supplies from Aswan at the beginning of the season, and communication with the outside world during the four months of excavation is slow and difficult. However, the Egyptian Antiquities Organization continues, as in the days of the International Campaign, to provide the expedition with houseboats, tugs, crews, and a communication service. Without this continued support the excavations at Qasr Ibrim could not proceed.

WIDENING HORIZONS

For those who were caught in the spell of Nubia during the Campaign there was a strong stimulus to explore further the surroundings of Nubia, following up lines of research into hitherto uncharted territories and unknown corners of African history.

The Combined Prehistoric Expedition has revised all previous ideas of Nubia's prehistoric development in the Nile Valley and its surroundings. Its experts analysed in detail the severe climatic changes in northeastern Africa and the successful adaptation of man to environments dictated by extremes of tropical rains or total drought. The analysis of the interrelations between these climatic changes in Africa and the glacial periods in northern Europe gives a deeper understanding of the mechanisms of the biosphere. These results were obtained by widening the horizons from Nubia to Ethiopia in the south, to Sinai in the north and from the Nile Valley deep into deserts which once were alive with game and human settlements.

Their more recent field work just north of Aswan has revealed the oldest traces of agriculture, possibly as much as 5000 years older than any previously known. Africa then, not Asia, would have been the place where man about 10,000 B.C. started to cultivate, to produce food instead of merely gathering it.

Another astonishing and recent development has arisen from the results yielded by different places in the Sudan which point to the existence of two immense so-called technocomplexes, that is to say, types of cultures with fundamentally identical technologies. One, dated to the 4th millennium B.C. is connected with the A-Group in Lower Nubia and its predecessor the neolithic "Khartoum Variant", both formerly regarded as local cultures restricted to rather small areas but now seen to encompass an area of Africa equal in size to western Europe.

The second, of the 3rd and 2nd millennia B.C., had its centre at Kerma in the Dongola province. There the Swiss archaeologist Bonnet found a large town surrounding two enigmatic brick complexes, known as the *deffufas*, excavated 60 years ago by the American archaeologist Reisner. Whereas the Eastern Deffufa located in the cemetery was assumed to be a funerary chapel or temple, the Western Deffufa was thought to be either an Egyptian stronghold or trading station or the palace of the Nubian ruler; its architectural history has now been clarified as well as its use as a temple serving the surrounding city, discovered by Bonnet. The Kerma culture can now be followed through centuries and it represented an African state of considerable importance and strength in the period between the Middle and Old Kingdoms in Egypt when the rulers of Kerma dominated Lower Nubia also. The pottery typical of this culture has great affinities to the pottery of the Lower Nubian C-Group and of the so-called Pan Graves; it has now been found over an immense area – from the Gash delta near the Red Sea to the Tibesti mountains deep in the Saharan desert, and even southwards to the territories of the Shilluk on the Upper Nile.

These sensational results are the consequences of the Nubian Campaign. They demonstrate the fact that northern Nubia really was the corridor to Africa and how important it was that this link in the chain from the known to the unknown, from Egypt to Africa further south, was not broken.

The scientific research in Nubia and the neighbouring areas has involved the collaboration of the most widely different categories of scholars and experts, and all kinds of methods and approaches. All have a common interest and of this a new science has been born: "Nubiology", internationally well organized and holding regular international symposia. In fact, two new sciences have been born of the Nubian Campaign as the Meroitists also, devoting themselves to the decipherment of the now computerized Meroitic texts, form a similar, albeit more restricted international group with a common scientific goal.

NUBIAN TREASURES

With the flooding of Nubia, many of its archaeological sites were destroyed, but its immense wealth of cultural treasure was rescued and brought to safety.

Many of the antiquities went abroad as ambassadors of Nubia and of Egypt and the Sudan, to museums across the world, to Member States of Unesco which had participated in the archaeological campaign. They kindle interest in Nubia and understanding of the kinds of problems involved in its history over the millennia, eternal problems, such as the adaptation of man to changing environments, the impact of human activities on natural resources, the meeting of different cultures, sometimes leading to conflict, sometimes to peaceful co-existence and cross fertilization of ideas and social devices.

The rest of the finds from Nubia remain in Egypt and in the Sudan. The National Museum of the Sudan in Khartoum is already a treasury of Nubian art, cherished by the Sudanese people, and a well-organized repository of scientific material for researchers everywhere.

In Egypt plans for a Nubia Museum in Aswan are being finalized in collaboration with Unesco through an Executive Committee. This body is a continuation of the Executive Committee of the Nubian Campaign and is also engaged in the creation of a new National Museum of Egyptian Civilization in Cairo.

Through these cultural treasuries Nubia will live on and the Nubians will to some extent be compensated for the loss of their "blessed land"; the world will be the richer because an essential part of the common cultural heritage was saved from destruction through Unesco's Member States demonstrating in practical terms their solidarity in a common cause.

The success in Nubia is ascribed in many publications and documents to many different people, but the decisive group is often forgotten.

It is the ordinary Nubian workmen.

The rescue operations could never have been achieved without their conscientious dedication, whether moving sand from one place to another, or engaged in work such as cutting monuments from the rocks or handling heavy blocks of brittle sandstone. There was hardly a job which a Nubian would not quickly learn to handle; even the most delicate of excavation work in tombs containing fragile objects could be entrusted to the Nubian workers, and the most precious finds could be left unguarded – the whole village guaranteeing their inviolability.

They were unschooled in many ways, but were well aware of the goals of the operations and that it was their own heritage which they were rescuing for generations yet unborn.

For them it was a very hard time. Most of the archaeological salvage operations coincided with the preparations for their own exodus and re-settlement in strange environments far from the Nile, but despite their anxiety for the future, they worked on faithfully. Those who had the privilege to work with these men, these friends, will never forget them.

And the land of Nubia itself – in his book *Nubian Rescue* – Rex Keating a former member of Unesco's Secretariat with a passion for Egyptology, who devoted much of his time over 10 years to the Nubian Campaign, wrote of it in these terms:

"Between the launching of the Nubian Campaign by Unesco's Director-General and the departure of the last expedition from that ill-fated land lie ten years of international endeavour such as the world has rarely witnessed. Nubia offered unusual possibilities to archaeology and those possibilities were amply fulfilled; it demanded of those who were there the meticulous care that modern archaeological methods impose on field work, yet at the same time all were driven in their efforts by the impending destruction of the scene of their labours.

"For those who sense such things, Nubia could cast a spell as hard to resist as it was difficult to pin down. There was the contrast between the Nile boiling through its Cataracts and the immobility of the deserts that enfolded it; there was the Nubian presence, calm and unhurried, in a pattern of living hallowed by practices as old as the river itself; there were the ancient settlements and places of worship, the fortresses and the graves, all indistinguishable in terms of time from the villages of our day, so that past and present, like life and death in Nubia, seemed never far apart. It was a disturbing magic because it induced a kind of topsy-turvydom, a feeling that this was the real world and that other world outside had no more substance than a half-remembered dream. Scattered around our problem-ridden planet are a few hundred men and women who had the good fortune to experience the unique flavour of Nubia in its closing years. I count myself favoured to have been among them."

Conclusion

The conservation and protection of works of art and monuments of history and science is one of the essential tasks laid on Unesco by its Constitution.

The international campaign to save the monuments of Nubia was the first major operation where this task was accomplished on a grand scale in practice and not just through recommendations and conventions. The principle of international cooperation for the conservation and protection of the world's common cultural heritage in the form of historical monuments was here applied to a concrete situation.

The Nubia Campaign was an outstanding success and the inauguration of the Philae temples following their salvage a moment of triumph in the history of Unesco. Not only had the great temples of Abu Simbel, Philae and Kalabsha been rescued in Egypt and the Sudan, some twenty other temples had also been brought out of danger, and those monuments which could not be removed had been fully documented. Moreover, the whole inundation area – over 500 km long and in some places up to 20 km broad – had been investigated and excavated by archaeologists more thoroughly than any (larger) district or country in the world. Monuments and objects of art and great beauty and historical importance had been saved for future generations and an important chapter in the history of Africa and of the world had escaped oblivion thanks to the archaeological investigations.

This success, achieved in so short a time and against unfavourable odds, with little time for proper preparations, often improvized and with no precedents, was brought about by world-wide cooperation, a result in which the governments of Egypt and the Sudan together with Unesco with its Member States played fundamental roles.

The mechanisms of this success are apparent from the development of the Campaign, from hesitant start to final triumph, and its continuation in the International Campaign for Egyptian Museums: the Nubia Museum in Aswan and the new National Museum of Egyptian Civilization in Cairo.

Here it must be said that during the Campaign operations even those most deeply involved sometimes asked themselves whether it was morally acceptable to collect millions of dollars for such a purpose in a world where millions of its inhabitants starve and innumerable children die of hunger or have no expectation of even a marginally decent standard of life. A private interview with the members of the Executive Committee, representing all varieties of Member States, East and West, rich and poor, and with widely differing political systems or religious creeds, showed that no one hesitated. All stressed the importance, not least for the developing countries with a colonial background, to establish their historical and cultural identity and to take care of their antiquities and monuments which are expressions of this identity. As the Sudanese delegate put it: "It is vital to know one's background and identity. Otherwise it is not possible to make the right choices in the modern world. Only those who care for their past, care realistically for their future. When you row a boat, you look backwards to arrive at the right point."

The Nubia Campaign clearly demonstrated that the rescue of antiquities and monuments is not only a moral duty towards future generations, but that the preservation of cultural treasures – objects of art, monuments or even entire landscapes – may be of importance also to economic and social development, especially in poor countries or zones. Excavations and salvage operations offer employment; in Nubia thousands of workers were employed in an area of unemployment or underemployment. And when the preservation works were completed, tourist traffic brought about by the attraction of the rescued monuments has resulted in growing financial advantages, just as Nubian antiquities and monuments in foreign museums are mute ambassadors of Egypt and the Sudan. In this respect the Nubia Campaign has changed the prevailing attitude towards salvage programmes. What were earlier often regarded as conflicting interests – the preservation of cultural values as opposed to technical or economic innovations – can indeed be reconciled and integrated into a single coherent scheme.

Looking back on the long and complicated history of the Campaign and the means which brought success, certain factors and circumstances stand out as especially important.

First, the personal element. It is doubtful if the Campaign would have been launched at all had it not been for the deep personal involvement of leading personalities in Egypt, in the Sudan and in Unesco. Thus the meeting between the Egyptian Minister of Culture and National Guidance, Dr. Okacha, with René Maheu in 1959 was of fundamental importance, as was the fact that Maheu shortly afterwards became Acting Director-General and then Director-General, thereby deepening Unesco's involvement and giving to the Nubia Campaign a higher priority. And what would the Campaign have been without the devotion, energy and diplomacy of Professor Paulo E. de Berrêdo Carneiro, the grand old man of the Executive Board of Unesco, not to mention all those others who were imbued with the "Spirit of Nubia", that extraordinary upwelling of enthusiasm to meet a great challenge and give of their utmost in a common cause?

The promotion campaign through the mass media and emissaries was also a central factor in the success story, whether directly organized or inspired by Unesco and the Egyptian and Sudanese authorities, or indirectly through the

National Committees in the Member States with their knowledge of specific local ways and means likely to bring about a positive response. The skilful advocacy of international responsibility for a common cultural heritage under the slogan "A Common Trust" was fundamental and became a leading theme in all later operations of a similar nature.

From the very beginning Egypt and the Sudan made it clear that they themselves felt a strong obligation to do their utmost to safeguard their threatened cultural heritage and that international support by no means diminished their obligation and duty. Such "Help yourself" attitudes, as well as being a clear demonstration that the threat to cultural treasures cannot be eliminated without the danger of provoking still bigger catastrophes, are necessary conditions for success in international campaigns of this nature. Thus in the case of Nubia it was important to show that the construction of the High Dam was inevitable and necessary for the welfare or even survival of millions of Egyptians. Otherwise it would have been possible to argue that if Egypt were so keen to save the Nubian monuments, the decision to construct the High Dam should be reconsidered!

When a State is assisted in its problems by acceptance of an international campaign it is hardly possible to be both national and international simultaneously. The State must show a positive attitude towards the international organization concerned and there must be close collaboration in a spirit of confidence and mutual respect. It was a considerable asset in the Nubia Campaign that the Executive Committee could report to the donors that the Egyptian and Sudanese authorities always respected the recommendations of the international bodies and that all important decisions were taken unanimously, in full harmony. The efforts to raise funds and other contributions were facilitated by the fact that collaboration with the local authorities was undisturbed by nationalistic complications and that the proper use of the funds could be guaranteed.

This latter implied not only a control of expenditure according to agreed allocations but also that the choice of salvage projects was the best possible; and that when chosen, a project should be financially and technically feasible and based on well conducted preliminary studies of all the methods likely to be used. Experience clearly showed that an international response could be obtained only when these conditions were met.

The operations in Nubia also demonstrated that contracts must be based on a comprehensive analysis of all details and possible complications and that a contract should be awarded only to firms with personnel, technical means and experience adequate for the completion of the work in the allotted time. Thus it follows that the contract should not automatically be awarded to the lowest bidder.

As for the archaeological aspect of the Campaign, the analysis of motivations and methods examined in a preceding chapter brings out points of special importance to be taken into consideration when planning similar large-scale international operations. Ideally a master-plan with well defined priorities and scientific goals should as far as possible be worked out in advance, an ideal which in practice may be hard to fulfil. Salvage archaeology is only too often haunted and hampered by shortness of time and lack of detailed advance knowledge of the scientific and logistic problems involved, but this does not diminish the need for as detailed and realistic planning as possible.

When soliciting participation, an appeal to feelings of general solidarity is hardly enough; it must be backed by solid scientific interest which, however, need not necessarily be centred on the area in question, but can equally well touch on fundamental and methodological problems. Very often the number of experts previously engaged in the specific problems of a circumscribed region or monument to be saved is insufficient for large-scale operations. Few archaeologists had any previous interest in or knowledge of Nubian problems before the Campaign started, and most of the work was done by scholars with an expertise based on experience drawn from entirely different fields of research. In the event, a good basic schooling in archaeological methods and general expertise proved quite adequate for the field work to be done effectively, while "outsiders" often imported a fresh impetus and introduced new methods and attitudes. The Nubian experience in this respect has also proved true in other, similar campaigns. It is mandatory that only good scholars and institutes of renown should be allowed to take on such responsibilities. In the Nubia Campaign concessions to survey or excavate were granted only to such institutions and never to private persons despite some tempting offers.

The Campaign drew attention in dramatic fashion to the new dangers to mankind's cultural heritage stemming from changing social and economic conditions. It also generated, forcefully, an awareness of the genuine need for the international community to participate in protecting cultural monuments which form part of the common heritage of mankind when threatened with destruction and when the country in which the property is located is unable to provide in full the resources necessary to ensure its proper protection.

This development, starting with the Nubia Campaign, has brought remarkable and heartening results both in the form of a large number of international salvage campaigns in many different countries which are administered by Unesco, and a series of international recommendations and conventions. Thus in June 1964 Unesco launched an International Campaign for Monuments "with a view to protecting the monuments that are mankind's heritage and enhancing their impact"; more than 50 countries took part in the Campaign.

On 19 November 1968 the General Conference of Unesco adopted a recommendation concerning the preservation of cultural property endangered by public or private works, in accordance with proposals made, among others, by those who were engaged in the Nubian project and were anxious to avoid at least some of the complications for future operations. The recommendation contains a large number of norms and principles covering the whole field and stipulates among other things that "the national or local authorities responsible for the safeguarding of cultural property should have adequate budgets to undertake the preservation or salvage of property endangered by public or private works" and that "costs of preserving or salvaging cultural property endangered by public or private works, including preliminary archaeological research, should form part of the budget of construction costs".

It is these principles of a common international responsibility – given substance in an exemplary way by the first international campaign launched by Unesco – which have been codified in the Convention concerning the Protection of the World Cultural and Natural Heritage. By adopting in 1972 this Convention, nations have recognized that each country holds in trust for the rest of mankind those parts of the world heritage that are found within its boundaries and that the international community has an obligation to support any nation in discharging this trust if its own resources are not equal to the task.

Annexes

Annex I

Direct Participation in Excavation and Preservation Work

ARGENTINA
: Three archaeological campaigns by the University of La Plata, in the Sudan.

AUSTRIA
: Six archaeological campaigns by the University of Vienna, in Egypt.
: Sending of an epigraphist to the DCC*, Cairo.

BELGIUM
: Sending of three experts to the DCC (architectural and epigraphic records).
: Photogrammetric and epigraphic records of five monuments, in the Sudan.
: Contribution to the cost of transferring the temple of Semna, Sudan.

CANADA
: One archaeological campaign by the Toronto National Museum, in Egypt.

CZECHOSLOVAKIA
: Five expeditions by the Institute of Archaeology of Charles University, Prague, in Egypt.

FINLAND
: General surveying to the south of Gemai, in the Sudan.

FRANCE
: Six campaigns by the "Institut français d'archéologie orientale", in Egypt.
: Two campaigns by the University of Strasbourg, in Egypt.
: Photogrammetric study of the Nubian temples.
: Sending of nine experts in various fields to the DCC.
: Removal and reconstruction of the temple of Amada, in co-operation with Egypt.
: Seven campaigns by the "Commission nationale des fouilles", in the Sudan.
: Payment of the costs involved in transferring the temple of Aksha.

FEDERAL REP. OF GERMANY
: Three campaigns by the German Institute of Archaeology, Cairo, in Egypt.

GERMAN DEMOCRATIC REPUBLIC
: Expeditions by the German Academy of Sciences to record the rock inscriptions and drawings and the ground-plan of the ruins of Attiri.

GHANA	Three campaigns by the University of Ghana, in the Sudan.
HUNGARY	One campaign by Budapest Museum, in Egypt.
INDIA	One campaign by the Archaeological Survey, in Egypt.
ITALY	Six campaigns by the University of Milan, in Egypt. One campaign by the University of Rome, in Egypt. Three campaigns by Turin Museum, in Egypt. Financial contribution by the city and Museum of Turin for the cutting out of the chapel of Ellesiya. Sending of three experts to the DCC by the University of Milan. Experimental work with sounding methods by the Lerici Foundation.
NETHERLANDS	Two campaigns by Leyden Museum, in Egypt. Preliminary studies for saving the Island of Philae. Contribution to the cost of saving the temple of Kumna (Sudan).
POLAND	One campaign by the Polish Centre for Mediterranean Archaeology, in Egypt. Sending of four architects to the DCC. Four campaigns by the Polish Centre for Mediterranean Archaeology and Warsaw Museum, in the Sudan.
SCANDINAVIAN COUNTRIES	Four campaigns by a joint mission (Denmark, Finland, Norway, Sweden), in the Sudan.
SPAIN	Four excavation campaigns and four campaigns to record and cut out rock inscriptions, in Egypt. Three excavation campaigns, in the Sudan.
SUDAN	Since 1960, successive expeditions by the Antiquities Service, led by a Unesco expert, for a general survey of Sudanese Nubia; excavations at some of the most important sites.
SWITZERLAND	One excavation campaign in co-operation with the University of Chicago, in Egypt. One excavation in co-operation with the French Institute of Cairo, in Egypt (both by the Swiss Institute of Architectural Research, Cairo). Architectural records of a temple and leadership of the Antiquities service expedition to cut out rock inscriptions in 1964.

Sending of an expert to the DCC by the "Fonds national suisse de la recherche scientifique".

ARAB REPUBLIC OF EGYPT

Five campaigns by the University of Cairo at Aniba.
One campaign by the University of Alexandria at Gebel Adda.
Eight excavation campaigns by the Antiquities Service on various sites.
Three campaigns by the Antiquities Service for cutting out rock drawings.
Removal of eight monuments, work in two others, dismantling of the front part of the temple of Amada and financial contribution to the work for saving this temple and those of Wadi es-Sebua, Beit el-Wali and Aniba.

UNITED KINGDOM

Four campaigns by the Egypt Exploration Society, in Egypt.
Two campaigns by the Egypt Exploration Society and the University of London for the general survey of Nubia.
Sending of two experts to the DCC.
Sending of an epigraphist (in co-operation with Brown University, Providence, USA).
Two excavation expeditions by the Egypt Exploration Society, in the Sudan.
Contribution to the dismantling of the temple of Buhen (Sudan).
Sending of an epigraphist (in co-operation with Brown University, Providence, USA).

UNITED STATES OF AMERICA

1. *In Egypt*
Four campaigns by the University of Chicago in Egypt, including one in co-operation with the Swiss Institute of Architectural Research.
Complete surveying and recording of a temple by the University of Chicago.
Four campaigns by Yale and Pennsylvania Universities.
Pre-history research on the Abu Simbel site by Columbia University.
Four campaigns by Yale University.
Sending of an epigraphist by Brown University (Providence) in collaboration with the Egypt Exploration Society.
Four campaigns by the Museum of New Mexico (pre-history survey).

Four campaigns by the American Research Centre.
Contribution by the United States Government for saving the temples of Beit el-Wali, Wadi es-Sebua and Aniba.

2. *In the Sudan*

Three excavation campaigns by the University of Chicago.

One pre-history survey campaign by Columbia University.

Three pre-history survey campaigns by the Museum of New Mexico.

Two excavation campaigns and one architectural survey campaign by the University of California.

Sending of an epigraphist by Brown University (Providence).

Three pre-history investigation campaigns by the University of Colorado Museum.

Contribution by the United States Government for the transfer and re-erection of the temple of Buhen.

USSR — One survey and excavation campaign, in Egypt.
General surveying and recording of rock inscriptions, in Egypt.

YUGOSLAVIA — Sending of two architects to the DCC.
Removal of Christian wall paintings (two experts), in Egypt.
Removal of Christian wall paintings (two experts), in the Sudan.

*Documentation and Study Centre for the History of the Art and Civilization of Ancient Egypt

Annex II

Unesco Organization

The *General Conference* consists of the representatives of the Member States of the Organization.

It determines the policies and the main lines of the work of the Organization. It takes decisions on programmes submitted to it by the Executive Board.

The *Executive Board* consists of 51 members elected by the General Conference among the delegates nominated by the Member States.

It meets in ordinary session at least twice a year.

It examines the programme of work for the Organization and corresponding budget estimates submitted to it by the Director-General and submits them with such recommendations as it considers desirable to the General Conference.

Between ordinary sessions of the General Conference, the Board takes all necessary measures to ensure the effective and rational execution of the programme by the Director-General.

The *Secretariat*, consisting of a Director-General and the staff he has appointed, carries out the approved programme and formulates proposals for appropriate action by the Executive Board and the General Conference.

DIRECTORS-GENERAL (1960–80)
1958–61 *Vittorino Veronese* (Italy)
1962–74 *René Maheu* (France)
1974– *Amadou-Mahtar M'Bow* (Senegal)

Annex III

Chronological Table of the Nubia Campaign

1955   *6 May* Creation of the Documentation and Study Centre for the History of the Art and Civilization of Ancient Egypt by the Egyptian Government with the technical assistance of Unesco (experts and material).

1956–64   The Documentation and Study Centre carries out photogrammetric (Institut Géographique National, Paris), architectural, photographic and epigraphic surveys of all the monuments of Egyptian Nubia.

1959   *6 April* The Egyptian Government requests Unesco assistance to save the sites and monuments of Nubia threatened by submergence as a result of the construction of the Aswan High Dam.

2 June The Egyptian request is examined by the Executive Board of Unesco (54th session).

1 October Meeting, first in Cairo then in Egyptian Nubia, of the group of international experts recommended by the Executive Board of Unesco, to study the problem of the safeguarding of the Nubian sites and monuments.

24 October The Sudanese Government requests Unesco assistance to save the sites and monuments of Sudanese Nubia.

27 Nov.–4 Dec. Fifty-fifth session of the Executive Board of Unesco. The Board adopts the principle of an appeal for international cooperation to assist the Egyptian and Sudanese Governments and authorizes studies preparatory to the work of safeguarding Abu Simbel and archaeological investigations of the sites in Sudanese Nubia to be undertaken as a matter of urgency.

1960   *9 January* Official Inauguration of work on the Aswan High Dam.

8 March The Director-General of Unesco launches an appeal to the international community for the preservation of the monuments of Nubia.

16–18 May First meeting of the International Action Committee in Paris.

22 May First meeting in Cairo of the Consultative Committee for the Campaign set up by the Egyptian Government in consultation with Unesco.

Summer months Dismantling and transfer of the temples of Debod and Taffa and the kiosk of Qertassi by the Egyptian Antiquities Service.

3–9 October Meeting of Sudanese Panel of Experts.

November Eleventh session of the General Conference of Unesco. The Director-General is authorized to continue and extend the International Campaign to save the monuments of Nubia.

1961–3   Dismantling, transfer and reconstruction of the temple of Kalabsha by the Federal Republic of Germany.

1962   *12–14 February* Experts meeting on the safeguarding of the monuments of Sudanese Nubia.

November–December Twelfth session of the General Conference of Unesco. Creation of the Executive Committee of the International Campaign.

1962–5   Dismantling, cutting and transfer of the temple of Beit el-Wali and Wadi es-Sebua and of the Tomb of Pennut at Aniba with a financial contribution from the United States of America; dismantling and transfer of the temples of Dendur, Dakka and Maharraqa. Work carried out by or under the supervision of the Egyptian Antiquities Service.

1963–7   Dismantling, transfer and reconstruction in Khartoum by the Sudanese Antiquities Service of:
–the remains of the temple of Aksha with a financial contribution from France;
–the temples of Buhen with a financial contribution from the United Kingdom and the United States of America;
–the temples of Semna East with a financial contribution from the Netherlands, and Semna West with a financial contribution from Belgium.

1963   *10–12 June* The Egyptian Government chooses the project to cut and transfer the two temples of Abu Simbel. The Executive Committee of the Campaign is satisfied with this choice.

5–9 November Meeting in Cairo of the Executive Committee of the Campaign and representatives of donor states. The Egyptian Government and Unesco on the one hand and Unesco and the donor states on the other sign agreements for carrying out the project of cutting and transferring the temple of Abu Simbel.

13 December Meeting of archaeologists convened by the Sudanese Government at Wadi Halfa.

1964   *Spring* Evacuation of population starts. Excavations finished up to Second Cataract.

April Beginning of work to save the temples of Abu Simbel (construction of the cofferdam).

14 May Diversion of the Nile to feed the turbines of the Aswan High Dam.

Summer months Cutting and dismantling of the temple of Derr; cutting of fragments of the temple of Gerf Husein and the chapels of Qasr Ibrim. Work carried out by the Egyptian Antiquities Service which also assisted Italy to cut the chapel of Ellesiya.

September–October The waters of the lake created by the Aswan High Dam begin to rise.

1964–5   Dismantling of the pronaos of the temple of Amada by the Egyptian Antiquities Service and transfer on rails of the sanctuary by France.

1965   End of the excavations in Egyptian Nubia (except for those on the promontory of Qasr Ibrim).

1966   *18–22 April* International Meeting on the Archaeological Survey in Sudanese Nubia.

1968   *Summer months* The Egyptian Government chooses the project of dismantling the temples on the island of Philae and re-erecting them on the neighbouring island of Agilkia.

22 September End of the work at Abu Simbel.

6 November Fifteenth session of the General Conference of Unesco. The Director-General launches an appeal to the international community for the safeguarding of the temples of the island of Philae.

1970   End of the construction of the Aswan High Dam.

3–4 December Eighteenth session of the Executive Committee of the International Campaign. The Director-General is authorized to sign agreements with the Egyptian Government and donor states for the safeguarding of the monuments of Philae.

19 December Signing of these agreements in Cairo.

1971   *6 May* The President of the Arab Republic of Egypt signs the agreement between the Egyptian Government and Unesco for the safeguarding of the monuments of Philae.

1972   Beginning of work to safeguard the monuments of Philae; levelling and widening of the island of Agilkia.

1973–4   End of excavations in Sudanese Nubia.

May 74 Completion of the cofferdam round the island of Philae. Beginning of pumping operations.

1977   *April* Beginning of reconstruction of the Philae monuments on the island of Agilkia.

1978   *November* Twentieth session of the General Conference of Unesco; the Executive Committee of the International Campaign is re-organized.

1979   *August* End of the work of transferring the Philae monuments.

1980   *10 March* End of the International Campaign to save the Monuments of Nubia.

Annex IV

Trust Fund for Safeguarding the Monuments of Nubia.
Final combined statement of contributions and other income
(expressed in US dollars)

Contributions	No. 1 Account EGYPT	No. 2 Account SUDAN	No. 3 Account (a) unspecified	No. 3 Account (b) Abu Simbel	No. 4 Account Philately	No. 5 Account Philae	TOTAL
I. GOVERNMENT CONTRIBUTIONS							
A. *In Currencies*							
Afghanistan	–	–	–	2,000.00	–	–	2,000.00
Algeria	–	–	–	105,016.07	–	–	105,016.07
Austria	–	–	–	25,000.00	–	12,031.67	37,031.67
Belgium	–	28,530.50	–	16,975.50	–	36,884.46	82,390.46
China	–	–	2,000.00	–	–	–	2,000.00
Cuba	–	–	–	160,000.00	–	–	160,000.00
Cyprus	–	–	1,400.12	1,306.24	–	2,394.90	5,101.26
Denmark	–	–	–	15,000.00	–	–	15,000.00
France	–	–	–	1,027,481.60	–	240,219.01	1,267,700.61
Germany (Federal Republic of)	–	–	–	62,495.47	–	615,670.23	678,165.70
Ghana	–	–	–	45,985.58	–	3,021.69	49,007.27
Greece	–	–	10,000.00	20,000.00	–	–	30,000.00
Holy See	–	–	10,000.00	25,000.00	–	–	35,000.00
Indonesia	–	–	–	10,000.00	–	–	10,000.00
Iraq	–	–	34,308.35	28,571.00	–	–	62,879.35
Italy	–	–	160,800.14	695,199.86	–	319,797.10	1,175,797.10
Japan	–	–	–	60,000.00	–	129,843.38	189,843.38
Kampuchea	–	–	–	4,976.39	–	–	4,976.39
Kuwait	–	–	50,008.42	50,000.00	–	5,000.00	105,008.42
Lebanon	–	–	33,333.33	–	–	6,644.51	39,977.84
Libyan Arab Jamahiriya	–	–	6,500.00	19,500.00	–	–	26,000.00
Luxembourg	–	–	1,997.78	–	–	–	1,997.78
Malaysia	–	–	–	13,003.14	–	1,136.36	14,139.50
Mali	–	–	2,040.00	–	–	–	2,040.00
Malta	–	–	–	–	–	239.98	239.98
Monaco	–	–	10,204.07	–	–	–	10,204.07
Morocco	–	–	3,960.39	–	–	–	3,960.39
Nepal	–	–	–	1,000.00	–	–	1,000.00
Netherlands	–	76,827.30	55,617.35	379,146.77	–	45,000.00	556,591.42
Nigeria	–	–	13,282.06	39,827.09	–	74,561.73	127,670.88
Pakistan	–	–	54,004.01	76,487.98	–	–	130,491.99
Philippines	–	–	–	10,000.00	–	–	10,000.00
Qatar	–	–	55,000.00	–	–	5,000.00	60,000.00
Saudi Arabia	–	–	8,000.00	–	–	–	8,000.00
Sierra Leone	–	–	2,800.00	–	–	–	2,800.00
Spain	–	–	–	325,000.00	–	200,000.00	525,000.00
Sri Lanka	–	–	1,000.00	–	–	–	1,000.00
Sudan	–	–	–	–	–	2,000.00	2,000.00
Sweden	–	–	–	500,000.81	–	–	500,000.81
Switzerland	–	–	–	229,994.11	–	102,223.36	332,217.47
Syria	–	–	–	2,555.20	–	149,936.32	152,491.52
Togo	–	–	–	815.20	–	–	815.20
Turkey	–	–	3,015.00	–	–	–	3,015.00
Uganda	–	–	2,800.34	2,796.59	–	–	5,596.93
United Kingdom	–	–	–	212,926.21	–	–	212,926.21
United States of America	2,382,132.53	118,825.21	–	12,000,000.00	–	4,000,000.00	18,500,957.74
Yugoslavia	–	–	64,571.00	161,429.00	–	–	226,000.00
Sub-total Currencies	2,382,132.53	224,183.01	586,642.36	16,329,489.81	–	5,951,604.70	25,474,052.41
B. *In Kind*							
India	–	–	–	373,333.33	–	41,214.45	414,547.78
Romania	–	–	–	4,830.00	–	–	4,830.00
Total Government Contributions	2,382,132.53	224,183.01	586,642.36	16,707,653.14	–	5,992,819.15	25,893,430.19

Contributions	No. 1 Account EGYPT	No. 2 Account SUDAN	No. 3 Account (a) unspecified	No. 3 Account (b) Abu Simbel	No. 4 Account Philately	No. 5 Account Philae	TOTAL
2. PRIVATE CONTRIBUTIONS							
A. Miscellaneous private contributions	166.48	10.20	13,352.52	935.01	–	21,370.30	35,834.51
B. American Committee for the Preservation of Abu Simbel	–	–	–	1,250,977.69	–	–	1,250,977.69
C. African Emergency Programme	–	–	–	–	–	20,717.65	20,717.65
D. Proceeds of Exhibitions							
Belgium	–	–	–	–	–	153,944.44	153,944.44
Canada	–	–	–	4,490.52	–	–	4,490.52
France	–	–	–	459,354.68	–	–	459,354.68
Germany (Federal Republic of)	–	–	–	–	–	1,207,653.62	1,207,653.62
Japan	–	–	–	1,089,050.75	–	–	1,089,050.75
Norway	–	–	–	–	–	6,471.22	6,471.22
Sweden	–	–	–	29,440.53	–	–	29,440.53
United Kingdom	–	–	–	–	–	1,600,613.51	1,600,613.51
USSR	–	–	–	–	–	1,602,351.15	1,602,351.15
Sub-total	166,48	10.20	13,352.52	2,834,249.18	–	4,613,121.89	7,460,900.27
3. OTHER CONTRIBUTIONS							
Sovereign Order of Malta	–	–	1,020.41	–	–	–	1,020.41
4. OTHER INCOME							
A. Tourist Tax (as reported by Government)	–	–	–	1,879,123.74	–	–	1,879,123.74
B. Interest and exchange adjustments	81,556.90	4,038.75	208,197.95	53,031.07	–	1,060,984.32	1,407,808.99
C. World Food Programme	–	–	–	–	–	3,517,557.57	3,517,557.57
D. Philatelic revenue and income from Philae Medals	–	–	1,975.00	–	65,690.64	45,000.00	112,665.64
Total other income	81,556.90	4,038.75	210,172.95	1,932,154.81	65,690.64	4,623,541.89	6,917,155.94
GRAND TOTAL	2,463,855.91	228,231.96	811,188.24	21,474,057.13	65,690.64	15,229,482.93	40,272,506.81

1. Transfers between sub-accounts of the trust fund have been eliminated.

2. The Government of Brazil contributed a sum of $12,848 which was utilized to meet part of the costs of the photogrammetric survey of the Monuments of Nubia undertaken by Unesco as part of the preliminary work of the Campaign. This contribution therefore has not been credited to the trust fund.

Annex V

The Temples of Abu Simbel

The four colossi of the façade of the temple depict the King, seated on the traditional throne, with the double crown of Upper and Lower Egypt. He is dressed in the royal loincloth and wears the beard of the divine sovereign of Egypt. In the time of Ramses II himself all these attributes of divine kingship already had millennial traditions.

The statues, in their serene grandeur, are not simply pictures of a divine ruler. They are divinities themselves, living representations of different aspects of the king's divinity. They have a cult of their own and their names are engraved on their shoulders – "The Sun of the Rulers" (Ré-n-heqau) and "The Ruler of the Two Lands" (Heqa-Tawy) are the southern ones, and "The Beloved One of / the God / Amun" (Mery Amun) and "The Beloved One of / the Sungod / Atum" (Mery-Atum) are to the north of the entrance.

The statues were the objects of a cult performed by the living king himself – not only at Abu Simbel but in other places also, and especially in the Ramesside capital, Piraramesses, in the eastern Delta.

His queens, Isisnofret and Nefertari, are sculptured on a smaller scale embracing his leg, and some of his numerous children appear here too and again on the terrace in front of the statues. At the southern end of this terrace is the famous stela which describes the marriage of Ramses II to a Hittite princess, and at its northern end is a small sanctuary of the sungod. It corresponds to a sanctuary of the god of wisdom, Thoth, cut in the front of the rock, just south of the terrace.

When passing the southern colossus next to the entrance one can see the oldest dated Greek text in Ionian "boustrophedon". It is the graffito left by Greek and Carian soldiers when an Egyptian army under Amasis launched a raid against southern Nubia in the reign of Psammetik II in the 6th century B.C. The graffito is high up on the leg, just under the knee. This shows why Abu Simbel was never mentioned in the Greek list of the Seven Wonders of the World; when this list was compiled the façade of Abu Simbel, and the entrance to the sanctuary, were already half buried in sand, and so the wonderful temple was never properly seen and justly appreciated in Greek times.

The passage leading to the entrance is flanked by splendid reliefs – kneeling foreigners from the north (on the northern side) and from the south (on the opposite side), the prisoners of the King whom he has "put under his feet". The thrones of the colossi next to the entrance door are adorned with a classical motive, the Niles of Upper and Lower Egypt tying the emblems of the Two Lands under the throne of the King, a symbolic representation of the King's domination of the united kingdom.

Over the high entrance is a picture of the sungod, with a falcon head and sundisk on his head, worshipped by Ramses II. Again, as in the case of the colossi, it is a way of symbolizing the divine king, as the sungod is here clearly identified with the king's divine "ego", to which Ramses offers a statuette of the goddess "Maat", who is the personification of the right order and truth.

The rising sun god, with his first rays, is thus greeted by a picture of himself and at the same time of the divine "ego" of the King, and at that moment the King on earth gives him "Maat", the right order of the newly created world of morning, after the night with its threatening powers of chaos which have been subdued by the cosmic power of the King.

The sunrays fill the passage through the first room – the courtyard hall with its procession of statues of the King adorning the pillars. He is here identified with Osiris, the dead but resurrected god of the Netherworld. Again the cult names to be found on the shoulders of the statues show the identity of King and god.

Behind the pillars on the north and south walls of the hall in the half-shadow we see wonderful reliefs depicting the glory of the King. To the right, on the northern side, is the famous monumental relief of the King's miraculous victory over the other Great Power of his time, the Hittite Confederation in Asia Minor, when he alone slaughtered their army at the Syrian town of Qadesh. He had been ambushed by the Hittites when pushing northwards ahead of his armies, but, thanks to the timely aid of his divine father Amun, the threatened disaster was transformed into victory when Ramses II, single-handed, drove his enemies into the River Orontes.

A modern visitor may smile at this representation of the King's overwhelming power, which to a non-believer seems ridiculous. But again we find here the notion of the King identified with the supreme god, the creator of the world. To conquer enemies was in the symbolic language of Egyptian theology another expression for the creation of cosmos out of chaos. When the god created the world he was alone, so the victorious King should also be alone in his triumph over his enemies, who symbolize the powers of chaos.

On the south wall we again find reliefs of a rare beauty and impressiveness: Ramses attacks in his chariot an Asiatic town, where the inhabitants in panic drive their cattle behind the height on which the town is built. Then the King kills his Libyan enemies, trampling one under his feet and dispatching another with his battleaxe. The Libyan is halted at the moment of his attack, like a wave breaking against a rock. The composition is outstanding and would seem to be the masterpiece of an original and creative artist, but as often in such cases, we are presumably mistaken – the same subject is met with long before in the Old Kingdom Period more than 1000 years earlier, where again the representation of the attacking Libyan, falling at the peak of his onrush, is one of the great achievements of the pictorial art of the Pyramid Age.

Only the last scene alludes to the south, to Nubia. Here we see the King in his chariot, leading a vividly depicted group of negro prisoners towards divinities on the adjacent wall. His tame lion runs near the chariot much more in the style of a happy hunting-dog or puppy rather than of the majestic king of beasts.

In the doorway to the next hall we again see the sungod with the disk on his head greeting the incoming sunrays and his celestial "ego". The rays also throw light on the reliefs of this hypostyle hall, where the procession of priests carrying the divine barque meet us on their way outwards. But more startling are the reliefs immediately inside the entrance to the right and left. On the southern side Ramses is offering to the Theban gods, Amun and his consort Mut. This was the original representation which was, however, changed later. Ramses the god was introduced as the third divinity, identified with the moongod Khons, but he was inserted between Amun and Mut – his divine parents and thus his superiors – that is to say, in front of the goddess Mut, whose legs are changed from a sitting to a standing position – the goddess has perforce to stand to make room for the king to sit! Similarly on the northern side the divine king has been introduced as an afterthought and as an object of the cult by the king on earth.

The same secondary introduction of the picture of the divine Ramses among other gods also occurs to the right and left of the inner entrance of the hall containing the Osirid Statues.

The sunrays pass the last doorway to penetrate the Holy of Holies, illuminating the altar on which once the sacred barque with the image of the god was installed. Behind the altar are four statues hewn in the rock – in the centre the principle deity of the Egyptian Empire, Amun of Thebes, and at his side the divine Ramses as a god. They are flanked by the gods of the two other main cult centres of Egypt in Ramesside times – Re-Harakhte from the city of the sun, Heliopolis, and Ptah-Tatenen from the oldest capital of united Egypt, Memphis.

The combination of these four divinities is not only a natural grouping of the most important gods of ancient Egypt; it is a manifestation of a politico-religious system – or as we would say today – the balance between state and "church", where Ramses represents the state and the other gods the official religion. Again within the "church" there is an equilibrium whereby the otherwise totally dominating principle god, Amun, is balanced against the two divinities of the two other most important administrative centres.

After peering into the large magazines to right and left of the main rooms of the temple, where the cult objects and other paraphernalia were stored, together with the offerings, we leave the courtyard of the Great Temple and pass through a stone doorway in its north wall of adobe. We proceed northwards to visit the smaller edifice dedicated to the goddess of love and maternity Hathor, with whom the royal consort Nefertari is identified.

The façade is again decorated with colossi depicting the divine Ramses, but here in a standing position. To the north is the pair "Sun of the Rulers" and "Beloved of Atum" and to the south "Ruler of the Two Lands" and "Beloved of Amun", separate individual divinities with their own cult names and objects of cult also from the side of the living king. Between these two pairs are statues of Queen Nefertari, shown here in the form of Hathor, with the horns of the sacred cow flanking a sundisk on her head; the sacred musical instrument of Hathor, the sistrum, is in her hand, lifted to her breast.

We enter the first room of the temple, what in most temples corresponds to the courtyard hall. The pillars are decorated with the sistrum of Hathor and the walls behind these pillars have wonderfully executed reliefs depicting coronation rituals and offering scenes.

On the entrance walls, to right and left of the main entrance, are representations of the king slaughtering his enemies, and behind him Queen Nefertari stands in adoration. This is the only scene alluding to the military and typically male side of the king. It has been said that the Great Temple is the sanctuary of the male aspect, of force and military triumph, whereas the Small Temple is that of the female counterpart, of charm, love and maternity. This contrast is reflected in the different styles of art in the two temples.

The vestibule in front of the Holy of Holies is decorated with reliefs connected with these typically feminine aspects. We see the Hathor cow coming forth from the mysterious papyrus marshes, place of birth of the young king and saviour-to-be. The most admired reliefs are those on the entrance walls. The northern half is decorated with a large anthropomorphic picture of the hippopotamus goddess Toeris, the divinity which protects women in pregnancy and ensures a happy birth. She is also the one who bestows pleasant dreams and sees to it that the sleeper is not harmed by evil powers. Thus pictures of Toeris are often to be found near the nuptial bed of the family and as an amulet among the women's adornments.

As a counterpart to this image of maternity and family love there is a masterpiece of Ramesside art, the perfect and adorable representation of Queen Nefertari being crowned by Isis, "The Mother of Gods", and by Hathor, "Mistress of Ibshek".

To an impressionable observer the first sight of the three figures can be overwhelming, as Rex Keating discovered:

"Cool and detached yet wholly alluring, Nefertari stands between the goddesses Hathor and Isis receiving their protection. The figures are life-size: their features are delicately coloured and they wear transparent robes of yellow linen. . . . They are nothing more than shapes chipped from the sandstone and coloured with ochres, yet such is the magic of their presence that it seems not only infinitely desirable but actually possible that they could become endowed with life and step down from the rocky wall into our space and time, with dignity and composure, and in all their peerless beauty." ("Nubian Twilight, 1962).

Hathor, "Mistress of Ibshek", who also occurs elsewhere in the temple, was the divinity of a wonderful and amazing place, not far from Abu Simbel, just south of the Sudanese border. One walks through the dunes at some distance from the Nile, and there suddenly is a little lake or pond in the midst of the surrounding sterility; it is as if a divine miracle had occurred. Alongside the water is a small rock with a sanctuary cut into it, with a relief by the Viceroy of Nubia in the reign of Ramses II. This tiny oasis was the holy place of the goddess Hathor, "Mistress of Ibshek".

The Holy of Holies is again dominated by the goddess Hathor, the divinity of femininity. It is a very small room where the holy cow of Hathor is depicted on the back wall as coming forth from the papyrus marshes. Hathor is also represented on the southern wall of the sanctuary, and on the north wall – as a kind of parallel to the reliefs in the Great Temple where Ramses is inserted as a divinity among other gods. Here Queen Nefertari is seated next to the deified Ramses and is adored by the king as priest, officiating to his own image and to that of his Queen, who thereby acquires a very special, divine character.

Today's visitors are by no means the first to regard Abu Simbel and its temples as a marvellous place. The Viceroys of Nubia, such as Iuny who lived under Sethos I and Ramses II, left their memorial stelae there together with those of other high officials; there is even one of a humble farmer, who lived under one of Ramses II's successors.

These ex-votos indicate that Abu Simbel was a place of considerable importance, but historians and archaeologists have found it difficult to explain the role not only of Abu Simbel but also of the other temples built in Lower Nubia by Ramses II. The odd fact is that the number of contemporary settlements and cemeteries is insignificant in relation to the majesty of the monuments. No town in Lower Nubia can be dated to this Ramesside period, nor any of the fortresses – at Buhen only the temple but not the town as such remained in use. The economic importance of Lower Nubia seems to have diminished in favour of Upper Nubia, where Ramesside towns and centres are found. Lower Nubia has become, it seems, a transit territory to richer and more important areas of Nubia further south and the temples seem to have marked the stations on this road southwards rather than having been focuses of importance in themselves.

Nevertheless, it remains a riddle why practically no traces have been found of the settlements which must have existed in the neighbourhood of the great temples where the daily rituals would have demanded the presence of a large number of priests and servants of the cult. And it is strange too that the tombs of temple personnel have never been found despite painstaking investigations. So far as the senior priests and officials were concerned this may be explained by the tendency of all Egyptians to arrange for burial in their homeland, loathing as they did the idea of internment abroad. Nubia was still regarded as a foreign country, despite the fact that it had been Egyptianized for centuries, to such a degree that archaeologists have great difficulty in distinguishing the Nubians from their Egyptian overlords when studying the tombs and the bodies found in them.

Annex VI

Philae – the Pearl of Egypt

Amelia Edwards, who visited Philae in 1873–4, described its appeal to her as arising not from "magnitude but perfect grace and exquisite beauty. The approach by water is quite the most beautiful. Seen from the level of a small boat, the island, with its palms, its colonnades, its pylons, seems to rise out of the river like a mirage. Piled rocks frame it on either side, and the purple mountains close up the distance. As the boat glides nearer between glistening boulders, those sculptured towers rise higher and even higher against the sky. They show no sign of ruin or age. All looks solid, stately, perfect. One forgets for the moment that anything is changed. If a sound of antique chanting were to be borne along the quiet air – if a procession of white-robed priests bearing aloft the veiled ark of the God, were to come sweeping round between the palms and pylons – we should not think it strange."

"It was an apt description" writes I.E.S. Edwards. "The buildings apart from their architectural elegance, were planned in scale with the small size of the island. In contrast with, for instance, the temple of Edfu, whose pylon exceeded 110 ft in height (33 m approximately), the pylons of the temple of Isis at Philae, which were roughly contemporaneous, were only 60 ft (approx. 18 m) and 40 ft (approx. 12 m) high and correspondingly less wide. The island itself, thanks to its surface-layer of silt, was covered with rich vegetation dotted with palm-trees and flowering shrubs. It was, in effect, a kind of oasis set in a background consisting of the river, granite rocks and the barren desert, and entirely unlike any other ancient site in Egypt.

"When the island of Philae is mentioned in the Egyptian texts, it is called Pireq, the Coptic equivalent of which (Pilak) means 'the island of (the) corner' or 'the island of (the) extremity' and thus describes its geographical position, either in the *corner* of a small bay in the east bank of the Nile or in the southern *extremity* of the cataract.

"Egyptian priests were in the habit of claiming that their local cults had originated in the remote past, even when, as in the case of Philae, their assertions had no basis in historical fact. Archaeological investigation has not brought to light any building earlier than a small kiosk of the twenty-sixth-dynasty king, Psammetichus II (595–589 B.C.) and a small temple of Amasis II (570–526 B.C.), which was dismantled in Ptolemaic times, many of its blocks being re-used in the second pylon and the columns of the hypostyle hall of the temple of Isis. One of the last native kings of Egypt, Nectanebes I (380–363 B.C.) also built a temple at Philae, but it soon collapsed owing to an exceptionally high Nile which flooded the island; eventually its entrance-hall was re-erected by Ptolemy II Philadelphus (285–246 B.C.) at the south-west corner of the island, not far from its original site. All the other monuments date from the Ptolemaic and the Roman periods.

"When Nectanebes I built his ill-fated temple at Philae, no one could have foreseen how prominently the island and its priesthood would figure in Egyptian politico–religious history for the next 1000 years. In 332 B.C., 31 years after the death of Nectanebes I, Egypt was conquered by Alexander the Great, and for three centuries following his conquest, the throne was occupied by rulers of Macedonian stock, all of whom bore the name of Ptolemy except the last, who was the famous Queen Cleopatra (51–30 B.C.). From the outset, they adopted the Egyptian religion, and in particular the cult of Osiris and Isis. Philae's principal monument, the temple of Isis, was built by Ptolemy II, Philadelphus (285–246 B.C.) and Ptolemy III, Euergetes I (246–221 B.C.), apart from the main doorway of the First Pylon which was a relic of the temple of Nectanebes. Philadelphus also built the temple of Imhotep, and Ptolemies IV and V, Philopator (221–205 B.C.) and Epiphanes (205–180 B.C.), constructed most of the nearby temple of Arsenuphis. The last of the Ptolemaic monuments at Philae, the temple of Hathor, was begun by Ptolemy VI, Philometor (180–145 B.C.) and completed by his successor, Euergetes II (145–116 B.C.). Other Ptolemies embellished with reliefs and inscriptions the temples built by their predecessors.

"It was not only in Egypt, however, that the cult of Isis and Osiris had advanced in popularity during the Ptolemaic Period. Greek settlers, many of whom were traders, had transported it to their native land and its dependencies, with the result that by the year 30 B.C., when the Mediterranean countries, including Egypt, were united under Roman rule, the cult was firmly established throughout the Aegean region. It had, moreover, reached Rome, where Isis acquired the reputation of being the protectress of mariners, and thence it spread to the remotest parts of the Empire. At first, Philae received no visible proof of imperial patronage, apparently because Augustus was disinclined to show partiality towards Isis, who had been the goddess of his enemy, Cleopatra, but eventually he relented and, in the 18th year of his reign (9 B.C.), he built a temple at the northern end of the island. Much of it is now lost, but those of its architectural elements which have survived show that it was once a fine edifice. Tiberius, Augustus' successor, and several later Emperors also left their mark at Philae, mostly by adding reliefs, and inscriptions to existing monuments, but four Emperors erected new buildings, namely Claudius (A.D. 41–54) – a temple to Harendotes, Trajan (A.D. 97–117) – the most celebrated of all Philae's monuments, the kiosk on the east side of the island, Hadrian (A.D. 117–38) – the gateway and vestibule near the temple of Harendotes, and probably Diocletian (A.D. 284–305) – the ceremonial gateway at the northern end of the island.

"While the cult of Isis was gaining adherents across the Mediterranean, it was also making headway in Nubia, even as far south as the kingdom of Meroë whose capital lay about 75 miles (120 km) north-east of present-day Khartoum.

One of the kings of Meroe, Ergamenes, enlarged the temple of Arsenuphis and travellers from Meroe left graffiti on the roof of the Birth-House of the temple of Isis. It was in Lower Nubia, however, that the cult of Isis made its greatest impact, especially in the so-called Dodekaschoenus, the territory extending southwards for 80 miles (130 km) from the First Cataract to Maharraqa. For the inhabitants of that region Philae became the religious metropolis, and more than one inscription states that all its products were dedicated to Isis and the priesthood of Philae. One of the gods of the Dodekaschoenus, named Mandulis, whose chief sanctuary lay at Kalabsha, was not only admitted by the Egyptian priests into the Osiris-Isis family as a son of Horus, but possessed a small temple at Philae built by Ptolemy II, Philadelphus, no doubt with a view to strengthening the ties between Philae and the Nubians. What seems to have been in origin another Nubian cult which was assimilated at Philae was that of a deified falcon. The bird is shown in relief on the First Pylon of the temple of Isis in an enthronement scene, with the gods Horus and Thoth performing the magic rites.

"Philae retained its privileged position even after the Emperor Theodosius I had issued his decree in A.D. 391 suppressing pagan worship throughout the empire. Political expediency was undoubtedly the chief reason for this act of toleration. Closure of the temples of Philae would have met with strong resistance from the inhabitants of Nubia, especially from the Blemmyes, the warlike people from the eastern desert who had long caused trouble to the Roman authorities by their raids on Upper Egypt. In A.D. 451–52 Maximinus, the general of the Emperor Marcian, led an expedition against them and defeated them. A treaty ensued, by which the Blemmyes undertook to keep the peace for 100 years and, in return, they were allowed to offer sacrifices at Philae and even to borrow the sacred image of Isis periodically for the purpose of obtaining oracles. Before the expiry of this pact, however, Justinian sent his general, Narses, c. A.D. 536, to put an end to the last outpost of paganism in the Empire. The temple of Isis was closed, the priests were disbanded and the statues were transported to Constantinople, apparently without serious opposition. Soon afterwards, the hypostyle hall was converted by Bishop Theodosius into a church, dedicated in the name of St. Stephen, and a Christian community settled on the island.

"During this new phase in Philae's history, which lasted until the 11th–13th centuries, very considerable damage was done to the monuments. Blocks were extracted from the monuments and re-used, some in the building of a Coptic church near the Harendotes temple and others in the construction of a street on the east side of the temple of Isis. The temple itself suffered comparatively little structural damage, but many of the figures of gods sculptured in relief on its walls were defaced and large Christian crosses were carved on its door-posts and elsewhere. Fortunately, the hieroglyphic inscriptions, both in this temple and in the other surviving buildings, have generally been spared deliberate mutilation. One text on the north wall of Hadrian's vestibule, in front of a figure of Mandulis, is dated by an accompanying note in Demotic to 24 August, A.D. 394; it is thus the latest datable example of the hieroglyphic script now known. The Christian iconoclasts also left undamaged many hundreds of Demotic and Greek graffiti, some written by priests and others by pilgrims who regularly came to Philae, either simply to pay homage to Isis or to seek her intervention in obtaining relief from their ailments. Here again, Philae has preserved the latest known examples of one of the three scripts in which the Egyptian language was written – in this instance Demotic, a cursive script ultimately derived from hieroglyphics. This graffito, which is dated 2 December, A.D. 452 (at about the time when Maximinus made his treaty with the Blemmyes), was written by a priest named Esmet on a wall of one of the Osiris chambers of the temple of Isis. It shows that knowledge of the ancient language was not completely lost as long as Philae continued to serve the needs of the worshippers of Isis.

"Philae, moreover, preserved one inscription which proved invaluable in the recovery of that knowledge after it had been forgotten for more than 1000 years. It was a Greek inscription on the pedestal of an obelisk which bore a hieroglypic inscription. The texts were not two versions of the same document, one in Greek and the other in Egyptian, but both mentioned Cleopatra III, a wife of Ptolemy VII, Euergetes II, and it was the recognition of her name in the hieroglyphic inscription of the obelisk, when combined with the previously uncorroborated identification of the name of Ptolemy on the Rosetta Stone, which provided the starting point in the decipherment of the hieroglyphic script."

Bibliographical Notes

The Nubian Campaign resulted in the publication of an immense wealth of books and articles and what can be given here are only references to further reading, some more important works or works relating to specific subjects treated in the book.

General

In 1977, Unesco published a bibliography, *Campagne internationale de l'Unesco pour la sauvegarde des sites et monuments de Nubie*, compiled by Louis-A. Christophe. It lists 718 books and articles.

For the years from 1977 onwards there is no similar bibliography, but most of the relevant publications can be found in Jean Leclant's annual reports, "Fouilles et travaux en Egypte et au Soudan" in *Orientalia* (Pontifico Istituto Biblico di Roma), and in the *Annual Egyptological Bibliography*, prepared for the International Association of Egyptologists by Jac J. Janssen and collaborators and from 1979 by L.M.J. Zonhoven and collaborators.

The acts of the regular meetings of Nubiologists also give up-to-date information on the progress of the scientific work with bibliographical references, which are also to be found in the monographs of the different archaeological expeditions.

In 1977, William Y. Adams published his *Nubia. Corridor to Africa* (London, Allen Lane, 1977) containing an extensive analytical description of the cultural development of Nubia based mainly on archaeological results from both the Campaign and earlier investigations. It gives exhaustive bibliographical references and is now considered as the standard work on Nubia.

During the Campaign several general works were published in different languages, giving information and illustrations of what was at stake – the monuments, treasures and cultural heritage of Nubia. Suffice it to mention here some of the more useful: Rex Keating, *Nubian Twilight* (London, Rupert Hart Davis, and Stockholm, Lars Hökerbergs, 1962) and *Nubian Rescue* (London, Robert Hale; New York, Hawthorn Books, 1975, and Budapest, Gondolat, 1980), Silvio Curto, *Nubia. Storia di una civiltà favolosa* (Novara 1965), Georg Gerster, *Nubien. Goldland am Nil* (Zürich, Stuttgart 1964), *The Nubian Monuments*, Special Supplement to the *Egyptian Gazette* (Cairo 1962).

The development of the Campaign itself can be followed through the relevant official reports issued by Unesco: UNESCO/CUA 103, 106, 107, 109, 113, 118, 127, and UNESCO/NUBIA/1 ff with appended working papers (on microfiche; full-size paper copies may be purchased).

Numerous brochures and articles have also been published by the Egyptian Documentation Centre and by Unesco (especially in the "Unesco Courier").

For the history of the Campaign up to and including the inauguration of the Abu Simbel temples an important and fascinating source is Saroite Okacha's *Ramsès re-couronné* (Dar Al-Maaref, Cairo 1974).

Reference may also be made to T. Säve-Söderbergh, *International Salvage Archaeology. Some organizational and technical aspects of the Nubian campaign.* (Annales Acad. Regiae Scient. Upsaliensis. 15/16, Stockholm 1972).

1 Prelude

GEOGRAPHY, ETC.

For the basic facts and bibliographical references see, in addition to the general works (especially Adams, *Nubia*), ordinary tourist guides (the classical *Baedeker* of 1927, *Guide Bleu*, etc.). Valuable information is also contained in Barbour, *The Republic of the Sudan* (London 1961) and the *Sudan Almanac* 1960 (Khartoum 1960).

HISTORICAL OUTLINE

For the history of all periods: J. Arkell, *A History of the Sudan* (2nd ed., London 1961); Bruce G. Trigger, *History and Settlement in Lower Nubia* (Yale 1965), as well as the introductions to the different expedition monographs such as *Memorias de la Misión Arqueológica en Nubia* (I ff) (Madrid 1963 ff) or *The Scandinavian Joint Expedition to Sudanese Nubia*. Publications 1–9 (1970 ff).

For individual periods see:

For Pharaonic times: T. Säve-Söderbergh, *Ägypten und Nubien* (Lund 1941) based on a combination of written sources and archaeological evidence; Walter B. Emery, *Egypt in Nubia* (London, Hutchinson, 1965) which emphasizes the archaeological results, and Bruce Trigger, *Nubia under the Pharaohs* (London 1976) which also covers the results of the International Campaign.

For Meroitic culture: P.L. Shinnie, *Meroë, A Civilisation of the Sudan* (London 1967), and for Roman Nubia: Ugo Monneret de Villard, *La Nubia Romana* (Rome 1941).

For Christian Nubia: U. Monneret de Villard, *Storia della Nubia Cristiana* (Rome 1938). (Cf. also the summary by Säve-Söderbergh in Scand. J. Exp. to Sud. Nubia, vol. 7. *Late Nubian Sites*, Helsinki 1970.)

For written sources on post-Pharaonic times: Woolley & MacIver, *Karanog* (Philadelphia 1910); G. Vantini, *Oriental Sources concerning Nubia* (Heidelberg, Warsaw 1975); id. The Excavations at Faras. *A Contribution to the History of Christian Nubia* (Bologna 1970).

HYDROLOGY

Karl W. Butzer, *Early Hydraulic Civilization in Egypt: a study in cultural ecology.* (University of Chicago Press 1976) with references.

TEMPLES

Les temples immergés de la Nubie (Service des Antiquités, Cairo 1909–38). H.B. Lyons, *A Report on the Island and Temple of Philae* (Cairo 1896); id., *A Report on the Temple of Philae* (Cairo 1908). Short surveys are contained in: *A Common Trust. Preservation of the Ancient Monuments of Nubia* (Unesco brochure, Paris 1960); Christiane Desroches-Noblecourt, *Temples de Nubie. Des trésors menacés* (Paris 1961); A.A. Tadema & B. Tadema Sporny, *Unternehmen Pharao. Die Rettung der ägyptischen Tempel* (Bilbao 1978, also in Dutch).

EARLIER ARCHAEOLOGICAL CAMPAIGNS

Are described in:

The Archaeological Survey of Nubia. Reports for 1907–11 by G.A. Reisner and by C.M. Firth (Cairo 1910–27). *Mission Archéologique de Nubie 1929–1931* (Service des Antiquités Egyptiennes); W.B. Emery & L.P. Kirwan, *The Excavations and Survey between Wadi es-Sebua and Adindan 1929–1931* (Cairo 1935); W.B. Emery, *The Royal Tombs of Ballana and Qustul* (Cairo 1938); G. Steindorff, *Aniba I, II* (Glückstadt 1935–37); Ugo Monneret de Villard, *La Nubia médioevale* (Cairo 1935).

Pennsylvania: Eckley B. Coxe, junior, *Expedition*, vols. 1–8 (Oxford, Philadelphia 1909–11).

Oxford Excavations in Nubia, reports by Griffith in *Annals of Archaeology and Anthropology*, Liverpool, vols. 8–15 (1921–8).

German expedition; Aniba (see above).

Austrian expedition: described by H. Junker in *Akad. d. Wiss. Wien phil. hist. Kl. Denkschriften*, 62:3, 64:3, 67:1, 68:1 (1919–26).

Pre-history: K.S. Sandford & W.J. Arkell, *Palaeolithic Man and the Nile Valley in Nubia and Upper Egypt* (Oriental Inst. Publ. Chicago, vol. 17, Chicago 1933).

THE HIGH DAM

The political background and official estimates are given in P. Mansfield, *Nasser's Egypt* (Penguin, 1969). *The Aswan High Dam and its Various Consequences* (VBB mimeographed edition 1976) by Lennart Berg is a thorough profit-and-loss analysis made available for this book.

MODERN NUBIAN CULTURE

R. Fernea, ed., *Contemporary Nubia* (2 vols. New Haven 1966); id. & G. Gerster, *Nubians in Egypt* (University of Texas Press, 1973); R. Herzog, *Die Nubier* (Berlin 1957); Marian Wenzel, *House Decoration in Nubia* (London 1972); L.-A. Christophe *Remarques sur l'économie de la Basse Nubie* (*Bull. Soc. Géogr. d'Egypte*, vol. 35, Cairo 1963).

Especially for the Sudan: A. & W. Kronenberg's preliminary reports in *Kush*, 11–13 (Khartoum 1963–4) and Hassan Dafallah, *The Nubian Exodus* (London, C. Hurst, 1975).

SUDANESE NUBIA

The general situation was well summarized in *Why excavate in the Sudan* (Khartoum 1959) published by J. Vercoutter and W.Y. Adams at the start of the Campaign.

For the Pennsylvania excavations at Faras, Buhen and in churches, see above.

For the fortresses of the Second Cataract see: Säve-Söderbergh, *Ägypten und Nubien*, pp. 80 ff and J. Vercoutter, *Mirgissa I* (Paris 1970), with references; G. Reisner's fieldnotes in *Kush*, VIII, 1960, 11–24; Dows Dunham & J. Janssen, *Semna, Kumna* (Boston 1960), and Dunham, *Uronarti, Shalfak, Mirgissa* (Boston 1967).

Abka: O.H. Myers, "Abka re-excavated" and "Abka again" in *Kush*, VI, 131–41; VIII, 174–81.

Gammai: Oric Bates, Excavations at Gammai (*Harvard African Studies VIII*) (Cambridge, Mass. 1927).

2 Launching the International Campaign

EXPEDITIONS 1958–9
See *Fouilles en Nubie* (1959–61) (Service des Antiquités, Cairo 1963), and *Annales du Service des Antiquités*, 61 (1973).

DOCUMENTATION CENTRE PUBLICATIONS
Collection Scientifique and *Brochures culturelles* (for details see Christophe's bibliography, 1977).

Christiane Desroches-Noblecourt & Ch. Kuentz, *Le petit temple d'Abou Simbel* (Mémoires du Centre etc., 2 vols., Le Caire, 1968).

ROCK DRAWINGS AND INSCRIPTIONS
F. Hintze, preliminary reports in *Kush*, 11–13 (Khartoum 1963–65); M. Almagro & M. Almagro Gorbea, *Estudios de arte rupestre, Nubia. Yacimientos situados en la orilla oriental del Nilo entre Nag Kolorodna y Kasr Ibrim (Nubia Egipcia)* (Memorias X. Madrid 1968); Zbyněk Žaba, *The Rock Inscriptions of Lower Nubia. Czechoslovak Concession* (Prague 1974); P. Hellström & H. Langballe, *The Rock Drawings* (Scand. Joint Exp. Publ. 1) (Odense 1970); B.B. Piotrowski, *Wadi Allaki* (in Russian) (Moscow 1983).

PREAMBLES, ORGANIZATION, ETC.
A vivid and full description of the events by Saroite Okacha in *Ramsès re-couronné* (Cairo 1974) supplements the official records.

The Unesco brochure "A Common Trust" (Paris 1960) contains the requests of Egypt and the Sudan, as well as (appended) the appeal of the Director-General of Unesco, Vittorino Veronese, with the messages from H.M. the King of Sweden Gustaf VI Adolf, H.E. the President of Egypt Gamal Abd el Nasser, H.E. the President of the Sudan Ferik Ibrahim Abboud, the Secretary General of the UN Dag Hammarskjöld, and the response by Mr. André Malraux, French Minister of Culture.

SUDANESE NUBIA
The section is based on a personal letter from Prof. J. Vercoutter (cf. also his articles mentioned in the Unesco Bibliography 1977).

3 The Salvage of Monuments

ABU SIMBEL
A richly illustrated, full description both of the temples and of the salvage operation is given in: Christiane Desroches-Noblecourt & G. Gerster, *The World saves Abu Simbel* (Vienna, Berlin, Verlag A.F. Koska, 1968; also French, German and Italian editions). The small temple: Chr. Desroches-Noblecourt & Ch. Kuentz, *Le petit temple d'Abou Simbel* (Mém. Doc. Centre Cairo 1968). A full documentation of the two temples in "Collection scientifique" of the Documentation Centre, Cairo.

The main sources concerning the preambles of the salvage operation are, in addition to the Unesco documents (CUA and Nubia), Saroite Okacha's *Ramsès re-couronné*.

For the salvage operation: *The Salvage of the Abu Simbel Temples. Concluding Report* (VBB 1971).

The speeches at the inauguration have been published by Unesco in a brochure.

Abu Simbel as a tourist attraction and future plans: *Lake Nubia. Tourism Development Study* (Egyptian Ministry of Tourism and Sudanese Tourism and Hotels Corporation. Final Report, Jan. 1979).

KALABSHA

H. Stock & K.G. Siegler, *Kalabsha. Der grösste Tempel Nubiens und das Abenteuer seiner Rettung.* (Wiesbaden, F.A. Brockhaus, 1965). G.H. Wright, *Kalabsha. The Preserving of the Temple* (Archaeol. Veröff. Deutsch, Arch. Inst. Kairo, Berlin, 1970). See also the "Collection scientifique" of the Documentation Centre and its "Educational Publications".

E. Winter & G.R. Wright & D. Arnold, *Die ptolemäischen Bauten von Kalabscha*.

AMADA

The text was contributed by J. Trouvelot. Cf. also Christiane Desroches-Noblecourt & R.P. du Bourguet and others, *Le déplacement du Temple d'Amada*. Suppl. aux *Annales de l'Inst. techn. du bâtiment et des transports publics* (Paris 1966). Documented in "Collection scientifique" of the Documentation Centre.

TEMPLES AS AMBASSADORS ABROAD

The temple of *Dendur*: For this temple see (in addition to "Temples immergés de la Nubie" and the "Collection scientifique" of the Documentation Centre), C. Aldred, *The Temple of Dendur* (Brochure of the Metropolitan Museum, New York 1978).

The temple of *Taffeh*: H.D. Schneider *Taffeh. Rond de wederopbouw van een Nubische tempel* ('sGravenhage 1979).

The temple of *Debod*: M. Almagro, *El templo de Debod* (Madrid 1971); id. *El templo egipcio de Debod en Madrid* (Anales de Historia Antigua y Medieval, vol. 17) (Buenos Aires 1972).

The speos of *Ellesiya*: S. Curto, *Il tempio de Ellesija* (Cahier No. 6, Mus. di Torino) Turin 1970. See also the "Collection scientifique" of the Documentation Centre.

THE MONUMENTS OF SUDANESE NUBIA

F. Hinkel, *Tempel ziehen um* (Leipzig, F.A. Brockhaus, 1966); id. *Auszug aus Nubien* (Berlin 1977); id. *Exodus from Nubia*, Berlin, Akademia-Verlag, 1978. Published with financial assistance from Unesco.

THE SALVAGE OF PHILAE

See: O.R. Rostem, *The Salvage of Philae* (Suppl. Annales du Service des Antiquités. Cahier 20), Le Caire 1955; W. Macquitty, *Island of Isis. Philae Temple of the Nile* (London 1976); and, especially, A. Giammarusti & Roccati, *File. Storia e vita di un santuario egizio* (Min. Affari Esteri) (Novara 1980). See also the brochures *Philae. A Pearl from the Waters* (Paris, Unesco 1975), *The Salvage of the Philae Monuments* (Condotte – Mazzi Estero S.P.A.) (1980?), *Salvage of the Philae Monuments, Aswan* (High Dam Co. for Civil Works. Min. of Irrigation, Egypt) (10 March 1980). *Nubia. A Triumph of International Solidarity* (Official Inauguration of the Temples of Philae and the Twentieth Anniversary of the International Campaign to Save the Monuments of Nubia. 10 March 1980), Paris, Unesco 1980.

4 The Archaeological Campaign

This chapter is based on interviews that the General Editor had with directors or responsible members of practically all the archaeological expeditions as well as on his own personal experience as head of the Scandinavian Joint Expedition to Sudanese Nubia; see T. Säve-Söderbergh, *The Scandinavian Joint Expedition to Sudanese Nubia* (Kgl. Danske Videnskabernes Selskab. Hit.-fil. medd. 49:§), Copenhagen 1979; and id. *International Salvage Archaeology* (see above under "General").

For the different expeditions and missions see Annex III and for their results J. Leclant's annual reports in *Orientalia*, and in the same journal P. van Moorsel, "Nubian Studies in Preparation" (vols. 43/1974, 228–36; 45/1976, 319–26; 47/1979, 321–31, etc.).

QASR IBRIM

Preliminary short reports in the *Journal of Egyptian Archaeology* (vols. 50/1964, 3 ff; 52/1966, 9 ff; 53/1967, 3 ff; 56/1970, 12 ff; 60/1974, 212 ff; 63/1977, 29 ff, etc.). For the necropolis, see A.J. Mills, *The Cemeteries of Qasr Ibrim. A Report on the Excavations conducted by W.B. Emery 1961* (Eg. Explor. Soc. Mem. 51), London 1982.

A RICH HARVEST
A Stone Age Massacre
The find was published in F. Wendorf (ed.), *The Prehistory of Nubia* (2 vols.) (Dallas 1968).

AN EARLY NUBIAN STATE
Br. Williams, *Excavations between Abu Simbel and the Sudan Frontier*, Keith C. Seele, Director. Part I: *Early Nubian Remains from Cemeteries L, W. S, V, Q, and T* (Oriental Institute Chicago Nubian Expedition, vol. III), cf. *Unesco Courier*, Feb./March 1980.

For this period and especially the A-Group, see N.A. Nordström, *Neolithic and A-Group Sites* (Scandinavian Joint Expedition. Publ. 3:1 and 2) Uppsala 1972.

AN OLD KINGDOM TOWN
Preliminary report by W.B. Emery in *Kush*, XI, 1963, 116–20.

THE PHARAONIC COLONY
For the Egyptian fortresses see especially W.B. Emery, H. Smith & A. Millard, *The Fortress of Buhen I. The Archaeological Report* (Egypt. Explor. Soc. Mem. 49), London 1979; H.S. Smith, *The Fortress of Buhen II. The Inscriptions* (Egypt Explor. Soc. Mem. 48), London 1976; J. Vercoutter et alii, *Mirgissa. La fouille du site par la Mission archéologique du Soudan*. Vols. I–II (Paris 1970, 1976), this publication also contains an excellent analysis of the Second Cataract fortresses with full bibliography. For preliminary reports on other fortresses, see *Kush*, VIII ff.

Analyses of Nubian contemporary "cultures" especially in M. Bietak, *Studien zur Chronologie der nubischen C-Gruppe – ein Beitrag zur Frühgeschichte Unternubiens zwischen 2200 und 1500 v. Chr.* (Wien Ak. Wiss. Phil. hist. Kl. Denkschr. 97) (Wien 1968); id. et alii, *Ausgrabungen in Sayala-Nubien 1961–1965 – Denkmäler der C-Gruppe und der Pan-Gräber Kultur* (ibid. 92) (Wien 1966).

For the interplay of cultures, see T. Säve-Söderbergh, "Die Akkulturation der nubischen C-Gruppe im Neuen Reich" (Zeitschr. d. Deutsch-Morgenländischen Ges. Suppl. I, XVII) (Wiesbaden 1969); id. *Kush*, IV, 54 ff and Scand. Joint Exp. Publ., vol. 4.

The tombs of the Nubian princes: T. Säve-Söderbergh, "The paintings in the Tomb of Djehuti-hotep at Debeira" (*Kush*, VIII/1960, 25 ff); id., "The Tomb of the Prince of Teh-khet, Amenemhet" (*Kush*, XI/1963, 159 ff). In full in Scand. Joint. Exp. Publ., vol. 5:2.

W.K. Simpson, *Heka-nefer and the Dynastic Material from Toshka and Arminna* (Pennsylvania–Yale Exp. to Egypt No. 1) (New Haven, Philadelphia 1963).

THE WONDER OF FARAS
Of the numerous monographs and articles see especially the series *Faras*, I–VII; K. Michalowski (with the collaboration of S. Jakobielski), *Faras. Wall Paintings in the Collection of the National Museum in Warsaw* (Warsaw 1974), and K. Michalowski & Gerster, *Faras, die Katedrale aus dem Wüstensand* (Zürich 1967).

WIDENING HORIZONS
Pre-history: F. Wendorf & R. Schild, *Loaves and Fishes. Prehistory of Wadi Kubbaniya* (Dallas, New Delhi 1980).

Kerma: An up-to-date account supplied by Ch. Bonnet; cf. his preliminary reports 1977–82 in *Genava*, nouvelle série XXVI ff.

Acknowledgements

A sub-committee was formed to assist me in my work as General Editor under the chairmanship of Dr. Ahmed Kadry and with Dr. Gamal Mokhtar, Mr. Marfaing, Mr. L. Monreal and the representative of Unesco, Mr. S. Naqvi, Director, Division of Cultural Heritage, as members. My sincere thanks go to this sub-committee with whose members I have had the privilege of collaborating for many years, both in the Nubia project and on other matters.

Mr. Rex Keating, who has followed and publicized the Nubia Campaign for more than two decades, agreed to scrutinize, on behalf of Unesco, the manuscript from the viewpoints of language, composition and contents. I thank him for the fruitful collaboration and final result.

As delegate of the Swedish Government to the Executive Committee and other committees during the whole Nubia Campaign I have had the opportunity of participating in the planning and execution of the Campaign. My text is thus based not only on official documents and working papers and on the overwhelming number of published accounts, but also on the discussions within the Committee, especially with its Chairman H.E. Professor Paulo de Berrêdo Carneiro as well as with the leading Unesco officials involved in the Campaign. I have also benefited from the collaboration and assistance of numerous other persons, first of all the officials of the Egyptian Antiquities Organization and the Sudanese Antiquities Organization. I have tried to give credit in the text to their role in the success of the Nubia project.

Among those who have contributed to this book I mention with gratitude, in addition to the members of the sub-committees of the Executive Committee, Dr. Shehata Adam, who provided me with a long and detailed text on the various aspects of the Campaign in Egyptian Nubia and kindly allowed me to use it freely as it proved impossible to insert it *in extenso* for lack of space. Dr. Nigmeddin Sharif, President of the Sudanese Antiquities Organization, was prevented by a serious car accident from making a written contribution, but I am indebted to him for a wealth of information.

Mr. Louis Christophe put at my disposal a comprehensive summary of the main events of the Campaign and I was able to benefit from his rich experience as a liaison officer of Unesco in Cairo.

Professor Jean Vercoutter, with whom I was in contact during the whole Campaign, sent me, in addition to published articles and works, most valuable data concerning the Sudan, especially in the initial stage when he was Commissioner for Archaeology in the Sudan and also later when he took a very active part in the archaeological field work.

Originally my task was conceived as that of a co-ordinator who should collect and harmonize a series of contributions from responsible officials, archaeologists and other experts. I therefore contacted by correspondence or through personal interviews a large number of persons, asking them for contributions on specific topics. However, it proved impossible to use these in their original form for lack of space in a short book which was intended to cover the 20 years of the largest salvage operation so far undertaken. It would also have been very difficult with this method to produce a harmonized and coherent account of all the events of those dramatic decades. So I have to apologize to all who responded positively to my demands either orally or in the form of detailed texts. Even if many of these contributions could not be used they have been a very valuable background to my efforts to do justice to the incredible amount of hard work, enthusiasm and professional skill involved in the Campaign.

Most of those who are or were in responsible positions concerning the rescue of monuments or archaeological remains have been contacted and I trust they will excuse me if I do not enumerate them all here.

In addition to the persons whose published works I have used lavishly, my special thanks are due to those who have permitted me to include, partly or *in extenso*, several, as a rule unpublished, texts: Mr. Lennart Berg (VBB, for an evaluation of the High Dam), Mr. Sven-Erik Frick-Meier (VBB, for the technical account of the rescue of Abu Simbel and other technical information), Mr. Jean Trouvelot (for a description of the salvage of Amada), Dr. Cathleen Keller of the Metropolitan Museum of Art, New York (for a text concerning the Temple of Dendur in New York). In this connection I also express my gratitude to the head of the Egyptian Department of the MMA, Dr. Christine Lilyquist, and to Professor Kelly Simpson (for a full documentation on the background and details of the US contributions); Dr. Hans Schneider (for the rebuilding of the temple of Taffa), Dr. I.E.S. Edwards (for the larger part of the text on Philae). Special thanks also are due to Professor William Y. Adams for his contributions on the basic problems encountered in the archaeological aspect of the Campaign, for his balanced evaluations and our many discussions which often clarified my own concepts.

As for the various archaeological expeditions I regret particularly that lack of space excluded the full use of many excellent texts put at my disposal – not least by Professor Harry Smith and Dr. A. Mills on the British contributions, by Professor Jean Leclant on the role of France in the field work and rescue of monuments; by Professor Shinnie on the Ghana expedition, and by Dr. Bonnet on recent investigations at Kerma, and many other colleagues and friends.

Finally, my indebtedness is of course great to a large number of other personalities and scholars for their publications on Nubian problems – specifically Dr. Saroite Okacha, Mrs. Christiane Desroches-Noblecourt, Mr. Hassan Dafallah, and Professor Robert A. Fernea to mention only a few – and to the photographers – professional and amateur – who have put illustrations at my disposal.

This enumeration of those who made this publication possible is by no means complete, for which I ask to be forgiven. Too many are those who are no longer with us, and cannot be reached with expressions of profound gratitude.

Torgny Säve-Söderbergh
Uppsala, September 1983

List of Illustrations

Colour plates

Monochrome plates

Figures

Index

Arabic numerals in italics are black and white illustration numbers; Roman numerals refer to colour illustrations.